I

977.803 P261
PARRISH
TURBULENT PARTNERSHIP: MISSOURI AND THE UNION, 1861-1865
FP
C.
5.50

2-3-75

Junior College District of St. Louis
Library
4386 Lindell Boulevard
St. Louis 8, Missouri

PRINTED IN U.S.A.

INVENTORY 1985

TURBULENT PARTNERSHIP
MISSOURI AND THE UNION
1861-1865

Missouri in 1860

TURBULENT PARTNERSHIP
MISSOURI AND THE UNION
1861-1865

William E. Parrish

With an Introduction by

Robert L. D. Davidson

President, Westminster College

UNIVERSITY OF MISSOURI PRESS
COLUMBIA, MISSOURI

Publication of this book
has been aided by the Ford Foundation program
to support publication,
through university presses, of work in the
humanities and social sciences

Copyright 1963 by

THE CURATORS OF THE
UNIVERSITY OF MISSOURI

*Library of Congress Catalog
Card Number 63-8072*

Printed and bound in the United States of America

For

KAYE

Acknowledgments

WITHOUT the generous assistance of numerous others, this book could never have been written. The staffs of the Manuscripts Division of the Library of Congress, the National Archives, the State Historical Society of Missouri, the Missouri Historical Society, and the Reeves Library of Westminster College have courteously rendered aid in the search for materials. A grant from the summer faculty research funds made available to Westminster College by the Danforth Foundation enabled me to spend a profitable summer in Washington. The pictures and map which accompany this study were made available by the State Historical Society of Missouri from its large collection of Missouriana. The excerpts from *Lincoln and the Civil War in the Diaries and Letters of John Hay,* edited by Tyler Dennett, are reprinted by permission of Dodd, Mead and Company (Copyright 1939 by Dodd, Mead & Company, Inc.).

Special thanks are due Professor James L. Bugg, Jr., of the University of Missouri, at whose suggestion this study was originally begun and under whose guidance the initial research was done; Professor Lewis E. Atherton, of the University of Missouri, who made numerous helpful criticisms at early stages of the project; Dr. Richard S. Brownlee, of the State Historical Society of Missouri, who read and criticized the entire manuscript and who, over the years, has exchanged numerous helpful conversations on Missouri's problems during the Civil War; and Dr. Robert L. D. Davidson, President of Westminster College, whose help in certain areas of research and whose constant interest in this project have been invaluable.

My final word of thanks goes to my wife, Kaye, without whose unfailing help and patience this work could never have been completed.

Fulton, Missouri
November, 1962

WILLIAM E. PARRISH

Contents

Contents

Illustrations

Introduction

JOHN WOOLMAN, writing of the Iroquois in 1761, made an observation of merit. As he recounted the histories of intertribal conflict he was "thinking of the innumerable afflictions which the proud, fierce spirit produceth in the world, also on the toils and fatigues of warriors in travelling over mountains and deserts; on their miseries and distresses when far from home and wounded by their enemies . . . of the restless, unquiet state of mind of those who live in this spirit . . . of the grinding squalor of those in the conquered areas; of those innocent who suffer the conflict about them; and the hatred which mutually grows up in the minds of their children."

Missouri in the Civil War was the stage for many plays and a multitude of roles. A slave state with considerable Whig leanings and the heritage of a thirty-year senator strongly Unionist, its people were largely Southerners. Yet it was in the throes of developing into a strong industrial and commercial economy with new railroad routes challenging the traditional Mississippi and Missouri waterways and with new citizens who "knew not the fathers" in the South. Hence, when men were faced with the choice much easier made in states to the south or north, Missouri became at once a loyal state, a state in the Confederacy, a battleground, invaded territory, a staging area, under military occupation, and a region devastated by guerrilla fighting and retaliation.

Professor Parrish has gathered for us here the stage settings and has picked out the various roles. With pressures from many sides—old friends, old loyalties, old customs—the hero tried to maintain his balance. A man who loved the Union but still wanted to preserve his state's institutions and character, Hamilton R. Gamble was willing to lend a hand to put down the rebellion but resisted the efforts to put the state under martial law, to deprive men of their rightful property (slaves), and to limit their constitutional rights. Yet, as Woolman knew so well, the passions of conflict brought with them the rise of the extremists; the attempt to maintain an even keel was impossible in the end.

Perhaps it is easier to understand if we attempt to play a role ourselves in this contumacious setting. Would you be a St. Louis shipper whose river trade with Memphis and New Orleans was your livelihood? Or a newly arrived German merchant, thrifty, educated, and despising tyranny in any form, of which slavery to him was an example? Would you choose to be a Boone or Callaway planter descended from Virginia and Kentucky planters? Or a Clay County farmer receiving the dreadful shock of the raiders from Kansas? How about the role of a former governor willing to stay with the Union so long as he was not required to fight against his Southern brethren?

The extremists were early in the minority. Jackson, Reynolds, Atchison, Price, and the rest of those who eventually chose the route of the secessionist were always a minority, and eventually, of course, were practically pushed off stage. Drake, Brown, Fletcher, and those whose Unionist sympathies drove them into the Radical camp with the sword of vengeance and the clean sweep of the new broom were, with the success of the Union, apparent victors. But the Blairs, the Rollinses, the Gambles, and the others who remained loyal to their old flag and at the same time loyal to the principles of justice and tolerance were the ultimate winners. For even as they were forced to the wings by the performance of the Radicals, they became the backbone of the return of moderation and common sense to the state.

A few examples of the "pressures" will suffice. In defense of a St. Louisan charged with disloyalty some contemporaries wrote: ". . . in Missouri it is exceedingly difficult to determine what is, and what is not loyalty, according to any standard. The late governor of the state [Gamble]—than whom a purer patriot never lived—was bitterly denounced as 'disloyal,' and the spotless beauty of his Christian character could not protect him, even in his grave, against cruel calumny and relentless detraction. The late Commanding General of the Department of Missouri [Schofield] was constantly declared to be 'disloyal'; members of the Cabinet at Washington are proclaimed, every day among us, to be 'disloyal,' and the President of the United States himself is charged with being a 'rebel sympathizer,' who ought to have been hanged long ago."

Attorney-General Edward Bates was told in 1862: "The Grand Jury now in session is disposed to indict a great number of persons—it is difficult to restrain them—and I think they are disposed to carry the matter too far. . . ." Bates, in reply, wrote: ". . . you will understand my policy in the matter of prosecutions. I would use indictments *for treason* sparingly—especially against small men. There are some magistrates, however, who are not now in the state, and may never be there again, against whom a pending indictment for treason might be made useful in the future. Such (for instance only) as Generals Polk and Pillow of Tennessee, Pike of Arkansas, Van Dorn, Clark, Parsons, Reid, etc., of Missouri, of course, not forgetting Price, Jackson, Thompson . . . when the war is mainly over it may be a good thing to have that hold upon them wherever they may be."

One more line from the players sets the tone of things perhaps more clearly. Written by a Confederate soldier in 1865, this verse speaks much:

Who shall portray the deep disgust
  Missourians feel when they are told
To trail their banners in the dust,
  Lay down their arms and be paroled?
Yield to the Yankee, Oh! that thought,
  Tears madly through my 'wildered head,
Give up the cause for which we fought,
  And humbly be base slaves for bread.

No more interesting stage is prepared for us than this period in Missouri. Rocked by fratricidal and internecine strife, governed either by a government in exile or one scarcely legitimate, belabored by intolerant military leaders or vacillation in policy from Washington, it was indeed a "turbulent partnership."

ROBERT L. D. DAVIDSON

1

Missouri Decides for the Union

THE ELECTION of 1860 was one of the most crucial in the history of the United States. As a result of the passage of the Kansas-Nebraska Act six years earlier, the winds of political fortune had begun to shift rapidly. The question of whether or not slavery should be allowed to extend into the territories had been in the air since 1820. Now it gained force and direction.

The dominant Democratic party, which had controlled the national government during most of the past thirty years, had tried at first to avoid the issue of slavery expansion and then had straddled it with the Compromise of 1850. After 1854, however, the party had come increasingly under the sway of its militant Southern minority. This minority felt the Compromise had been betrayed by the passage of Northern personal liberty laws. Strong in their desire to make Kansas a slave state, they had accepted the Dred Scott decision gladly as their justification for attempting to bring the party into line through a strong proslavery plank in the 1860 platform. Failing in this, many of them bolted the regular party to nominate candidates on their own platform. The once mighty Democratic party split asunder, North and South. The supporters of Senator Stephen A. Douglas assumed control of the regular party organization and nominated their hero for the Presidency on a platform advocating popular sovereignty as the solution to the slavery question in the territories; the Southern dissidents nominated Vice-President John C. Breckinridge.

The ruptured Democratic party of 1860 faced formidable opposition. The rapidly growing Republican party, emerging swiftly on the currents of Northern discontent over the Kansas-Nebraska Act, owed its existence to its strong stand against the extension of slavery. The party had made steady strides forward in the heavily populated North during the past four years, and it now stood in a highly challenging position. With a broadened platform promising many things to many people, especially in the economic realm, it nominated Abraham Lincoln for the Presidency. Relatively unknown until recently, Lincoln had gained considerable stature in the 1858 Illinois senatorial race, although he had lost it to Douglas.

The old Whig party, seldom in its history able to take a united stand on any given issue, had at last foundered on the treacherous rock of the Kansas-Nebraska Act. Its diverse membership left the sinking ship to join whatever other party better suited the immediate interests of each. Many former Whigs along the border and some few elsewhere were unable to accept the strong antislavery views of the Republicans. Not wishing to join forces with their ancient Democratic enemies, they found a haven in the American, or Know-Nothing, party with its antiforeign appeal. The new targets provided by this party allowed them to concentrate on something other than the slavery question, and in the heightening tensions of 1860, these old-line Whigs transformed the organization into the Constitutional Union party. To minimize the slavery issue along typical Whig lines the new party adopted the vague slogan, "The Union, the Constitution, and the enforcement of the laws." It nominated for the Presidency Senator John Bell, an old-line Whig from Tennessee with a wide following along the border.

Missouri, too, had been in the midst of political turmoil during the 1850's. Long the fief of Thomas Hart Benton and his Democratic organization, the state stood at the gateway to the West. When Benton took a strong stand against the extension of slavery into the new territories in 1849, the Missouri Democratic party broke into quarreling factions. With the help of the proslavery Whigs in the legislature, the anti-Benton Democrats ousted "Old Bullion" from the United States Senate in 1851 and accepted a Whig in his place. The following year, the two factions patched up their quarrel sufficiently to elect a Democratic governor, Sterling Price, and with his help the anti-Benton forces secured control of the party machinery. "Old Bullion's" followers had sufficient strength in the legislature, however, to prevent the re-election of David R. Atchison, the anti-Benton leader and a strong proponent of slavery extension, to the Senate in 1854. A deadlocked legislature allowed this seat to remain vacant for two years. The final showdown between Benton and his enemies came in 1856 when "Old Bullion" ran a poor third for the governorship on an Independent Democratic ticket. Following this defeat, his followers either drifted back into the regular Democratic party or moved into the meager ranks of the Republicans.

With a strong majority in the legislature, the Democrats chose James S. Green, a staunch anti-Benton ex-congressman, to fill the Senate seat left vacant two years earlier. They also sent their newly elected governor, Trusten Polk, to Washington to fill a regular vacancy in that body. This move necessitated a special gubernatorial election in 1857 which developed into a hotly contested battle. All of the anti-Democratic elements united behind James S. Rollins, who came within 329 votes of wresting the governorship from the majority party.

The Democrats suffered their most serious losses, as a result of their quarreling, in the Congressional races in the 1850's. Whereas the Whigs had been able to elect only two congressmen prior to 1850, after that date seven of their number secured election to the national House of Representatives from Missouri.

In addition, four Know-Nothings went to Congress from Missouri in this same period. Benton served one term in the House as a Missouri Compromise Democrat, and his chief disciple, Frank Blair, Jr., was elected in 1856 as a Free-Soiler from the St. Louis district. Invariably in the 1850's, Congressional races were three- or four-way affairs, with the Democratic forces split sufficiently to allow the opposition candidate to hold the balance of power and secure a plurality.

The 1860 Missouri Democratic convention met early in April, the proslavery element of the party still in firm control of the organization machinery. The convention nominated Claiborne F. Jackson, the party's state chairman, for the governorship, and Thomas C. Reynolds for lieutenant-governor. Both had been active leaders in the anti-Benton struggles. The platform strongly supported the Southern view that slavery could not be excluded from the territories either by Congress or by the territorial legislatures. The delegates chosen to attend the national Democratic convention at Charleston, South Carolina, later in the month were committed to this platform.

As he began his canvass early in the summer of 1860, Jackson found that he was being followed by Sample Orr, a farmer from Greene County who had announced his independent candidacy for the governorship. When Robert Wilson, the first choice of the Constitutional Union party, declined the nomination, Orr received the support of most of the group and became its candidate. Orr was a conservative thinker who advocated compromise in the same vague sense as did his national party. He proved a dogged if not well-known opponent. Jackson haughtily ignored Orr's challenge to debate the issues of the day, but he soon discovered the political unknown appearing at his rallies to address the people after he had finished. Gradually Orr gained ground as he preached the moderation many Missourians wanted to hear.

Jackson's most serious difficulty lay in the situation which had developed in the national Democratic canvass. Following the break in the party at Charleston and the subsequent nomination of two sets of rival candidates, Jackson found himself being pressed by both sides for an endorsement of their respective nominees. His natural proclivities were to the South. The state platform on which he had been nominated expressed the Southern stand on the slavery extension issue. Yet Jackson and Reynolds correctly surmised that having been nominated as regular Democrats it would be difficult for them to repudiate the nominees of the regular party on the national level with any hope of success. After much deliberation and consultation, both endorsed the Douglas ticket at a rally in Fayette early in July.

The Democratic State Central Committee promptly deposed the two men as the party's candidates on the ground that they had betrayed the state platform in endorsing Douglas. While continuing to sustain all of the other nominees for state office, of whose loyalty to the Southern cause they had no doubt, the committee nominated Hancock Jackson and Monroe M. Parsons as replacements for Jackson and Reynolds at the top of the ticket. The new choice for governor was a former occupant of that post and a cousin of Claiborne Jackson. A number of key Breckinridge men refused to accept this arrangement because of their fear that a party split would allow Orr to become governor. Led by popular Senator James S. Green and aided by the custom of holding the state election in August prior to the national balloting in November, they endorsed and actively campaigned for the Jackson-Reynolds ticket.

Their action saved the day for the regular Democratic nominees. Claiborne F. Jackson was chosen governor over Sample Orr by a vote of 74,446 to 66,583; Hancock Jackson ran a very poor third with only 11,416 votes, while James B. Gardenhire, the Republican candidate, garnered only 6,137. Most of the Republican strength centered around the St. Louis area with its strongly antislavery German population.

The results of the national election in Missouri seemed to justify Green and his followers in their stand. The vote for President in November was even closer than the count in August, but significantly it held to the same trend. Douglas barely carried the state by a margin of 429 votes (58,801 to 58,372) over Bell. The united pro-Southern Democrats produced 31,317 votes for Breckinridge, while Lincoln ran a poor fourth with 17,028. The outcome of this election clearly indicated that the great majority of Missourians were conservative and desired no extreme solution to the slavery question. Rather, they hoped for compromise and had difficulty choosing between the popular sovereignty of Stephen A. Douglas and the vague, middle-ground assurances of John Bell. The conservative strength in Missouri as represented by the Douglas-Bell vote amounted to 70.7 per cent of the total vote cast.[1]

The Twenty-first Missouri General Assembly convened at Jefferson City on December 31, 1860, in an atmosphere fraught with uncertainty because of the secession crisis. Interestingly enough, this body's membership did not reflect the voting in the recent gubernatorial and presidential elections. The Breckinridge Democrats dominated with sixty-two members in House and Senate as compared with forty-six Douglas Democrats, forty-four Constitutional Unionists, and thirteen Republicans. This alignment included fourteen holdover Breckinridge senators. Most of the other proslavery Democrats came from sparsely settled counties which enjoyed representation in the House equal to that of more heavily populated counties. Recognizing the need for at least nominal unity, the two branches of the Democratic party united on John McAfee of Shelby County, a pronounced proslavery Breckinridge Democrat, for speaker and elected him easily. In the upper house, one of the staunchest secession sympathizers in the state, Lieutenant-Governor Thomas C. Reynolds, presided.[2]

Five days after convening, the two houses in joint session witnessed the inauguration of Governor Claiborne F. Jackson. Although elected as a conservative Douglas Democrat, Governor Jackson in his inaugural address left little doubt as to where his real sympathies lay. He requested the legislature to convene a state convention to consider Missouri's relationship with the Union and stated his position on this question by affirming:

> The destiny of the slave-holding States of this Union is one and the same. . . . The identity, rather than the similarity, of their domestic institutions—their political principles and party usages—their common origin, pursuits, tastes, manners and customs—

> their territorial contiguity and intercommercial relations—all contribute to bind together in one brotherhood the States of the South and South-West. . . . Missouri, then, will in my opinion best consult her own interest, and the interest of the whole country, by a timely declaration of her determination to stand by her sister slave-holding States, in whose wrongs she participates, and with whose institutions and people she sympathizes.[3]

The new governor insisted that this did not necessarily foreshadow disunion, but he asserted that it did mean the time had come for the conflicting sectional views of the nation to be reconciled. In any compromise agreement the Northern states would have to make the greater concessions.

The next day Jackson's supporters introduced measures into the General Assembly which would give the Governor extraordinary powers in marshaling the forces of the state to meet any emergency which might arise. Despite pressure for speed, the legislature proceeded slowly. Time and again the compromise element moved successfully to delay and postpone. By the time the legislature adjourned on March 22, only one emergency measure had passed. This act removed the home rule of St. Louis over its police force and placed it under the control of a board of four commissioners appointed by the Governor, with the Mayor serving ex officio as a fifth member. The act provided that this board should have control of the volunteer militia of St. Louis, the sheriff, and "all other conservators of the peace." Jackson appointed three ardent pro-Southern men and one conservative to the board—a group which indicated its true sympathies in a number of ways in the weeks which followed.[4]

The major accomplishment of the legislature at this session was the calling of a state convention "to consider the then existing relations between the government of the United States, the people and governments of the different States, and the government and people of the State of Missouri; and to adopt such measures for vindicating the sovereignty of the

State and the protection of its institutions, as shall appear to them to be demanded." Little opposition to this proposition manifested itself once it had been amended to provide that should the action of the convention result in an ordinance of secession, that measure would be referred to a vote of the people. The citizens of Missouri would have to approve the ordinance of secession before it could become effective. Inclusion of this provision had been hotly contested in both houses before it prevailed by 17 to 15 in the Senate and by 81 to 40 in the House. The provision served as a check upon any rash decision by a group of delegates who might be swayed by the prevailing temper of a moment. Yet, few doubted that the people would support the convention should it decide for secession.[5]

Passage on January 18 of the bill to call a state convention came as no surprise. Most of the state's newspapers had been advocating it; their pages carried the resolutions of numerous meetings across the state supporting such a move. This interest in a convention did not indicate large-scale support of secession, but merely a desire that the issue be discussed fully and settled. The bill provided for a special election one month from the date of passage, with the convention scheduled to meet on February 28. Three delegates were to be chosen from each of the State's thirty-three senatorial districts.[6]

Campaign plans for the election of delegates began to take form even before the legislature passed its measure. Because such an early date was set for the election, little time existed for an extensive canvass. Missouri's weekly, and predominantly partisan, press barely managed to get out two or three issues on it. Three rather distinct groups soon emerged to contend for seats: the Unconditional Unionists, who came largely from the ranks of the antislavery Germans and their friends in St. Louis; the States' Rights or Anti-Submission men, who believed strongly in secession; and the Conditional Unionists (Constitutional Unionists in St. Louis), who occupied a broad range of middle ground opposing both secession and war in varying degrees, depending upon the circumstances.

Missourians felt keenly the gravity of their decision. The campaign did not run along partisan political lines. It attracted many candidates of substantial, conservative, business and professional backgrounds—men who would not ordinarily seek office. The *Missouri Republican* at St. Louis, probably the state's leading conservative newspaper, set the tone. It argued that secession constituted folly and would bring economic ruin upon the state. Pointing out that such a course would leave Missouri surrounded by free territory, the *Republican* indicated that this situation would provide a fine inducement for Missourians' slaves to run away. The most profitable use for Missouri slaves was the production of hemp, but a Southern free trade policy would destroy this industry. At the same time, the South did not have the capital to develop the mineral resources of the state. This could be done only by Eastern money—and only if Missouri stayed in the Union. Others took up this theme, and it became a major argument in the campaign.[7]

While the Confederacy inaugurated Jefferson Davis as its president at Montgomery on February 18, Missourians went to the polls to determine the future course of their state. Although there had been some fear of violence, particularly among the more radical German element, the election came off peacefully. The Unionists carried the day strongly. Some 110,000 votes were cast for both Conditional and Unconditional candidates, while the secessionists garnered only about 30,000. Indeed, reliable sources indicate that no avowed candidate of the States' Rights, or Anti-Submission, ticket secured election. Again Missourians had expressed their desire for a moderate course.

Of those elected, a fairly even distribution existed between Conditional and Unconditional Unionists. A large percentage had belonged to the Whig party in the 1850's or had supported Bell in the recent election. Only four known Republicans were chosen, all of whom were from St. Louis. Not a single Breckinridge

Democrat secured a seat, so far as is known.[8] Undoubtedly the results greatly disappointed many officials at Jefferson City.

The convention delegates assembled on Thursday, February 28, in the Cole County courthouse at Jefferson City. The General Assembly remained in session at the Capitol, a circumstance which prevented the convention from using those more auspicious quarters. Of the ninety-nine delegates, better than half were of Virginia or Kentucky descent; all but seventeen were natives of slave states. The group chose former Governor Sterling Price as president of the convention. He received the support of most of the Unionist elements; only a scattering of ultraconservative votes went to his opponent.

Once organized, the convention considered the quarters in which it found itself. There could be little doubt of their inadequacy for a group of this size and importance. Furthermore, many Unionists feared that if the convention continued in Jefferson City it might fall increasingly under the sway of the prosecession elements in the capital. Consequently, they prevailed on Samuel M. Breckinridge to telegraph the Mercantile Library Association of St. Louis for permission to use its facilities. Upon receiving the association's invitation and an offer from the Pacific Railroad to transport the delegates to St. Louis without charge, the Unionists made their move. William A. Hall of Randolph County introduced a resolution to adjourn the convention for the purpose of reconvening in St. Louis. In so doing, he contended that the courthouse provided inadequate quarters for discharging the business at hand. Assured by Breckinridge that the Mercantile Library afforded better facilities, including individual desks, the delegates resolved to recess over the weekend and reconvene in the new quarters the following Monday.[9]

While the eyes of most of the nation turned toward Washington for the inauguration of a new President on Monday, March 4, 1861, the delegates of the Missouri state convention were convening in the festively decorated chamber of the Mercantile Library Association at St. Louis. Here they were to determine their state's future relationship with the rest of the Union. A visitor entering the hall might have assumed that the room was the site of a patriotic rally: oversize American flags had been placed on either side of the chamber, and red, white, and blue bunting decorated the large alcove at the west end of the quarters leading into the anterooms. This assumption would have been strengthened when, as the meeting opened, a large American eagle was carried into the hall amid the applause of the delegates.[10]

With preliminaries accomplished, the convention settled to the business at hand. Hamilton R. Gamble of St. Louis introduced a resolution calling for a seven-man committee to prepare a report on the existing relations of Missouri and the Union. Debate revolved around the question of the size of such a committee. It was finally set at thirteen. The instructions to this group reflected the general antisecession feeling of the convention by asking them "to suggest guarantees for the future, as shall under it [the Union] be fraternal, permanent, and enduring."

The convention selected the committee members by ballot, with Gamble receiving a unanimous vote for the chairmanship. Henceforth, he was the dominant figure in the convention. Gamble, a prominent St. Louis attorney and former judge of the Missouri Supreme Court, was a conservative ex-Whig who had received the nomination of both Union tickets for a place in the convention. He was now sixty-two, older by at least ten years than any other member of the committee. From the very outset the strength of his personality manifested itself in their deliberations. He was determined that the committee's report should leave no doubt as to where Missouri stood.[11]

The convention meanwhile settled down to a round of speechmaking. Luther J. Glenn of Georgia requested permission to address the convention. One of several commissioners from the newly created Confederate States to the states of the Upper South, Glenn had been sent to help persuade these slaveholding sisters that their best interests lay in joining the Confederacy. He was freshly arrived from Jefferson City where he had been given a warm reception by the legislature.

A lengthy and lively debate ensued as to whether Glenn should be accorded the privilege of speaking. Sample Orr sarcastically inquired whether the Georgian came as a commissioner or an ambassador. If he came in the latter capacity, Orr thought Glenn should go to Washington, as the states could not officially receive foreign diplomats. If he came as a commissioner, the delegates need not hear him, since the United States Constitution forbade any state to enter into a treaty or alliance with other states. A majority decided that the Georgian should be heard, however, inasmuch as his message pertained to the work of the convention.

Beginning with Missouri's struggle for admission to the Union, Glenn retraced historically the bitterness engendered over the years by the antislavery movement. He denounced President Lincoln and the Republicans for their firm stand against slavery expansion. Georgia, he reported, had determined on "peaceable separation" because she believed the differences between North and South could never be reconciled. He invited Missouri to join Georgia and the other Southern states in their stand, and then retired amid a mixed reaction of applause and hissing.[12]

The Committee on Federal Relations reported through Chairman Gamble on March 9. It submitted several resolutions for the consideration of the convention. By far the most important of these was the first, which firmly announced: "At present there is no adequate cause to impel Missouri to dissolve her connections with the Federal Union, but on the contrary she will labor for such an adjustment of existing troubles as will gain the peace, as well as the rights and equality of all the states." Supplementing this, a second resolution pledged Missouri to labor for an adjustment of the differences between the states and reaffirmed the devotion of her people to "the institutions of our country."

The committee approved the Crittenden Compromise, which Congress had just rejected, and urged the state legislatures to take proper steps for calling a national convention to amend the federal constitution so as to guarantee slavery. In this latter regard, the committee recommended that the convention elect delegates to the Border States Convention called by Kentucky. Still another resolution strongly urged that neither the federal government nor the seceded states take military action to redress their grievances against each other.[13]

Gamble made a strong plea for the proposals and indicated quite plainly that they were primarily his work. "I am responsible for every word and sentence in the report, for I wrote it," he affirmed. And in the ten days of debate which followed, he guided the report through the convention with the skill and adroitness of a veteran floor manager.

Much of the debate centered around two amendments. The first came from George Y. Bast of Montgomery County. He sought to pledge Missouri "to take a firm and decided stand in favor of her sister slave States," should the North decline a settlement of the issues on the basis of the Crittenden Compromise and the other border states then secede. Defeated 70 to 23, the amendment attracted the support of many of those who later went South. Most of the opposition developed from an unwillingness by the majority to assent to anything which might appear as a threat or ultimatum to the North.[14]

Thomas Shackelford of Howard County proposed the second amendment, which advocated that federal troops be withdrawn from "the forts within the borders of the seceding States where there is danger of collision between the State and Federal troops." Ultimately this amendment was adopted, 54 to 39, with Gamble's approval, to become the only amendment of substance to the entire report.[15]

When the final vote came on the different resolutions, the convention displayed near unanimity. Only George Y. Bast voted against the first resolution, while the amended fifth met opposition from six members primarily because of the Shackelford proviso.[16]

In this manner, the people of Missouri spoke in favor of the Union and of compromise through their chosen delegates. Fortunately for the state the convention did not adjourn sine die, but set the third Monday in December, 1861, as the date for a second session. At the same time, it established a committee of seven members, a majority of whom could call the convention into session at any time should an emergency arise prior to the time scheduled for the next meeting. With its work completed, the convention adjourned on March 22.[17]

2

Union Military Strength Asserts Itself

IN THE southern part of St. Louis stood the United States arsenal. Within its walls were stored 60,000 stand of arms and various other materials of war. Throughout the winter, the arsenal had been marked as a prime military target by the secessionists should Missouri withdraw from the Union. It appeared that taking the facility would be a rather easy task; Major William H. Bell, the arsenal commander, was a Southern sympathizer who had agreed to hand the area over to state troops if Missouri seceded. Although this officer was replaced late in January because of the alertness of some of the Union men in St. Louis, it soon became evident that his successor also sympathized with the Southern cause.[1]

Both the Unionists and the secessionists were recruiting military companies in St. Louis. The latter organized the "minute men," who were mustered under military law and incorporated into the state militia of the district. The Union men, under the leadership of Frank Blair, established the Home Guards and set up a Union Committee of Public Safety to supervise their organization.

Blair, who had served as Thomas Hart Benton's chief lieutenant during the political struggles of the 1850's, had taken the lead in organizing the Republican party in Missouri toward the end of that decade. A close friend of Abraham Lincoln, he had just been elected to Congress from Missouri's first district. Fully aware of Governor Jackson's inclinations, Blair strongly believed that St. Louis, with its German population and the arsenal nearby, was the key to maintaining Missouri for the Union and planned accordingly.[2]

On February 6, a company of United States regular troops arrived in St. Louis from Fort Riley, Kansas, to reinforce the arsenal. The importance of this event lay not in the eighty men added to the strength of that area but in the presence of their commander, Captain Nathaniel Lyon. Few Missourians realized the significance of Lyon's arrival at the time. During the next six months, this outspoken career officer was destined to play a major role in the struggle to keep Missouri in the Union, for Nathaniel Lyon, more than any other one man, was responsible for driving Governor Claiborne F. Jackson and his followers into exile. Thereby he brought civil war to Missouri, with all its attendant strife and bloodshed.

The new arrival, a New Englander by birth, was an ardent antislavery Unionist. While stationed at Fort Riley, he had witnessed with great revulsion the attempts of Missourians to impose slavery on Kansas in the 1850's. Lyon had participated in the Kansas Free-Soil movement as actively as his position allowed. Less than two weeks before his transfer to St. Louis he had revealed his inner feelings with prophetic vision in a letter to a friend:

> It is no longer useful to appeal to reason but to the sword, and trifle no longer in senseless wrangling. I shall not hesitate to rejoice at the triumph of my principles, though this triumph may involve an issue in which I certainly expect to expose and very likely lose my life. I would a thousand times rather incur this, than recall the result of our Presidential election. We shall rejoice, though in martyrdom if need be.[3]

Lyon met with Frank Blair and the Union Safety Committee soon after his arrival. He realized that Major Peter V. Hagner, who commanded the arsenal, had secessionist leanings. Learning that, technically, he outranked Hagner (whose commission as major was by brevet), Lyon at once laid plans to have himself placed in command of the arsenal. This he hoped to accomplish through Blair's influence with Lincoln, once the change in administrations took place.

Lyon eventually obtained his objective with Blair's help in mid-March. Then new complications arose as he found his plans for control of the arsenal restricted by Brigadier General William S. Harney, the commander of the Department of the West at St. Louis. Under Harney's interpretation of the War Department directive, Lyon commanded the men at the arsenal, but Hagner continued to have charge of the buildings, arms, ammunition, and other stores. In order to obtain any matériel, Lyon had to secure a requisition from Harney.[4]

Thus matters in Missouri and in St. Louis stood when, on April 12, the Confederates opened fire on Fort Sumter in Charleston Harbor. President Lincoln promptly issued a call for 75,000 men to put down the rebellion. The Secretary of War notified Governor Jackson that Missouri's quota was 4,000 men, but the state's chief executive refused to provide a single man to the nation's forces on the grounds that they would no doubt be used to "make war" upon the people of the seceded states. The Governor termed Lincoln's request "illegal, unconstitutional, and revolutionary; in its objects inhuman and diabolical."[5] Numerous meetings were held throughout the state to draft resolutions supporting Jackson's action. Quite probably the majority of Missourians agreed with the Governor's stand. They did so, not from any desire to aid the South, but simply because they wished to avoid involvement in any conflict.[6]

Frank Blair returned to St. Louis from Washington on the same day that Governor Jackson issued his stinging refusal. He brought with him a War Department order giving Lyon 5,000 stand of arms from the arsenal, to be used in arming loyal citizens. Upon learning of Jackson's action, Blair wired the Secretary of War for authority to muster into service the Home Guards of St. Louis. This levy would quickly fill the state's quota.[7]

Rumors floated around St. Louis that the secessionists were laying plans to seize the arsenal. Without consulting Harney, Lyon anxiously wrote Governor Richard Yates of Illinois on April 16. He suggested that the Governor communicate with Washington about holding in readiness for use at the arsenal the six regiments that Illinois was to furnish the Union cause. He further recommended that Yates requisition a large supply of arms from the arsenal, thereby preventing their falling into unfriendly hands.[8]

Before the Governor of Illinois could secure the necessary orders, swiftly moving events had considerably changed the situation at St. Louis. The fear of an attack prompted Lyon to send patrols beyond the walls of the arsenal to sound an alert should secessionists attempt a night raid. The presence of patrols in the streets of the city caused the pro-Jackson police board of St. Louis to protest to General Harney. He not only ordered the practice stopped, but fearful of inciting the Southern element in the city to an explosion, withheld permission for Lyon to distribute the arms placed at his disposal under the requisition which Blair had brought from Washington.[9]

Following his telegram of April 17 offering to muster troops, Blair wrote Secretary of War Simon Cameron a lengthy letter questioning Harney's general fitness to serve as mustering officer. Blair did not question the General's loyalty, yet he feared that Harney might find himself in an embarrassing position because of his Southern background and Missouri connections. He consequently suggested that it might be wise to transfer the department commander to a less sensitive post and replace him with General John E. Wool. When, later that same day, Harney restricted Lyon's movements and use of arms, Blair no longer had any doubts that the General had outstayed his usefulness. Blair dispatched a special emissary to Washington to accomplish Harney's removal and implored his brother Montgomery, Lincoln's Postmaster-General, to aid the cause.[10]

Action came quickly. The War Department issued orders on April 21 relieving Harney of his post and calling him to Washington for consultation. At the same time, a dispatch hummed over the wire to Lyon, who now temporarily assumed command of the forces around St. Louis. He was now authorized to muster into United States service the four regiments which the Governor had refused to furnish.[11]

With the departure of Harney, Lyon and Frank Blair mustered the Home Guards, marched them to the arsenal, and distributed arms to them. In Illinois, Governor Yates had received orders to send two or three regiments of militia to the St. Louis arsenal. The circumstances at St. Louis having changed, however, the Illinois troops were kept east of the Mississippi to prevent what might be interpreted by Missouri secessionists as an invasion.

Early on the evening of April 25, Captain James H. Stokes of the Illinois militia appeared at the arsenal. He carried Governor Yates's requisition for arms and ammunition for 10,000 men. The purpose of his visit was well suspected, and Stokes found quite a crowd of civilians gathered at the arsenal gates when he arrived. In order to decoy them, Lyon sent a few boxes of old flintlock muskets up to the levee as if he were preparing to load them on a steamboat. The crowd followed, seized the muskets, and carried them away to hiding places in the city, believing they had a quantity of serviceable weapons.

Shortly before midnight, another steamboat was warped to the levee in front of the arsenal, and Lyon and Stokes quickly loaded it with the requisitioned arms. The latter suggested that it might be wise to send the arsenal's surplus arms over into Illinois. Lyon, ever fearful of attack, readily fell in with the idea. Thus, 11,000 additional stand of arms were taken from the arsenal without requisition or authorization for shipment across the river. The hastily loaded boat proved so heavy, however, that it stuck in the mud along the levee, and it was necessary to shift a part of the cargo to the stern before it could proceed to Alton on the east bank of the Mississippi. From there the arms were transferred to a train and carried inland.[12]

Now in full command of the situation at the arsenal, Lyon began preparing it for a possible assault or siege. On April 30, he hurriedly dispatched a message to The Adjutant General at Washington, informing him that volunteers were still being mustered and would be until countermanding orders arrived. "The State is doubtless getting ready to attack Government troops with artillery," he warned. He had sent four companies to occupy buildings outside the arsenal "which the secessionists had intended to occupy themselves, and upon which they openly avowed they would plant siege batteries to reduce this place."

That same day extraordinary orders were being cut in Washington at the instigation of the President. These authorized Lyon to enlist under his personal command up to 10,000 men "for the protection of the peaceable inhabitants of Missouri." They also gave him permission to proclaim martial law in St. Louis if he and the Union Safety Committee deemed it necessary. This action owed its inception to the Blairs, who had been appealing for more authority. General Winfield Scott endorsed it with one terse sentence: "It is revolutionary times, and therefore I do not object to the irregularity of this."[13]

Governor Jackson had not been idle. On the same day that he refused to furnish the United States with troops, the Governor conferred with leading secessionists at St. Louis. Foremost among them stood Major General Daniel M. Frost, commander of the state militia for the St. Louis district. Frost previously had outlined a plan for a militia encampment overlooking the arsenal, from which he could make his preparations to take that place. The Governor considered this plan quite audacious. Lacking artillery sufficient for the task, Frost suggested dispatching envoys to the Confederacy to obtain clandestine aid. Others at the meeting endorsed the idea, whereupon Jackson sent two militia officers to Jefferson Davis, requesting siege guns and mortars for an assault on the arsenal. A similar request went to Virginia, which had just seceded.[14] Jackson followed this action publicly, five days later, with a proclamation calling the General Assembly into special session early in May "to place the State in a proper attitude of defense." At the same time he ordered the state militia to assemble in their respective military districts for six days of instruction and drill, as provided by law.[15]

Upon learning that the arms which they had hoped to capture had been removed from the arsenal, state officials ordered the quartermaster general of the militia to St. Louis to secure all the arms and ammunition he could find. He acquired several hundred hunting rifles, seventy tons of gunpowder, and other miscellaneous equipment, which he shipped to Jefferson City. State militia already had seized without authorization the small federal arsenal at Liberty on the western border. Here they found four brass guns and 1,500 stand of arms.

Prompt assurances of aid came from the Confederacy. Jefferson Davis wrote Jackson on April 23 that "our power to supply you with ordnance is far short of the will to serve you." He directed that two 12-pound howitzers and two 32-pound guns be dispatched to Frost at St. Louis to aid in taking the arsenal; he agreed that this was an important target. "We look anxiously and hopefully for the day when the star of Missouri shall be added to the constellation of the Confederate States of America," Davis assured the Governor.[16] When the Confederacy sought a Missouri regiment for service in Virginia a few days later, however, Jackson found it necessary to demur. "Missouri, you know, is yet under the tyranny of Lincoln's Government, so far, at least, as forms go." To soften his refusal, he informed the Confederate Secretary of War that he felt confident the legislature would soon give him authority to act. If the Confederacy could arm them, Missouri would eventually put 100,000 men in the field for the Southern cause. "We are using every means to arm our people," the Governor asserted, "and, until we are better prepared, must move cautiously."[17]

Lyon's disposal of the arms from the arsenal removed Frost's object for encamping at St. Louis. Nevertheless, the militia commander went ahead with his plans. On Monday, May 6, he established Camp Jackson, named in honor of the Governor, in a wooded valley known as Lindell Grove just west of Grand Avenue. The hills overlooking the arsenal, where he had intended to camp originally, had long since been occupied by Lyon. Realizing that Lyon's position effectively prevented the launching of any surprise attack, the secessionists, through their

St. Louis police board, formally demanded of Lyon that same Monday that he withdraw all United States troops from the buildings and grounds outside the arsenal. They sought to justify their demand on the grounds that these areas belonged to Missouri and that Lyon's occupation of them was usurpation. Lyon, of course, refused to accede to the demand, which ended the matter.[18] Thus, he took the step which rendered Camp Jackson virtually harmless so far as accomplishing its original purpose.

Two days after the establishment of Camp Jackson, the arms and ammunition which the Governor had requested from the Confederacy arrived. They had been procured from the federal arsenal at Baton Rouge when the Confederates seized that post. They had been brought up river to St. Louis in boxes of various sizes marked "marble Tamaroa." Meeting the boat as it docked that Wednesday evening, militia officers quickly unloaded the "marble" and took it to Camp Jackson, where the boxes remained unopened.[19]

Lyon now decided that he must capture Camp Jackson to thwart an attack by Frost. The ridiculousness of this idea will readily be seen when it is remembered that, with the removal of the arms to Illinois, Frost no longer had any reason for attacking the arsenal; the militia had but 700 men against Lyon's 10,000; the location of Camp Jackson and Lyon's occupancy of the heights overlooking the arsenal made it impossible for Frost to make a surprise move against that post; had the militia made an attack, they could have expected little help from the Confederacy, for neither Arkansas nor Tennessee, the nearest Southern states, had yet seceded. On the other hand, Union forces in Illinois, Iowa, and Kansas could have moved quickly into Missouri, had they been needed.

Learning of the arrival of the guns, however, Lyon decided that he could afford no further delay. Around four o'clock on the afternoon of Thursday, May 9, the members of the Union Safety Committee received notes requesting them to meet with the Commander at seven. When they arrived, Lyon outlined his proposal and sought their acquiescence. He told them that he had toured Camp Jackson that afternoon in an open carriage, disguised as Frank Blair's blind mother-in-law, and had seen considerable activity. The loyalties of the camp were indicated by the small Confederate flags which flew from some of the tentpoles, and the names of two streets in the camp's layout—"Davis" and "Beauregard" avenues. The meeting continued until midnight while a storm raged outside. Not all of the committee members were convinced of the legality of the move. When Lyon stressed that the arrival of stolen armaments could not be ignored, they agreed. But they proposed that the Commander first get a writ of replevin for government property and serve it on Frost. A vote was finally taken; four of the six members sided with Lyon. Unhappy over the outcome of the vote, one of the dissidents, Samuel T. Glover, returned to his law office, where he prepared a writ which he delivered to the United States marshal with the instruction to take it to Lyon. When that officer went to the arsenal the next morning, he was denied admittance, so that Glover's legal device remained unused.[20]

Friday, May 10, 1861, was to become one of the most significant dates in Missouri history. Early that morning, a letter arrived at the arsenal from General Frost: he had heard that Lyon planned an attack upon Camp Jackson; he hoped that the rumors were unfounded; he denied that his camp had been set up for other than lawful purposes. Lyon refused to receive this message. That afternoon he moved out with his men against Camp Jackson. Surrounding the area, Lyon demanded Frost's surrender within one-half hour on the ground that the camp represented a threat to the United States Government.

Frost had no alternative except certain destruction. He quickly complied—though not without protest. The Union forces placed the militia under arrest and marched them out of camp. A crowd which had gathered along the road to watch the procedure soon became unmanageable. They began throwing rocks and brickbats with cries of "Damn the Dutch!" and "Hurrah for Jeff Davis!" A shot came from the crowd; a soldier fell dead; an officer gave the command to return fire. In the ensuing melee, twenty-eight persons were killed, and many others fell wounded. In subsequent investigation of the event, Lyon disclaimed any responsibility for this incident.[21] Regardless of the instigator, war had come to Missouri.

Terror quickly spread among the secessionists in St. Louis. That night the streets were filled with rioting, angry men. Uriel Wright, one of the foremost opponents of secession at the recent state convention, stirringly addressed a great throng from the steps of the Planters' House: "If Unionism means such atrocious deeds as have been witnessed in St. Louis, I am no longer a Union man." A mob formed and began a march on the offices of the *Missouri Democrat,* the newspaper organ of the Union committee. A platoon of thirty policemen blocked their way with fixed bayonets. The mob moved to the *Anzeiger des Westens* building, which housed the German press. Here, too, they found police and in addition, a regiment of Home Guards to thwart their plans. Police and troops could not be everywhere, however, and rioting continued throughout the night.[22]

At Jefferson City, the General Assembly had convened on May 2, pursuant to the call of the Governor. It had accomplished little by the tenth of the month because of the obstructionist tactics of the more adamant Union members. On that sultry Friday afternoon it had under consideration the military bill which would give the Governor almost absolute power over the state militia. This force was to include every able-bodied man in Missouri. There seemed little prospect of action.

Into this stalemate rushed Claiborne F. Jackson toward evening with his excited announcement of the capture of Camp Jackson. After recovering from their initial shock, the members of the legislature pushed through the military bill and other legislation which the Governor had been trying to get adopted since the beginning of January. Among the bills passed were finance measures switching funds from the state's charitable institutions and schools to the militia. The legislature authorized a loan of $1,000,000 from Missouri's banks as well as the issuance of $1,000,000 in state bonds.

When later word from St. Louis indicated that Frank Blair and three regiments of Germans were on their way to Jefferson City, real panic set in. The legislators armed themselves to the teeth while continuing their session. Governor Jackson sent officers out along the railway to St. Louis with orders to destroy the Gasconade and Osage river bridges, if necessary, to obstruct the advance. Although the defenders found no enemy, part of the bridge over the Osage River was destroyed in the excitement.[23]

In the midst of this confusion, General Harney returned from Washington to resume command of the department. He had had quite an adventurous time during his absence from Missouri. The Confederates captured his east-bound train at Harpers Ferry, Virginia, and took Harney to Richmond in the hope of persuading him to join their cause. When he declined in emphatic fashion, the Confederates released him. He continued his trip to Washington, where he persuaded General Scott, a close personal friend, and the War Department that his firm but conciliatory policy would keep Missouri in the Union. This assurance, with his recent stand at Richmond, brought his reinstatement.[24]

On May 13, two days after his arrival in St. Louis, Harney issued a proclamation denouncing the military bill just passed by the General Assembly. He approved the capture of Camp Jackson by the federal forces and promised to maintain order within the city. Gradually the terror subsided. Although avoiding a declaration of martial law, Harney took possession of the city with troops and sent a request to General Scott for 10,000 additional stand of arms for issuance to "reliable Union men." Harney also asked that the governors of Minnesota and Iowa be directed to furnish him 9,000 reinforcements.[25]

Despite General Harney's official approval, the Camp Jackson affair was in fact a colossal blunder. Instead of suppressing secessionist sentiment, the move strengthened it. Before the action at the camp, the state government had little chance of removing Missouri from the Union, notwithstanding all its grandiose ideas for doing so. After this incident, the possibility that the state's star would shine in the Confederate flag became much greater, for the action at Camp Jackson drove many Conditional Unionists into the secession camp. Uriel Wright's shift in allegiance has been mentioned already. Among others of prominence swayed by this event were Sterling Price, former governor and the president of the state convention, and Congressman John B. Clark of Fayette. Both men hastened to Jefferson City and offered their services to the Governor.

Under the persuasion of Lieutenant-Governor Reynolds, Jackson appointed Price as Major General of the new Missouri State Guard, provided for under the Military Act. Jackson had been distrustful of Price at first but yielded to Reynolds, who believed the former governor could furnish both military and political prestige to the new program. To complete the State Guard organization, the Governor announced the appointment of eight brigadier generals—one for each military district of the state—with orders to enroll the men of their respective districts at once. Already over 1,000 men from the surrounding countryside had gathered at Jefferson City, eager to be enrolled and mustered into the State Guard. Camped at the nearby fairgrounds, they were armed with the supplies gathered earlier at St. Louis and with the arms taken from the United States arsenal at Liberty.[26]

Much to the consternation of the conservatives, their ability to control affairs seemed about to vanish. Civil war appeared imminent within the state. In spite of the increasing threat of war, some of these men did not give up hope of maintaining Missouri's neutrality in the national struggle. They sent James E. Yeatman of St. Louis to Washington to outline their views to the President. A wire went to Hamilton R. Gamble, then near Philadelphia, imploring him to join Yeatman.

The two men secured an interview with Lincoln through Attorney-General Edward Bates. They presented a petition, largely the work of Gamble, which asked the President to call a board of inquiry to look into the rioting which had followed the capture of Camp Jackson. They also requested that regular federal troops be used in patrolling St. Louis rather than the German Home Guards, whom the general populace detested.[27] Lincoln agreed to take the matter under advisement, but when action was taken, the conservatives discovered that the President placed greater reliance upon the Blairs and their friends.

With the return of Harney to St. Louis, Lyon had been relegated once again to a subordinate position. All of his plans to squelch the secessionists became subject to the General's approval. Lyon's disgust at this turn of events found its way into a dispatch of May 12 to Adjutant General Lorenzo Thomas at Washington:

> It is with great delicacy and hesitancy that I take the liberty to observe that the energetic and necessary measures of day before yesterday . . . require persevering and consistent exertion to effect the object in view of anticipating combinations and measures of hostility against the General Government, and that the authority of General Harney under these circumstances embarrasses, in the most painful manner, the execution of the plans I had contemplated, and upon which the safety and welfare of the Government, as I conceive, so much depend. . . .[28]

Without waiting to see what course Harney might take, Frank Blair sent his long-time agent, Franklin A. Dick, to Washington to press for the General's removal a second time. Dick emphasized Harney's Southern background as being prejudicial to his taking a strong stand at this crucial moment, and he hinted that a number of the General's relatives in St. Louis had become avowed secessionists. Dick requested a brigadier general's commission for Lyon, who had been elected to that rank by the Missouri volunteers whom he had mustered. In all of this, the Blair forces pressed for a free hand for Lyon to carry out the suppression of secession sentiment.

Dick arrived in Washington at about the same time as the conservative Yeatman and Gamble, who obviously opposed any coercive policy such as Lyon apparently had in mind. These conflicting views precipitated a division in the Cabinet over what should be done. Attorney-General Bates, a conservative St. Louis lawyer and Gamble's brother-in-law, sided strongly with the conciliationists in seeking the retention of Harney. Postmaster-General Montgomery Blair backed his brother. Secretary of War Simon Cameron apparently had some reservations about Lyon's competency for a full command, but Dick and Blair overcame these with the subtle argument that Lyon alone could save Missouri.[29]

In the end Lincoln decided, with some reservations, to go along with the Blairs. The War Department prepared an order on May 16 removing Harney a second time and granting him an indefinite leave of absence. The order was transmitted to the Postmaster-General for forwarding to his brother with instructions that it be held in abeyance for the time being. It was to be delivered only if, in the younger Blair's judgment, Harney's removal seemed absolutely necessary.

To make sure that Frank Blair could have no misunderstanding of his desires in the matter, Lincoln wrote him two days later of his doubts as to the propriety of the order. The President revealed that his misgivings had increased the more he pondered the affair. He feared that the Administration might be accused of vacillation, and that the move would "dissatisfy a good many who otherwise would be quiet." In all of this he continued to trust the Blairs, for he closed by stating: "Still if, in your judgment it is *indispensable* let it be so."[30]

Frank Blair received the President's letter on May 20. That same day a special messenger arrived with the order for Harney's removal and a cover letter from the Postmaster-General. These communications had been held up to await the drafting of a second order—one from the Secretary of War appointing Lyon as Brigadier General of Missouri Volunteers.[31]

While these events had been transpiring, the conservatives had arranged a meeting between the federal and state military commanders in an effort to effect a truce. Held at St. Louis on May 21, the meeting resulted in the Harney-Price agreement by which the former pledged (in effect) that the federal government would respect the neutrality of the state. Both governments were to help maintain peace. Price was to have active control, with Harney's troops being used as a reserve force when needed outside St. Louis.

General Harney accompanied the printing of the agreement with a proclamation in which he called upon the people "to observe good order, and respect the rights of their fellow-citizens, and give them the assurance of protection and security in the most ample manner." Three days later Price ordered all troops at Jefferson City to return home to be organized by the commanders of their respective districts as the law required. Only one company was exempted from this order. It remained on duty at the capital.[32]

The promulgation of the Harney-Price agreement caused the Unionists in St. Louis considerable alarm. Writing for the Union Safety Committee on May 22, James O. Broadhead complained to Montgomery Blair: "We fear that no good will come of the arrangement but that it will only result in putting off the evil day until such time as the enemy will be better prepared to make resistance." He strongly recommended that the full force of the federal government be used to insure the peace of Missouri.

The following day Frank Blair wrote Secretary of War Cameron: "The agreement between Harney and Price gives me great disgust and dissatisfaction to the Union men; but I am in hopes we can get along with it, and think that Harney will insist on its execution to the fullest extent, in which case it will be satisfactory."[33]

Blair's hopes quickly disappeared in the days which followed. Letters began pouring into St. Louis from all corners of the state. Their writers complained of mistreatment at the hands of the secessionists and of military preparation and organization being carried on by the state government. President Lincoln became alarmed when these reports were relayed to him. On May 27, he directed The Adjutant General to remind Harney that it was his duty to prevent such outrages regardless of whether they continued from the inability or from the indisposition of the state authorities to suppress them. "The authority of the United States is paramount, and whenever it is apparent that a movement, whether by color of State authority or not, is hostile, you will not hesitate to put it down."[34]

Harney had been keeping the telegraph operator busy with messages to Price, seeking reassurance that the state authorities were keeping their part of the agreement to maintain peace. He intimated that he might send a regiment of federal troops to Springfield to protect the peaceable citizens there. Price replied that the reports which had alarmed Harney were false rumors; he promised to carry out the agreement faithfully. These assurances satisfied the federal commander, and he wrote Frank Blair to this end.[35]

Blair now became convinced that the Union cause could no longer afford to retain Harney in command of its forces in Missouri. To him the indications of violations of the Harney-Price agreement were too strong to be overlooked, so he delivered the removal order to the General on May 30. At the same time he forwarded to Lincoln his reasons for doing so.

Lyon now assumed temporary command of the Department of the West and wired the Secretary of War for reinforcements from Illinois and Iowa. With Blair's having asked for authorization to enroll citizens in the interior of the state into the federal army, all seemed prepared for the outbreak of hostilities. Price, upon learning of Harney's removal, decided that the agreement between the two had been broken. He sent instructions to his district commanders to hasten the enrollment of the State Guard in order that the expected invasion might be met.[36]

The conservatives were unwilling to resign themselves to open conflict within the borders of Missouri. Some sought to reverse the President's orders and to secure Harney's reinstatement. On May 31, the General wrote the Secretary of War that he had the situation under control. He asked for another chance.[37]

When it became evident that the Administration had no intention of reversing itself again, Congressman William A. Hall and several others sought to bring the opposing leaders together in an attempt to work out a new compromise. Under persuasion from Frank Blair and Thomas T. Gantt, a prominent jurist, Lyon agreed to give Jackson and Price safe conduct to "visit St. Louis on or before the 12th of June, in order to hold an interview for the purpose of effecting, if possible, a peaceable solution to the troubles of Missouri."

The two state officials, accompanied by Thomas L. Snead, Governor Jackson's aide, arrived late on the afternoon of Tuesday, June 11. That evening they conferred at the Planters' House with Lyon, Blair, and Major Horace A. Conant, the latter's secretary. The men argued for more than four hours about the relations between state and nation, Lyon dominating the discussion. Unfortunately, no agreement could be reached. Finally, Lyon rose. With little passion, he deliberately and emphatically closed the meeting with this declaration:

> Rather than concede to the State of Missouri the right to demand that my Government shall not enlist troops within her limits, or bring troops into the State whenever it pleases, or move its troops at its own will into, out of, or through the State; rather than concede to the State of Missouri for one single instant the right to dictate to my Government in any matter however unimportant, I would see . . . every man, woman, and child in the State, dead and buried. *This means war.* In one hour one of my officers will call for you and conduct you out of my lines.[38]

The three state officials did not wait that long. They immediately proceeded to the railroad yards, where they secured a locomotive. They headed at full speed for Jefferson City, stopping only long enough to fuel the engine and burn the bridges over the Gasconade and Osage rivers. Immediately upon their arrival in Jefferson City, Governor Jackson issued a proclamation to the people of Missouri. He reported the interview and its failure and called for 50,000 volunteers to fill the ranks of the State Guard. This proclamation he quickly dispatched to all parts of the state.[39]

At the same time orders went out to the district commanders. They were to assemble their men immediately at some convenient place and prepare them for instant service in the field. Brigadier General John B. Clark was ordered to report with his men to Boonville. Here Jackson and Price joined him with their staffs and the one militia company from Jefferson City in the belief that Boonville could be defended more easily than the capital.[40]

Lyon embarked at St. Louis with about 2,000 men on Thursday afternoon, June 14, just as the last remnants of secession left Jefferson City. Moving up the Missouri River, he occupied the capital without opposition the following day. He left three companies there for garrison duty and advanced on Boonville. The state troops were driven from that city on Monday, June 17. During subsequent weeks, various skirmishes followed between the opposing forces, and in July the scene of action shifted to southwest Missouri.[41]

Thus, by the early summer of 1861, the duly elected state government of Missouri was in flight from its capital, pursued by the forces of the federal government of which it was still a part. The efforts of the vast majority of Missourians to remain neutral in the great struggle which was rending the Union asunder had been of no avail. Missouri had embarked on a bloody voyage which would not end until the national conflict came to a close.

3

The Provisional Government Is Established

THE FLIGHT of Governor Claiborne F. Jackson with much of the state government from Jefferson City created a power vacuum at the capital. For almost two months there was no official in the city who could supervise the necessary day-to-day operations of government and assist local officials in their efforts to promote stability. With federal armies overrunning large areas of the state, some kind of civilian responsibility needed to be established in order to coordinate the efforts of the federal government with those of Missouri's loyal citizenry, who still formed the bulk of her population.

Some Union men are said to have suggested that the President appoint Frank Blair as military governor. But this proposal did not seem generally satisfactory, and Blair himself wisely discouraged it. Rather, most of Missouri's pro-Union leaders began to talk about the possibility of reconvening the state convention. Before its adjournment on March 22, that body had appointed a committee of seven members with the power to call the convention into special session should a majority of the committee decide an emergency existed. Following the retreat of Jackson's forces into the southwest corner of the state, five of the committee members decided that such an emergency did exist. They issued a proclamation on July 6, calling the convention to assemble in Jefferson City on July 22.[1]

Governor Jackson, still claiming the full exercise of his executive powers, continued to hope that he could take Missouri out of the Union. Following the victorious battle of Carthage early in July, he left General Price at Cowskin Prairie to reorganize and prepare his raw recruits for further combat. Accompanied by former Senator David R. Atchison, Jackson made the long trek to Richmond, Virginia, to seek aid from the Confederacy. The two men arrived in the Confederate capital on July 26, and held a number of conferences with Jefferson Davis during the next few days. These meetings resulted in the Confederate president's promising Jackson and Atchison financial aid to pay Missouri's troops in the field as soon as the money could be appropriated by the Confederate Congress.[2]

By the time the two men returned to Missouri, the state convention had met and deposed the Governor. Early in August they arrived at New Madrid, then occupied by Confederate forces, and found Lieutenant-Governor Reynolds awaiting them. There followed a thorough discussion of the military and political situation in the state, with Jackson and Atchison informing Reynolds of their accomplishments at Richmond. The three decided the situation called for definite political action to establish a legal basis for negotiating with the Confederate government. Consequently, on August 5, Governor Jackson issued a proclamation declaring Missouri an independent and sovereign state. The Governor justified his action on constitutional grounds by listing the violations of the United States Constitution and Missouri's sovereignty by federal authorities.[3]

The following month, Jackson issued another proclamation from Lexington, calling the Twenty-first General Assembly to meet at Neosho on October 21 to approve his action. This body had been deposed by the state convention in July. However, a number of members (their exact number and identity undetermined to this day because of scattered records) appeared at the Newton County seat on the appointed day. Protected by Price's army, they deliberated the now moot question of secession and passed an ordinance severing Missouri's ties with the Union. Jackson signed the ordinance at Cassville on November 3. It was thus that Missouri's government-in-exile marched into the arms of the Confederacy.[4]

Governor Jackson had sent Thomas L. Snead and Edward C. Cabell to Richmond to negotiate a more definite agreement with the Confederacy, a mission they completed on October 31. Their agreement provided for Missouri to be admitted as a full partner in the Confederacy as soon as her legislature should pass an act of secession and ratify the Confederate Constitution. Under this arrangement the Jackson government continued to function throughout the war even though driven from the state shortly after being admitted to the Confederacy. It sent senators and representatives to the Confederate Congress and cooperated with the Confederacy in every way possible. When Jackson died late in 1862, Lieutenant-Governor Reynolds became head of the government-in-exile and maintained a phantom administration until the end of the war.[5]

This narrative must turn back, however, and take up the story of another government, the one established by the state convention, for this Provisional Government of Missouri was to rule the state until almost the close of the war. Around its efforts to coordinate federal-state policy the remainder of this study will center.

The members of the state convention converged on the Capitol at Jefferson City from all corners of Missouri on July 22. By evening sixty had arrived, a sufficient number to constitute a quorum. After requesting the state printer to furnish them with copies of the laws and journals of the current legislature, they turned to reorganization. The convention adopted, 54 to 21, a resolution declaring the presidency of the group vacant inasmuch as Sterling Price was now at the head of the secession forces in southwest Missouri. It then proceeded to elect unanimously Robert Wilson of Andrew County, the vice-president of the first session, to fill the vacancy. Aikman Welch of Johnson County became vice-president, also by unanimous vote.[6]

The debate soon made it evident that many Southern sympathizers had not followed Price into the Southwest. The number of negative votes on the question of unseating the absent president were but an indication of what was to come. Following the election of Wilson and Welch, some of the more ardent Unionists attempted to unseat the pro-Southern doorkeeper of the preceding session. A bitter debate ensued between Uriel Wright of St. Louis, the apparent leader of the Southerners, and John B. Henderson of Pike County, one of the more rabid Union men. The convention solved the issue temporarily by referring the matter to a committee of three.[7]

With the question of organization temporarily resolved, James O. Broadhead of St. Louis offered a resolution calling for the appointment of a committee of seven to report what action should be taken under the existing circumstances. Amended to require that the committee membership include one representative from each of the state's seven Congressional districts, the motion passed without difficulty. The convention elected Broadhead, Henderson, William A. Hall of Randolph County, Willard P. Hall of Buchanan County, William Douglass of Cooper County, Littleberry Hendrick of Greene County, and Joseph Bogy of Ste. Genevieve County to the committee. None of these men could be considered as a representative of the pro-Southern group led by Wright. Four of them had served on the Committee on Federal Relations at the previous session.[8]

The following day saw resolutions introduced by both sides outlining the steps which should be taken. The Southerners presented one calling upon the convention to leave unchanged the status of the state government as it existed at the time of the February election. This resolution asserted that the administration at Washington should acknowledge at once the independence of the Confederacy. The border slave states should be allowed to hold voluntary elections to determine which side they would join.

The Unionists, on the other hand, offered resolutions which declared that the executive branch of the state government had "expatriated" itself and committed treason in opposing federal forces. They wished the executive offices declared vacant. This group maintained that the convention represented the people in a constitutional capacity, with full power to act as it saw fit. All resolutions were referred to the committee of seven.[9]

Broadhead presented the report of that committee on the fourth day of the session. In it were summarized the events in Missouri leading up to that moment, as they concerned the convention. Now the state government had abandoned the capital and was inciting opposition to the government of the United States. In this situation, the committee solemnly declared:

> It is the duty of this Convention to do something, if possible, to remedy these evils—to restore peace to the country and establish the relations which have existed between this State and the Government of the United States—to consider, in the language of the act of the legislature . . . the "relations between the Government and people of the State of Missouri" and to adopt such measures for "*vindicating* the sovereignty of the State, and the protection of its institutions," as may appear to be demanded by the occasion.

Drawing upon the language of this act and the provisions of the thirteenth article of the state constitution[10] as a warrant for their power, they made the following recommendations: (1) that the offices of governor, lieutenant-governor, secretary of state, and members of the General Assembly be declared vacant; (2) that the first three offices be filled by the appointment of the convention, the appointees to have full powers until the election of successors in August, 1862; (3) that such an election be held; (4) that the membership of the state Supreme Court be increased to seven; (5) that the governor elected by the convention appoint four judges to the Court in addition to the three already serving, all of whom would hold office until the August, 1862, election. All of the above were proposed as amendments to the state constitution.[11]

The committee further recommended the abrogation of the Military Act passed by the late legislature and the re-enactment of the Militia Act of December 31, 1859, for the purpose of providing the state with troops. Another proposal was to place the amendment changing the Supreme Court before the electorate in August, 1862. Also, the governor appointed by the convention should be authorized to call a special election to fill the vacancies in the General Assembly if he deemed it necessary.[12]

The convention placed the report on the table until the next day and voted to add Hamilton R. Gamble, who had just arrived, to the membership of the committee of seven. Gamble, who had dominated the first session of the convention, returned belatedly from the East at the urging of Edward Bates and other friends. The Attorney-General had written that he believed Gamble's presence in the convention would "be of very great importance." He recommended "a bold & judicious course" which "may at once restore law & order." Bates had spelled out this course earlier in a letter to Broadhead as including the deposing of the executive and legislative members of the state government. The election of replacements should be controlled, he thought, by requiring the voters to take an oath of allegiance.[13]

From the moment of his arrival, Gamble again became the dominant figure in the convention. He obviously desired some revision of the committee's report to make it more acceptable to the majority of conservatives, and he told Broadhead so. Deferring to Gamble, Broadhead moved to recommit the committee report in order to enable the group to perfect it. This simply meant that Gamble would rewrite the report. This move disgusted Broadhead's partner, Samuel T. Glover, who impatiently wrote that too much time had been wasted already. While he agreed that Gamble should be placed on the committee and flattered and praised because of his influence, Glover warned "much delay may ruin us."[14]

Gamble also realized the importance of time. He completed his work quickly, and the committee submitted the revised report on July 29. The revision differed from the original in that it made no mention of the Supreme Court, with which ex-jurist Gamble no doubt hesitated to tamper. It advanced the date of the state election from August, 1862, to the first Monday in November, 1861; added certain election procedures, including a test oath; and recommended that the entire work of the convention be submitted to the people for their approval.[15] Gamble and the other members of the committee obviously hoped that the revised report might prove more palatable to those who had not yet committed themselves to a definite position.

The Southern element lost little time in attacking the proposals. Uriel Wright led the fight with a bitter denunciation of the proposed usurpation of the power of the people to select their officials. "We have no power to vacate offices," he emphasized, "for it requires just as much power to vacate an office as it would to make a Constitution." To this Gamble replied that the original state constitution rested upon the sole authority of the convention which had adopted it, as it had never been submitted to the people for ratification. With regard to the convention, Gamble declared: "It is a body assembled by the people, directed by the people themselves in their original capacity." He reminded his colleagues that they met "under peculiar circumstances; we are a peculiar body, and we are to act upon peculiar questions." When a convention assembles, Gamble reiterated, "it has all the power that the people could have if they had all assembled in one vast plain, unless there has been some limitation upon the power."

Wright remained adamant and warned his hearers:

> I know the people of Missouri will stand a great deal. They have foreborne in many instances; but there is a time when forebearance ceases to be a virtue, and I do not think the people will stand your dictation of a government. They won't stand the government you make for them. They will question you very closely about what authority they ever gave you to unmake a Legislature, to oust men from their seats whom they, in the exercise of their sovereignty, sent there.[16]

James H. Birch, who had been quite active in the proslavery anti-Benton ranks during the 1850's, tried to placate Wright.

He thought the convention "competent and necessary to provide for the temporary suspension of the functions of certain officers, in order to promote the tranquility of the State." In so doing, the convention merely protected "the untrammeled exercise of the elective franchise which is to be invoked as the legitimate *final* verdict." Obviously, the changes Gamble had made were affecting Birch and others who valued the ultimate sovereignty of the people. Birch had also served on the Supreme Court. He and other lawyers would have little sympathy for any tampering with the judiciary.

Yet, a number of Southern sympathizers remained unconvinced. E. K. Sayre of Lewis County maintained that instead of creating a rival government, the convention should persuade the Jackson administration to return and work peacefully with the military authorities. The ridiculousness of this idea was obvious. Nevertheless, Sample Orr closed the day's debate by accusing the committee of requesting the convention to take action against the state officials without presenting definite proof that they had disqualified themselves. Presentation of such proof, he thought, was only their just due.[17]

The next day, P. L. Hudgins of Andrew County made perhaps the soundest contribution to the entire Southern argument when he pointed out:

> . . . I call the attention of the members of this body to that provision of the Constitution which declares that the power to impeach the Executive belongs alone to the Legislature of the State of Missouri. If he is impeached by that body, he is condemned, and his office is made vacant. We are neither the lower House nor the Senate of Missouri. . . . This being the case, and we having sworn to support that Constitution, we should look well before attempting, on the part of ourselves, the violation of it. . . . Our Constitution provides further, that when a vacancy occurs, the people themselves shall fill that vacancy on three months' notice. . . . These are the provisions of the Constitution which we have sworn to support.[18]

Herein the group opposing the committee report had its best legal argument. The remainder of the debate concerned itself largely with present conditions and past events in the state.

When the voting began later that same day, the convention agreed to consider the report one section at a time. It vacated the offices of governor, lieutenant-governor, and secretary of state by a vote of 56 to 25 and deposed the General Assembly, 52 to 28. The opposition came largely from the counties along the Missouri River and in the southeastern corner of the state, representing about 20 per cent of the state's total white population in 1860.

Having vacated the state's three top executive offices and all the seats in the General Assembly, the convention proceeded, by a vote of 54 to 27, to declare itself the agent of the people to fill the vacancies. The provision for the November, 1861, election was then adopted, 55 to 23. The remaining sections passed without a division.

The convention next abrogated the Military Act of 1861 and reinstituted that of 1859 by a vote of 52 to 21. Only the question of the submission of the convention's work to the people remained unsettled. On this the group agreed unanimously, indicating that all the members of the convention considered their exercise of sovereignty as only temporary.[19]

Significantly, the entire revised report of the committee of eight was approved without change. Certainly this stands as a tribute to the moderating influence of Hamilton R. Gamble. He had amply rewarded the faith which Bates and others had shown in urging him to go to the convention. Accurately gauging the mood of the group, he retained all the features of the original report except the questionable ones on the judiciary, which many conservatives considered sacrosanct; he added those provisions designed to emphasize the ultimate sovereignty of the people; and he included the test oath, which appeased the more ardent Union men.

Throughout the two days of debate which preceded the final vote, Gamble quietly dominated the proceedings. He was always ready to supply an answer or to drive home a point. John F. Phillips, a member of the convention, recalled many years later that Gamble never made a set speech and disliked overt display. Not an orator in the popular sense, "his eloquence was that masterful logic, deep, sincere earnestness, that overwhelms sophistry and convinces intelligent judgment."[20] In the end, Gamble won over the undecided middle group and carried the day. The hard core of some twenty Southern ultras remained fairly constant. Their consistency indicated that only surrender on basic points could have wooed them away from their position.

On July 31, the ninth and final day of the session, the convention proceeded to fill the vacancies it had created. Only three men were nominated to fill the three offices. All were elected unanimously. The pro-Southern members were excused from voting, because they declared the proceedings illegal. They still contended that the convention had no right to vacate the offices. The convention made the obvious choice in selecting Gamble as governor. Although reluctant to hold public office, he accepted, undoubtedly in part because he anticipated serving only a short time. The convention named Willard P. Hall of St. Joseph as lieutenant-governor and Mordecai Oliver of Greene County as secretary of state.[21]

All three men had long been active in state affairs. Gamble, a native Virginian, had received his academic education at Hampden-Sydney College. He studied law and was admitted to the bar of three states before attaining the age of twenty-one. He first came to Missouri in 1818, three years before its admission as a state, and settled in St. Louis as a deputy circuit clerk under his elder brother, Archibald Gamble. Within a short time, the young lawyer moved farther west, to Old Franklin. Here he became prosecuting attorney of Howard County, which then covered much of the interior portion of Missouri. In 1825, Governor Frederick Bates appointed Gamble secretary of state, but his tenure in this position was brief. The Governer died soon after his inauguration, and Gamble resumed the practice of law in St. Louis. He became a prominent member of the bar of that city, for a time enjoying a partnership with his brother-in-law, Edward Bates.

Although elected to a single term in the Missouri House as a Whig in 1844, Gamble generally avoided political office. He much preferred to devote his full energies to his legal practice. When the state amended its constitution to provide for the popular election of judges in 1850, the people literally drafted Gamble, a persistent critic of the appointive system, to run; he was elected by an unprecedented majority, even though a member of the minority Whig party. His associates on the court selected him to serve as its president, and he soon built a reputation as an eminent jurist. It was during his service on the state bench that the Dred Scott case came before that judicial body, and it was Gamble alone who upheld Scott's right to freedom.

Ill health forced his resignation from the bench in November, 1854. Once again Gamble returned to his law practice in St. Louis. Having accumulated a small fortune, he went into semi-retirement in 1858. He settled at Norristown, Pennsylvania, near Philadelphia, to supervise the education of his children. He was still in the East early in 1861 when Missourians began talking of a state convention to determine the issue of secession. At the urging of his friends, Gamble returned to St. Louis to become a candidate for election to that body. He delivered a stirring address at a Union rally in the rotunda of the courthouse on January 12. This catapulted him to the forefront of those advocating a levelheaded policy. In the election which followed, he received a vote larger by one-third than that cast for any other candidate. And in the convention, as already seen, he quickly became the dominant figure.[22]

Willard P. Hall, although of Massachusetts Puritan ancestry, was also a native of Virginia. Graduating from Yale College in

1839, he came to Missouri the following year to read law under his elder brother, William A. Hall. He practiced briefly at Sparta before moving to St. Joseph in 1843, where he made his home throughout the remainder of his life. When the Mexican War broke out, Hall enlisted as a private in Doniphan's expedition. While in the service he had primary responsibility for drafting the code of civil government adopted for the new territory of New Mexico.

He returned to take a seat in Congress, where he asserted active leadership in the movement to secure the organization of Nebraska Territory. An ardent anti-Benton Democrat, Hall voluntarily retired from Congress in 1853 and resumed his legal practice in St. Joseph. When Abraham Lincoln, with whom he had served in Congress, spoke at Elwood, Kansas, across the river from St. Joseph, in 1858, Hall served as his host. Hall did not accept the Republican's credo, however, for in 1860 he supported Douglas for the Presidency.

Hall had been a conciliatory force in the state convention sessions of 1861. He was Gamble's personal choice for the lieutenant-governorship. The newly elected chief executive wanted a younger man on whom he could rely in this post because of his own poor health. Hall's record served as a firm recommendation.[23] In the turbulent days which followed, Hall amply rewarded Gamble's faith in him. During Gamble's frequent absences from the state, Hall exercised full powers as acting governor with patience and firmness. Gamble died early in 1864, but Hall had secured the necessary experience to move quickly ahead with the work of the Provisional Government during its final year.

The last of the trio elected by the convention, Mordecai Oliver, was a native Kentuckian. Moving with his parents to Missouri at an early age, he received a common school education, studied law, and was admitted to the bar at twenty-three. He secured election to Congress in 1852 on the Whig ticket as a result of the split in the ranks of the Democratic party. Oliver served two terms in that body and distinguished himself largely through service on the Howard Committee, which investigated the electoral difficulties in Kansas Territory. Declining to stand for re-election in 1856 because of his opposition to the Know-Nothing infiltration of the Whig party, he returned to his law practice. A staunch Unionist, he was the only one of the three newly elected state officials selected from outside the convention ranks.[24]

The inauguration of the new officials occurred in the evening of the same day on which they were elected. In his inaugural address Governor Gamble made it clear that he had not sought the office. His words are worth careful study, for they represent the sincere thoughts of a man who was eventually to give his life for his state. Said Gamble:

> It is the yielding of all my own schemes, of all my own individual wishes and purposes, when I undertake to assume this office. I could give you, gentlemen of the Convention, no better idea of my devotion, to what I believe to be the interest of the State, than I do now, if you could only understand the reluctance with which I accept the election with which you were pleased to honor me. . . . It is utterly impossible that any one man can pacify the troubled waters of the State. . . . I feel I have a right to ask that when you have by your voice placed me in such a position, that you shall unite with me your efforts and voice, instead of endeavoring to prevent the result we all desire. Unite all your efforts so that the good which is desired may be accomplished; and with the blessings of that Providence which rules over all affairs, public and private, we may accomplish this end for which we have labored and which shall cause all the inhabitants of the State to rejoice. If you desire the peace of the State—if you earnestly desire it, then give this experiment fair trial. . . .
>
> Gentlemen, if you will unite with me, and carry home this purpose to carry it out faithfully, much can be accomplished, much good can be done; and I am persuaded that each one of you will feel that it is his . . . individual duty . . . to do all he can for the welfare of the State. . . . I have come now to express to you my earnest desire that we shall be found co-operating for that same common good in which each one

> of us is equally interested; that, although differing as to modes and schemes, we shall be found united in the great work of pacification.[25]

It is the tragedy of the Provisional Government that many soon forgot this declaration of devotion and plea for unity.

Before adjourning, the convention issued an address to the people of Missouri in which it outlined its actions and the reasons for them. This statement clearly set forth the authority upon which the convention had decided its power rested:

> It is one of the fundamental principles of our government that all political power resides in the people, and it is established beyond question, that a Convention of delegates of the people, when regularly called and assembled, possesses all the political power which the people themselves possess, and stands in the place of the assemblage of all the people in one vast mass. If there be no limitation upon the power of the Convention, made in the call of the body, then the body is possessed of unlimited political power.[26]

The leading conservative journals of the state praised the action of the convention and heaped praise on Gamble. Said the *Missouri Statesman* of Columbia in its editorial columns: "It is most fortunate for the people that Judge Gamble was prevailed upon to accept the position and to bring his great talents, ripe experience and tried conservatism to the task of restoring peace to the State."[27]

Edward Bates wrote his brother-in-law: "You better than any extreme man, can tranquillize the State. . . . The internal peace of Missouri and its security in the Union . . . will do more towards the suppression of the insurrection in the border states, than 100,000 of our best men in the army. You see the prize before you, and God bless you in your efforts to win it."[28]

Even Uriel Wright, the leader of the pro-Southern faction in the convention, did not hesitate to praise the selection of Gamble. Although he and his followers had refrained from voting for him in protest against the convention's action in deposing Jackson,

Wright asserted through the *Missouri Republican*: "There is no man in the limits of the State upon whom I more readily confer the important trust which must devolve upon a chief executive. . . . I know of no man . . . who challenges more unqualified approbation than Hamilton R. Gamble."[29]

The steps taken by the state convention in July of 1861 were of great importance for Missouri. In spite of its declaration of power, the legality of the convention's action is highly questionable. The argument of P. L. Hudgins opposing the convention's power of impeachment was probably the soundest which was advanced. Yet, that body faced a great crisis brought on by extraordinary times. The condition of Missouri was deplorable. Action was necessary to insure that responsible authority should manifest itself in handling the affairs of the state. Missouri was still a part of the federal Union, yet its governor, Claiborne F. Jackson, stood in rebellion against that government. Therefore, it became necessary to set up a state administration which could work with the federal authorities in restoring peaceful conditions in Missouri. In such circumstances expediency won out.

President Lincoln immediately recognized the Provisional Government as the legal governing body of Missouri. As such, it administered the affairs of the state from the time of its inception until January, 1865, when it was superseded by a duly elected set of officials. It constituted a unique experiment, the only government in the entire history of the United States to be established by a convention legally in existence for an entirely different reason. During its tenure the Provisional Government saw its authority continually questioned by different groups ranging from secessionists to radical Unionists. It frequently ran into conflict with the military authority emanating from the commander of the Department of the Missouri at St. Louis and his subordinates in the field, which made its work much more difficult. Yet, its officials never gave up in their efforts to carry out the task set for them by Governor Gamble in his inaugural address.

4

The Provisional Government Survives Frémont

THE CAREER of Brigadier General Nathaniel Lyon as commander of the Department of the West proved short-lived. The conservatives in Missouri were not pleased by his appointment; their representative at Washington, Attorney-General Bates, backed by General Scott, demanded a more experienced commander. This agitation, together with Secretary of War Cameron's misgivings about the general competence of Lyon to command, led the President to place the department under Major General George B. McClellan, operating in western Virginia. Lincoln's decision, however, greatly irritated the Blairs. They wanted Lyon to have an independent command in Missouri. Unexpectedly, however, the change left Lyon great freedom of action. McClellan, who had his hands full directing a campaign in the East, could not pay much detailed attention to affairs in Missouri.[1]

General conditions in the Mississippi Valley during the summer of 1861 prompted the governors of the Northwest to meet. They urged "the appointment of a competent commander who might organize the immense resources of the West, and make them effective in a grand campaign southward to open the Mississippi." Having failed to secure the independent command for Lyon, the Blairs pressed for the removal of Missouri from under the wing of McClellan. They considered the situation critical and wished the appointment of someone who could take direct control of affairs.

The man chosen by the Blairs as their candidate for the command had spent the past winter in Europe. After the outbreak of the war, John Charles Frémont returned home to offer his services to the Union. He was an old friend of the Blair family. As the son-in-law of the late Thomas Hart Benton, he had a considerable acquaintance in St. Louis and seemed the ideal choice for commander in that area. His many explorations had made him famous as "the Pathfinder of the West." Upon his arrival in New York on July 1, the President appointed him a major general in the regular army and assigned him to the command of a new Department of the West with headquarters at St. Louis. This department consisted of Illinois and all the states and territories west thereof between the Mississippi River and the Rocky Mountains.[2]

Instead of quickly accepting the command and hastening to his post, Frémont waited until mid-July before agreeing to take the assignment. Even then he failed to proceed to St. Louis although ordered to do so by General Scott. Montgomery Blair daily urged him to leave for the West in the belief that his presence there was badly needed. But Frémont continued in the East, seeking military supplies for the department and assembling his staff. He did not reach his post until July 25. His instructions from President Lincoln were not detailed. In essence they called for the "clearance of all rebels from Missouri, and a movement down the Mississippi upon Memphis." Frémont later reported that the President told him: "I have given you *carte blanche*; you must use your own judgment and do the best you can."[3]

Six days after Frémont's arrival in St. Louis, Hamilton R. Gamble became provisional governor of Missouri. During the next one hundred days his administration received its "baptism under fire." Gamble was determined to stand upon his constitutional rights and do whatever he felt was necessary to bring peace to Missouri. As the Governor saw it, loyal Missourians could keep order in their state better than outsiders. But the impetuous and ambitious Frémont had little intention of allowing the Governor much authority in his new domain. Inevitably the two men clashed, and a controversy arose which found its way to the desk of the President. He tried to get the Governor and the General to work together but failed. In the end, Frémont departed and Gamble stayed, establishing a pattern of change in Missouri's military command and stability in its civil leadership which four years would not alter.

When Gamble assumed office the state was in turmoil after nearly two months of political anarchy. As his first official act, he published a proclamation on August 3, announcing the action of the convention and asking all citizens to work for peace. The Governor promised that military intervention in the state would be stopped as soon as possible. He declared it the intention of the Provisional Government to protect all peace-loving citizens regardless of their political beliefs, and assured the people that his administration had no intention of interfering with the institution of slavery. He called upon citizens to surrender any secret caches of military supplies so that they could be used by the state in its efforts to restore order. Then, in a final effort to secure unity and peace, Gamble promised amnesty to all those who had taken up arms with Jackson and Price but now desired to return peacefully to their homes and occupations. In this last move, the Governor received the prompt backing of President Lincoln, who desired the restoration of peace to Missouri as much as he.[4]

General Frémont had arrived in St. Louis to find "this command in disorder, nearly every county in an insurrectionary condition, and the enemy advancing in force by different points of the southern frontier." He complained to Lincoln: "I am sorely pressed for want of arms. . . . Our troops have not been paid, and some regiments are in a state of mutiny, and the men whose terms of service have expired generally refuse to enlist."[5] This latter situation threatened to become an increasing problem. The original ninety-day enlistments of the early volunteers expired at the same time that their hopes and enthusiasm for a short war went a-glimmering.

The new commander found himself harassed on two sides by

calls for more men. General Lyon had advanced to Springfield in southwest Missouri on July 13. There he faced what he believed to be an overwhelming force of Price's State Guard supported by Confederates moving up from Arkansas under Brigadier General Ben McCulloch. Lyon, with only 7,000 men, had been making repeated requests for reinforcements and supplies from the East with little success. Following Frémont's arrival, Lyon besieged the headquarters at St. Louis for additional troops. His messengers met with delay and red tape in their attempts to reach the Commander through his aides. One of them finally burst in upon Frémont, unannounced, and presented Lyon's demands. The Commander promised help, but it failed to materialize. John M. Schofield, Lyon's adjutant, later wrote in his memoirs that the General was greatly depressed by his inability to secure the reinforcements and supplies he considered essential to his campaign. He apparently had a strong conviction that he was being sacrificed to Frémont's ambition.

Governor Gamble did his utmost "by application in writing and in person" to secure reinforcements for Lyon, even though he did not agree with all the latter had done. The Governor feared that a successful Price in southwest Missouri might try to reoccupy Jefferson City and restore Jackson to office. But Gamble's efforts to aid Lyon also proved in vain. Frémont's adjutant informed one of the Governor's emissaries early in August that "they are just notified Lyon & Sigel have men enough" although he understood "they purpose to send more men in that direction as soon as possible." Dispatches for this period fail to bear out the adjutant's contentions.[6]

While Lyon cried for reinforcements in the southwest, Brigadier General Benjamin M. Prentiss urgently requested additional troops in southeast Missouri. He reported that Major General Leonidas Polk was moving on Cairo, Illinois, the key to the upper Mississippi, with a large Confederate force. Prentiss anticipated difficulty if not reinforced. In this situation, Frémont decided to reinforce Prentiss with 4,000 men. He personally conducted them down the Mississippi. Upon Frémont's arrival at Cairo, the Confederates apparently became frightened and departed, for no engagement occurred.[7]

Frémont hoped to secure more troops from Illinois and Indiana. En route to Cairo, he sent Lyon an order to fall back upon the railhead at Rolla and await reinforcements if he did not think himself strong enough to maintain his position at Springfield. Lyon received the dispatch early on the morning of August 9. He replied that he would hold his position as long as possible, in the belief that he could resist any attack if not surrounded.

Lyon believed his army offered the only hope against disaster befalling the Union people of southwest Missouri. He called in Franz Sigel, his second in command, shortly after receiving Frémont's letter. They made plans to move forward against Price before new orders might come, forcing their withdrawal. The next morning at dawn Lyon's army attacked the numerically superior force of Price and McCulloch at Wilson's Creek near Springfield. The attack was repulsed, and in the fray Lyon lost his life. Forced to retreat to Rolla, the federal forces abandoned southwest Missouri with its large Unionist population to the Confederates.[8] Although the federal troops withdrew at this time this region was to see much more fighting and devastation before the war's end.

Lyon's heroics in Missouri had caught the imagination of a North eager for action. Now he became the Union's first martyr. The Governor of Connecticut, his home state, wired Gamble asking that Lyon's body be preserved for transportation to his birthplace at Norwich, where he was to be buried with full military honors. Missouri's chief executive complied. En route, large crowds gathered wherever the funeral train stopped. When it became known that Lyon had bequeathed his life savings of $30,000 to the United States Government for the prosecution of the war, the martyr's crown glowed even brighter. Congress passed a resolution enabling each regiment which had fought at Wilson's Creek to embroider "Springfield" on its colors in gold.[9]

The blame for Lyon's fate fell on Frémont from all sides. Lack of action at Cairo undermined the Commander's excuse of reinforcing that point at Lyon's expense.[10] The disaster at Wilson's Creek marked the beginning of constant complaints of various sorts which plagued the noted "Pathfinder" in Missouri.

The Confederate victory at Springfield greatly depressed Union men in Missouri. It left the way open for many secessionists to join Price's army. Brigadier General John Pope, in charge of Union forces in north Missouri, encountered considerable guerrilla activity and little success in restoring order because of the fear or apathy of the population. "When troops were sent out against these marauders, they found only men quietly working in the field or sitting in their offices, who, as soon as the backs of the Federal soldiers were turned, were again in arms and menacing the peace. To such an extent had this gone that there was no safety of persons or property in North Missouri except to the secessionists, and the Union men were too timid or too much in the minority to offer the least resistance."[11]

Pope decided to make the people in each locality responsible for law enforcement in that area, as his troops could not be everywhere at once. On July 31, he issued Special Order Number Three in which he decreed that a committee of public safety be established in each locality to maintain order. This local group should call out the citizenry for militia purposes any time the area became menaced by marauders. If the local citizens refused to perform this police function, federal troops would be used to keep order. The latter were to be paid by a levy assessed against the county or community, and that area would have to provide quarters, subsistence, and transportation for them while so engaged. Pope assured Robert T. Van Horn: "I am satisfied that peace can be kept if the people will interest themselves in keeping it & I have therefore furnished them with a very strong inducement to do so."[12]

Trouble quickly followed. In those instances where the local citizenry failed to take action and it became necessary to send in troops, the latter conscripted supplies from Unionist and secessionist indiscriminately. By August 17, J. T. K. Hayward, President of the Hannibal and St. Joseph Railroad, was writing Gamble: "The Union cause in our section of the State is being greatly injured by the bad management of our military affairs. The outrages committed on the people by the soldiery . . . are all causing Union men to leave."

Hayward had welcomed Pope's policy at first, because it meant better protection for his trains. Now he complained to Frémont that the actions of the Union troops, especially those from Kansas and Illinois, simply aggravated and intensified guerrilla activity because of the outrages being perpetrated. Hayward also wrote numerous letters to John W. Brooks, one of the railroad's officials in Boston, who forwarded them to the Secretary of War. These spelled out in vivid detail the terror being visited upon the populace by troops who seemingly considered all Missourians as "rebels." General Pope, nevertheless, continued to defend his policy as the only one which would "keep North Missouri quiet with the smallest force."[13] Efforts were continually made to tighten control over these out-of-state troops, but trouble of this sort cropped up frequently throughout the war. A large part of the difficulty can be attributed to the desire of many Missourians with strong Southern sentiments to remain neutral in a conflict which brooked no neutrality.

All of these conflicts, civil and military, made the position of the new Provisional Government extremely difficult. The state convention had abrogated the military measures of the Jackson administration in reinstituting the Militia Act of 1859. As conditions in the state deteriorated rapidly, Governor Gamble issued a proclamation on August 24, calling for 42,000 volunteers to fill the ranks of the militia for six months. Only 6,000 men answered the call, a most disappointing response. With the Confederates victorious in southwest Missouri, few Missourians wished to join what appeared to be a losing cause. If they were disposed to enlist, Frémont's recruiting officers could offer regular pay, while the depleted state treasury held little but promises for those who joined the militia.

The task of organizing the new militia fell to George R. Smith of Sedalia, Gamble's newly appointed adjutant general. Smith set up headquarters at St. Louis and proceeded to muster the volunteers into regiments. He had little with which to work, as most of the records and supplies for his office had been taken by the Jackson forces when they departed.[14]

Gamble wrote President Lincoln on August 26, outlining his action and reviewing the sorry state of the depleted treasury. Describing the deplorable internal condition of Missouri, the Governor laid at least a part of the blame at the door of the Home Guards. Originally recruited by Frank Blair among the Germans, this outfit was maintained by Frémont as a special unit. They had little sympathy for those Missourians who did not share their radical Union enthusiasm, and were therefore a source of constant friction with the civilian population. Gamble recommended that the Home Guards be either disbanded as such and integrated with regular United States regiments or placed under state control. The Governor also complained of the out-of-state troops brought into Missouri. Their lack of understanding of the situation within Missouri caused them to assume that all Missourians were disloyal. In such circumstances, clashes with civilians were inevitable, and cooperation unlikely.

Gamble assured Lincoln that he would have no difficulty raising a sufficient force to keep order in the state if he could but secure the means to sustain them. Such a force would be doing the work now attempted by federal troops. These could then be released for needed service elsewhere. Under the circumstances, the Governor thought it only fair that the national government provide for sustenance of the state militia in the form of money and material.[15]

Gamble emphasized the urgency of his request by going to Washington at the end of August to seek a personal interview with the President. He already had two strong advocates there laying the groundwork for his negotiations. Attorney-General Bates had written William G. Eliot of St. Louis on August 19 that he had been working for months to secure the concentration of a force in Missouri which would "look down" opposition and prevent insurrection. Bates was ably supported in this by Charles Gibson of St. Louis, Gamble's nephew, who had recently become solicitor of the United States Court of Claims. These two worked constantly in Washington to obtain recognition of Missouri's problems. As a result of their efforts, Gamble was well received by President Lincoln. He obtained the promise of arms for the use of his troops and a loan of $200,000 from the federal government. The latter would come from an appropriation made by Congress in July for the purpose of aiding the loyal citizenry of rebellious states.[16]

The Governor's order calling for the enrollment of the state militia had greatly irritated Frémont, who believed that Gamble was usurping his authority. The Governor had had no such intention and later explained to Frémont: "I thought that if I could bring into the field a body of troops acquainted with the country and with the rebels themselves, they would perform service which troops from other States could not perform." Learning of Gamble's visit to Washington, the General wired Lincoln a brief message: "Will you allow me to suggest that for the present no authority be given to Governor Gamble to raise regiments in Missouri?"[17] The aid which the Governor received during his visit to the capital effectively answered Frémont's "suggestion."

Gamble had come into conflict with General Frémont almost from the outset of his administration. "The Pathfinder" had no desire to let any authority prevent his carrying out the steps he deemed necessary to keep Missouri loyal to the Union. In this respect his personality closely paralleled that of Lyon, although the motives of the two men were not the same. Frémont desired personal advancement and saw Missouri as but a step to greater things for himself. With the backing of his ambitious wife, the daughter of Thomas Hart Benton, the General apparently was already eyeing the possibility of another presidential nomination in 1864. Frémont's policy undoubtedly was influenced by the radical German element in St. Louis. Strongly antislavery, they disdained any course of moderation as weakness. Moreover, the General had nothing to gain and much to lose by catering to the pro-Southern element in Missouri.

Governor Gamble, on the other hand, firmly believed that the state constitution must be upheld at all costs, even if it prevented his doing some things which he would have liked to do. He had been one of the leaders of the conservative group in Missouri from the very beginning of the war. As such he had advocated consistently a policy of moderation toward the pro-Southern group. He believed that, if treated properly and fairly, many of the Southern sympathizers would return to their former allegiance to the Union and the task of pacifying the state would be made easier. This moderate, conciliatory attitude had been manifested in his inaugural address and in his proclamation to the people on August 3. He had no desire to set forth upon a radical program of spectacular measures and changes. Yet the policy of moderation he sought to carry out could succeed only with the backing of the military commander at St. Louis. Such support was not forthcoming from General Frémont.

On August 2, the General wired Gamble through his assistant adjutant, requesting that he make no appointments in the state volunteer regiments until Frémont could write him. The next day the Commander himself wrote Gamble. He enclosed a list of certain officers he wished appointed to head these battle groups. The Governor replied that his power of appointment was narrowly limited by the state constitution, which permitted each regiment to elect its own command. He agreed to appoint the men suggested by Frémont for the posts of adjutant general and quartermaster general if they would accept the appointments in spite of the low pay of those offices.

This response did not satisfy Frémont. He replied on August 12, through another aide, assuring the Governor that it was his privilege to make the appointments under the act of Congress regulating volunteer regiments. He urged Gamble to follow the previous suggestions as closely as possible. There is no record that this letter received a reply from Gamble.[18]

Within the week Frémont wrote the Governor two more personal notes. The disunionist police board of St. Louis, which had been appointed by Governor Jackson, remained in office. Frémont suggested the removal of its members and their replacement with four men of his own choosing. These new members could be expected to cooperate better with him in keeping order in the city. Again Gamble felt powerless to comply under existing law. To his knowledge, the members of the police board had done nothing to give him just cause for their removal. Shortly after this, however, a vacancy occurred on the board through resignation. The Governor promptly appointed one of Frémont's nominees, at the same time asking him to examine the records of the board in order to find cause for the removal of the others. The nominee hesitated; but the board itself, hearing of Gamble's desire to examine their records, sent them to the Governor. He quickly found the cause he sought and removed them. Frémont's nominees were appointed in their stead.[19]

The Commander's other note of mid-August requested the appointment of Frank Blair as brigadier general of Missouri volunteers. "In organizing my force for the field I am embarrassed by the want of superior officers to whom important trust may be confided," Frémont confessed. Gamble quickly informed Blair that he could not make the appointment within the limitations of the state constitution. He requested that Blair write the President and get him to issue commissions. Frank wired Montgomery instead, asking him to bring the matter to Lincoln's attention.[20] The Administration held up action on the matter, pending the arrival of Governor Gamble for consultation on militia matters. By the time Gamble made his trip at the end of August, Frank Blair had become disillusioned with Frémont and began to seek the General's removal on grounds of incompetence. Indeed, the Governor became an emissary between the Blairs, carrying a note to Montgomery in which Frank outlined his complaints.[21]

Frémont later claimed that his break with Frank Blair stemmed from difficulties over his refusal to grant contracts to Blair's friends. Apparently though, the rupture had its beginnings in an interview which Blair and Major John M. Schofield had with "the Pathfinder" toward the end of August. Schofield had come to St. Louis to report on the events at Wilson's Creek. He and Blair sought an interview with Frémont. After being kept waiting for some time, the two men were ushered into the General's presence. Much to their surprise, Frémont asked not one question about the battle in which the valiant Lyon had so recently been slain. Rather, he engaged in an enthusiastic one-sided conversation about his coming campaign against the Confederates in south Missouri. The two men came away somewhat dazed and agreed that the General left much to be desired.[22]

Certainly Frank Blair's letter of September 1 to his brother, a follow-up of the one sent through Gamble, reflected this opinion. Blair complained that Frémont had become unapproachable. His subordinates neglected their duties and kept the Commander misinformed. Messengers with important dispatches were kept waiting while Frémont, engrossed in his own plans for a future campaign, neglected present conditions. To make the situation worse, there was an utter want of discipline in the camps around St. Louis.

"Oh! for one hour of our dead Lyon," Frank cried. While not disposed to blame Frémont entirely for the martyr's fate, Blair affirmed that had reinforcements been sent to Lyon, his disaster might have been averted even as the attack on Cairo had apparently been so thwarted.[23]

Montgomery Blair showed the letter to the President. Similar messages had come from James O. Broadhead, John How, and Lincoln's good friend, Samuel T. Glover. Attorney-General Bates also passed on to the President reports he had been receiving from Missouri.[24]

Hard pressed by censure from all sides and strongly influenced by the radical antislavery German element of St. Louis, Frémont decided it was necessary for him to take matters into his own hands. This decision resulted in his famous proclamation of August 30, which began: "Circumstances, in my judgment, of sufficient urgency render it necessary that the commanding general of this department should assume the administrative powers of the State." Accordingly, Frémont proclaimed martial law throughout the state and declared that anyone found with arms within Union lines would be shot upon being found guilty by a court-martial. The most disturbing features of the new policy dealt with the property of those who had taken up arms against the Union. The proclamation declared that property of such persons would be confiscated and their slaves freed.[25]

There had been no preliminary warning. The whole country, including President Lincoln, learned of the proclamation through the newspapers. Governor Gamble's first inkling of the new policy came when he alighted from the train at Washington and bought a paper. He had stopped to see Frémont en route to the capital but had been unable to obtain an interview because the General was absorbed in the formulation of his proclamation. There is no record of what his feelings were as he read of Frémont's action or what he may have said to Lincoln on the matter. There can be no doubt that the policy ran counter to his own. Certainly he preferred civil law and government as the agencies for keeping the peace, and certainly he felt them adequate to the situation. Less than a month previously, in his proclamation of August 3, the Governor had declared that "no countenance will be afforded to any scheme or to any conduct calculated in any degree to interfere with the institution of Slavery existing in the State."[26]

Union leaders in the border states were greatly alarmed by this last aspect of Frémont's proclamation. Heretofore the war had been fought to restore the Union. To turn it into a crusade for Negro liberty would make it extremely difficult for these men to hold their states in that Union. The Unionists in Kentucky were especially concerned with the implications of the proclamation. They wrote Lincoln urging him to repudiate the act.[27]

Both the *Missouri Democrat* and the *Missouri Republican* supported Frémont in his emancipation policy. The former contended that the proclamation would act as a "powerful preventative and sedative" to those who were disposed to or were laboring under "the delirium of secession." The *Republican,* not aware of the real implications of the proclamation, reported that it felt Gamble and Frémont were in agreement in that the emancipation policy did not refer to those who had accepted the Governor's amnesty. It denied a statement by the *New York Independent* that the proclamation was tantamount to complete emancipation in Missouri.[28]

President Lincoln lost no time in making known his feelings in the matter. On September 2, he dispatched a letter to Frémont by special messenger. The President feared most keenly the order to shoot those taken with arms. If carried out, it would lead to retaliation by the Confederates. He therefore ordered that no such action be taken without his consent. He requested Frémont to modify his emancipation policy to conform with the act of Congress passed on August 6. This act limited emancipation to those slaves who were forced to take up arms or otherwise actively participate in the war against the Union. The patient Lincoln closed significantly: "This letter is written in a spirit of caution and not of censure."[29]

Unfortunately, Frémont did not heed the admonishment. In replying to the President's letter, he explained his actions in part as follows:

> Between the rebel armies, the Provisional Government, and home traitors, I felt the position bad and saw danger. In the night I

> decided upon the proclamation and the form of it. I wrote it the next morning and printed it the same day. I did it without consultation or advice with any one, acting solely with my best judgment to serve the country and yourself, and perfectly willing to receive the amount of censure which should be thought due if I had made a false movement. . . . If upon reflection your better judgment still decides that I am wrong in the article respecting the liberation of slaves, I have to ask that you will openly direct me to make the correction. . . . If I were to retract it of my own accord, it would imply that I myself thought it wrong, and that I had acted without the reflection which the gravity of the point demanded. But I did not. I acted with deliberation, and upon the certain conviction that it was a measure right and necessary, and I think so still. In regard to the other point of the proclamation to which you refer, I desire to say that I do not think the enemy can either misconstrue or urge anything against it, or undertake to make unusual retaliation.[30]

It is interesting to note the lack of regard with which Frémont held the newly established Provisional Government. No public statement was forthcoming from any official of that administration at the time, but it soon became apparent that Gamble and his associates were working actively for Frémont's removal.

President Lincoln issued his final order in the matter in a letter to General Frémont, dated September 11. He directed that the proclamation be modified to conform with previous Congressional action. The General had not waited for Lincoln's reaction to his reply before beginning to carry out the provisions of the proclamation. On September 12, he granted deeds of manumission to two slaves of Thomas L. Snead, the aide of Governor Jackson, because their master had taken part in the insurrection.[31] These were the only slaves liberated before the President's second letter arrived to stop the practice.

Frémont's proclamation had long-range significance for Missouri. To the Radicals who later agitated the emancipation question, it marked the beginning of the attempt to bring freedom to Missouri's Negroes.

Martial law was the one aspect of Frémont's policy which remained in force throughout the war. Each succeeding federal military commander in Missouri considered it necessary to help maintain order. This did not affect the civil courts where conditions were such that they could operate efficiently. In many areas guerrilla warfare and general turmoil made it impossible to maintain an impartial judicial system. Here martial law was the only answer. It had its abuses, to be sure, but conditions in Missouri rendered it imperative.

Governor Gamble returned from Washington on September 11 just as the controversy over Frémont's proclamation was reaching its climax. Immediately, Gamble sent the Commander a note requesting an appointment and stating that he bore a letter from the President. Frémont responded promptly that he would see the Governor any time it might be convenient. Thereupon Gamble decided to call that same afternoon.

Upon handing Frémont the President's letter, Gamble informed him that he knew its contents which indicated "a want of cordiality" between them. The Governor told Frémont that if such existed he had been unaware of it. He assured the General that he had not gone to Washington specifically to oppose his proclamation, as Frémont had supposed. The proclamation had been issued after his departure, and he did not know of it until his arrival in Washington. The General, however, seemed primarily interested in knowing when Gamble would carry out his requests concerning appointments. The Governor replied that he had written on August 6 of his inability to do so under the state constitution. Frémont could recall having seen the letter, but he did not remember its contents. Again, Gamble explained his position. He also pointed out that he had honored the General's request concerning the St. Louis police board as soon as he could legally do so.

Frémont remained silent at the end of this explanation. Gamble then brought up the subject of state troops. The President's letter requested Frémont to give the Governor all the help possible in recruiting and equipping the state militia. Gamble tried to assure the General that he had had no desire to irritate him by calling out the militia without prior consultation. He had simply thought that in so doing he would be following the very course of action Frémont desired. These troops could better than any other forces rid the state of rebels because of their familiarity with the countryside and the places where secessionists might be hiding. Furthermore, their use would release the regular troops for service elsewhere. When the Governor informed him that the Secretary of War had agreed to accept fifteen militia regiments, Frémont muttered something about lack of cooperation between state and federal forces. The Governor hastened to assure him that in all instances the state troops would be subject to the command "of those carrying on the military operations of the United States."

As the conference broke up, Frémont told the Governor that he would like to think about the matters which they had discussed and would communicate further. Gamble asked if "on the points discussed all unfavorable impressions had been removed from his mind."

"Oh, yes," Frémont replied vaguely, "let that all go."

The one positive assurance from the interview for Gamble seemed to be the promise of Frémont that he would send the Governor 10,000 stand of arms within sixty days. But Gamble wired Charles Gibson that he did not expect to get them. And in this surmise he was correct.

The next day Frémont sent his judge advocate, Major R. M. Corwine, to Gamble's quarters. The two discussed matters at some length. The Governor assured Corwine of "a disposition on my part for a hearty cooperation," whereupon the Major said he was sure that Frémont would want to see Gamble again. The Governor delayed his departure for Jefferson City two days, waiting for an appointment. When a time was finally set, Gamble made his appearance at Frémont's headquarters promptly on the hour. He sat in the anteroom nearly an hour without gaining admittance to the General, who was obviously in his office. Disgusted, the Governor arose and left. Asked by one of Frémont's aides if he would call again, Gamble replied that he might if he found time before going to Jefferson City, but he did not return.[32]

The arms and money which Lincoln had promised the militia were slow in coming. Gibson wired Gamble on September 18 that it would be impossible to act upon his request for arms until the result of his interview with Frémont was known. The Governor immediately wired a brief résumé of the conversation with the promise that a more detailed letter would follow promptly. The letter, prompt in arriving as Gamble had promised, gave a full account of his encounter with the General and the events that followed. It showed only too clearly that the Governor had been deeply hurt by his treatment at the hands of Frémont. From this time on, Gamble's friends in Washington spared no effort to secure the General's removal.[33]

With the receipt of Gamble's telegram of September 19, the Administration began to implement its promise of arms for the militia. William M. McPherson, a prominent St. Louis broker, was serving as Gamble's agent while on a trip in the East. He wrote the Governor that he had reached Washington on the 18th to be whisked before a full Cabinet session within four hours of his arrival. There he explained his business on behalf of the Provisional Government, only to have the President complain that Gamble had not yet relayed the requested details of his interview with Frémont. McPherson consequently was forced to wait two days before receiving an order from Lincoln for 4,000 guns. He went to New York to procure these but found that the arsenal there had only 2,810 guns available. These he shipped by express before going on to Hartford, Connecticut, to continue his search for adequate supplies.

Five days later McPherson could report to Gamble that he had secured eighty additional carbines, eighty-five pistols, and other miscellaneous arms. These he was forwarding immediately. He advised the Governor to pay for the arms out of state funds, since they were not regulation issue, and the federal authorities might not approve of them. McPherson promised to keep searching for more guns, but indicated that arms were difficult to obtain because of the heavy demands from all quarters. Attorney-General Bates wrote Gamble in a similar vein on September 27 after receiving a letter from the Governor which showed his obvious irritation over the delay. Bates reported that the federal government was not entirely to blame for the arms shortage, as the demand was great in Kentucky and Tennessee.[34]

The money promised by the Administration was also slow in arriving. Gamble urged Bates to look into the matter and to bring pressure in the right places. Replying, the Attorney-General said that he had seen the Secretary of the Treasury, who informed him that an order for the money had been issued and that it was assumed that Gamble had received it. The Secretary promised to look into the matter, and the money eventually arrived.[35]

In spite of the shortage of arms and the lack of regular pay, the state militia undertook the protection of Missouri. Most of the 6,000 men who volunteered for service came from the interior of the state. They were interested in protecting their homes and families from roving bands of Confederate marauders and served within their own counties for the most part, seeking out guerrilla camps. In addition, they frequently acted as guides and scouts to the several bodies of federal volunteer troops in various parts of the state.[36]

Frémont, in the meantime, faced a new crisis. Following his victory at Wilson's Creek, Sterling Price moved slowly north toward Lexington. As early as August 15, certain citizens of the area wrote Frémont that they needed troops badly, as they lived in the heart of secession country. Dispatches from Colonel Jefferson C. Davis, commanding at Jefferson City, began coming into the St. Louis headquarters on September 12. These indicated that an engagement was imminent and that Price had between 10,000 and 15,000 men with him. Colonel James

A. Mulligan had been sent to Lexington with a small force but, obviously, he could not hold off the secessionists very long.

Governor Gamble added his plea for action in a note to Frémont on September 13. Should Lexington fall, he warned, "it would be a great disaster, giving control to the enemy of the upper country." He urged that the troops under Generals John Pope and Samuel D. Sturgis in northeast Missouri be hastened by rail to reinforce Mulligan's command. In a postscript he added significantly that he had learned that the bank vaults at Lexington had $750,000 in coin which Price and the Jackson government badly needed.

Frémont underestimated the danger and urgency of the situation and did not order sufficient reinforcements until the 14th. To compound his error in judgment, various delays and mishaps prevented the troops from arriving where they were needed. Although Pope promised he would have 4,000 men at Lexington by the 19th, none ever arrived because of confusion in the transportation facilities. Davis set out from Jefferson City, but through some mischance, in the darkness, his troops fired into each other's ranks. Sturgis came closer to Lexington than the others, but hearing reports of Price's "overwhelming" force, retired. He returned whence he had come without making any effort to aid Mulligan, who held out until September 20.[37]

The loss of Lexington, while not directly Frémont's fault, added to the already growing discontent with him in Missouri. Gamble wrote Gibson: "He [Frémont] is incomprehensible to me. We have lost Lexington. We will soon lose the whole State." A friend of Secretary of War Cameron, visiting the central Missouri area, warned that if a change did not occur in the department soon "it will require double the number of men to do what could be done now with a proper man at the Head." Others echoed these sentiments. When the St. Louis *Evening News* criticized Frémont editorially for his failure to reinforce Lexington in time, the General suppressed the paper and arrested its editors. This action did not increase his stature with those many St. Louisans who had protested his earlier ban of critical Eastern papers.[38]

Nevertheless, the blow at Lexington goaded "the Pathfinder" into more concerted action. In reporting the defeat to headquarters at Washington, Frémont revealed that he had finally decided upon a definite course of action. "I am taking the field myself," he declared, "and hope to destroy the enemy either before or after the junction of forces under McCulloch. Please notify the President immediately."

General Scott replied that Lincoln was glad to hear of Frémont's decision and expected him to "repair the loss of Lexington" quickly. Once decided on his course, Frémont organized his forces rapidly. He moved out of St. Louis on September 27, his immediate destination being Jefferson City. In so doing, he gained a temporary reprieve. Bates informed Gamble in very despondent tones the same day: "Genl Fremont is not to be removed, at least until he has had a full opportunity to retrieve his fortunes, or to ruin our state utterly & endanger our cause."[39] The movement to secure Frémont's removal as commander of the Department of the West nevertheless had gained considerable momentum by this time. It was to reach its culmination before "the Pathfinder" could return to St. Louis.

Although Frémont did have some positive accomplishments to which he could point, he did not seem to understand the problems of Missouri. He particularly did not concern himself sufficiently with the outstate situation. Most Missourians, aside from the German radicals, failed to see the necessity of the strong entrenchment he built around St. Louis. Neither did they appreciate his grand schemes for a drive down the Mississippi while guerrillas infested the interior of Missouri and Price roamed through the western half of the state with little apparent hindrance.

Frémont's inaccessibility was another factor which galled those who sought action. They resented the General's surrounding himself with foreign officers who wore gaudy uniforms and bore fantastic titles in ostentatious display. Shocking irregularities existed in the issuing of commissions and the letting of contracts. The Administration at Washington became appalled at the costs being run up in the department.[40]

Early in September, during the proclamation controversy, President Lincoln became alarmed at the reports emanating from Missouri. The President's action at this time took the form of a letter to Major General David Hunter, a long-time regular army officer, then stationed at Chicago. Revealing his keen insight, Lincoln wrote:

> General Frémont needs assistance which it is difficult to give him. He is losing the confidence of men near him, whose support any man in his position must have to be successful. His cardinal mistake is that he isolates himself, and allows nobody to see him; and by which he does not know what is going on in the very matter he is dealing with. He needs to have by his side a man of large experience. Will you not, for me, take that place?[41]

Hunter went, accompanied by Montgomery Blair and Quartermaster General Montgomery C. Meigs, Blair's brother-in-law, who had brought him the President's message. The latter two were sent to St. Louis ostensibly to arrange for the Overland Mail; their real mission centered upon a friendly investigation of Frémont's activities.

The men arrived in St. Louis on Thursday evening, September 12, the day after Gamble's interview with Frémont. Blair quickly arranged a conference with the General. "He seems satisfied & almost unconscious, & is doing absolutely nothing," the Postmaster-General reported to Lincoln two days later. Blair consulted others, including his brother Frank and Governor Gamble, still waiting for a new appointment with Frémont. All of them considered Frémont "unequal to the task of organizing the defences of the State." Blair consequently recommended the General's removal and immediate replacement with Meigs. Lincoln bided his time, having received a message from Frémont which indicated action was forthcoming.[42]

Jessie Benton Frémont, bearing the General's reply to the President's first letter on the proclamation, crossed the path of Blair and Meigs on her way to Washington. She hoped to lay her husband's case personally before Lincoln. Arriving late on the evening of September 10, after two nights and two days on the train, she immediately sent the President a note. She asked for an interview "with as little delay as possible."

Lincoln granted her request that same evening, although the hour was quite late. A thorough discussion of the Missouri situation followed. The two participants disagree as to exactly what was said, but Lincoln apparently told her he would consider things overnight. When she did not call the next day, he sent Frémont his final letter rescinding the emancipation policy.

Failing to hear from the President by the morning of September 12, Mrs. Frémont dispatched a note to the White House begging an answer to the General's letter so that she could return quickly to St. Louis. Then, pondering what appeared to be a strange delay, she wrote a second letter without waiting for a reply to the first. This letter revealed that Francis P. Blair, Sr., had called on her the previous day. In the course of the conversation he let drop the information that his son Frank had written a letter concerning Frémont's conduct of the Department of the West which had been submitted to the President. The elder Blair further implied that his son's letter had prompted Lincoln to send the Postmaster-General to St. Louis to investigate conditions. Jessie now demanded, on behalf of her husband, all correspondence relative to the "investigation."

Lincoln's reply, when it came, assured her that Montgomery Blair had gone to St. Louis only as a friend to see if he could help her husband. The President declined to furnish her letters in his possession without the consent of the authors. He also informed her that he had replied to Frémont directly by mail on the emancipation question.[43]

Jessie Frémont soon left Washington and again crossed the path of Blair and Meigs on their way back to the capital. Undoubtedly she had harmed her husband's cause more than she helped it. Reaching St. Louis, she informed Frémont of all that had happened in Washington and showed him the Lincoln note.

In the midst of these revelations a letter appeared in the pages of the *Missouri Republican* which, with Jessie's goadings, brought Frémont to take an action which made any reconciliation with the Blairs virtually impossible: he arrested Frank Blair and charged him with insubordination. The letter in question had been addressed to the editors of the *Missouri Democrat*. In it Blair accused the editors of stirring up a nonexistent quarrel between Frémont and himself. The apparent crusher came in the last paragraph with Blair's announcement that he was not frightened by "the pompous threats which appeared in your columns, but whose unfamiliar garb betrays another origin [Frémont]." Seeking to tie down his case, Frémont now wired the President asking for a copy of the Blair letter which Jessie had heard about. He requested Lincoln to secure the necessary consent of the writer if he had not done so already.[44]

The President showed Frémont's wire to Montgomery Blair, who quickly telegraphed Frémont: "I will send Franks letter. It is not unfriendly. Release him. This is no time for strife except with the enemies of the country." In dispatching the letter the following day, Blair reiterated his contention that he did not consider it "unfriendly." "But," he continued, "as I am aware that men do not readily suppose that others honestly change their opinions of their ability & that my relations to the writer do not admit of any profitable discussion of his motives with you I do not propose to do so."[45]

Lincoln apparently thought seriously at this time of a face-to-face interview with "the Pathfinder." The Robert Todd Lincoln Collection in the Library of Congress contains the following telegram dated September 19, from the War Department to Frémont: "The President desires to discuss certain matters of public business with you, personally. Please place Major General Hunter, temporarily, in the command of the Western Department of the Army, & come hither without unnecessary delay."[46] The telegram does not appear anywhere in the *Official Records of the War of the Rebellion*. For some reason, having had the message drawn up, Lincoln changed his mind and decided not to send it. Had he done so, such a conference might have alleviated the situation in Missouri for all concerned and would have stemmed much of the bitterness which continued to build up on both sides.

In all of this affair, the Blairs saw the hand of "Genl Jessie." According to Montgomery, "Jessie threatened the old man that Frémont should hold Frank personally responsible" for his difficulties. To this the elder Blair replied that "the Blairs did not shirk from responsibility." So, Montgomery continued, "she went back to make a military offense of it."[47]

Frank Blair would have preferred remaining a prisoner in the hope of seeing his charges sifted in a public trial, but Frémont agreed to release him after Montgomery's intercession. The malcontent Blair promptly filed formal charges against the Commander with The Adjutant General. He charged neglect of duty, disobedience to orders, gross extravagance, mismanagement and misapplication of the public funds, and despotic and tyrannical conduct. Frémont promptly had him rearrested.[48] The Blairs now worked harder than ever to bring about "the Pathfinder's" removal.

Others also labored energetically to secure this end. As seen earlier, Governor Gamble and his associates had become irritated by the General's behavior. They now became quite active in the efforts to rid the state of him. Charles Gibson sent Gamble's letter of September 20 to the President. He wrote the Governor that he had requested, on his own initiative, the removal of Frémont.

Attorney-General Bates informed James O. Broadhead: "I have demanded the recall of Genl Frémont, possibly with too much emphasis & too often repeated." He had thought the task accomplished a few days previously, but circumstances arose which altered the situation. Writing to Gamble a day earlier, Bates intimated that the President had decided to give Frémont a chance to redeem himself through direct action against the enemy.[49]

With Frémont in the field, reports flowed into Washington that he was encountering numerous difficulties in getting his campaign underway. A great deal of money had been spent already in the department. Senator Lyman Trumbull, after a visit to St. Louis, wrote the President on October 1 that he found things there in a deplorable condition. "Thousands of his [Frémont's] men have no arms, others are ragged & half clad, & there was yesterday no money at the command of the Western Department, not enough even to pay for scout service." Congressman John A. Gurley, who had been serving on Frémont's staff, came east with instructions to "ask for money and arms." He warned Lincoln that if these were not immediately forthcoming the entire state of Missouri, including St. Louis, might fall before the secessionists.[50]

The President became thoroughly alarmed with the situation. He realized that if he continued to let matters drift, total demoralization might result. Consequently he issued an order on October 7 for Frémont's removal. Rather than implement it immediately, he entrusted it to Secretary of War Cameron who, with Adjutant General Lorenzo Thomas, proceeded to Missouri to make a personal investigation. The final decision on whether the order should be delivered rested with Cameron.

The two men arrived at St. Louis on October 11. They promptly consulted with Brigadier General Samuel R. Curtis, who had recently assumed command of Benton Barracks at St. Louis. Cameron gave Curtis a letter from the President which instructed him to talk frankly and confidentially with the Secretary about Frémont. Curtis did so in strong terms. He had come, somewhat reluctantly, to the conclusion that Frémont "lacks the intelligence, the experience & the sagacity necessary to his command." The next day, in writing his views to Lincoln, Curtis sagely reminded the President: "Public opinion is an element of war which must not be neglected."[51]

Leaving St. Louis on October 12, Cameron and Thomas arrived at Frémont's camp near Tipton the following day. The Secretary of War immediately went into conference with the Commander, during which he presented Frémont with the order for his removal. The General, greatly shocked, asked for a chance to prove himself in the field, and Cameron granted his request. A dispatch to Lincoln outlined the arrangement: Should Frémont fail to intercept the enemy, he would resign at once.

Cameron also consulted with General Hunter at Tipton. This officer, who had been sent to Missouri to assist Frémont and to serve as a counterbalance to the General's vagaries, considered "the Pathfinder" incompetent. Although Hunter was second in command, Frémont never consulted him as to his plans.[52]

While Cameron made his investigation, Adjutant General Thomas did not hesitate to make inquiries of his own. Upon their return to Washington, he submitted a caustic report to the Secretary. This precipitated a Cabinet showdown on the question of the General's removal. Bates confided to his diary that Lincoln seemed to think that Thomas' report, backed by Hunter's testimony, indicated the need for a change; but Seward, Cameron, and Chase counseled delay so "the President still hangs in painful and mortyfying [*sic*] doubt."[53]

Lincoln had been receiving increasingly adverse reports from Elihu B. Washburne, chairman of a Congressional subcommittee investigating government contracts in St. Louis. Conditions in that city were deplorable. Many prominent Unionists, including Governor Gamble, stood "under the ban" while "a gang of California robbers and scoundrels rule, control and direct everything." John G. Nicolay, the President's secretary, reported from Springfield, Illinois, on the 21st: "The universal opinion is that he [Frémont] has entirely failed, and that he ought to be removed." And Ward H. Lamon, Lincoln's close friend, wrote the same day from Frémont's camp at Tipton that things there were "in a terribly unorganized state."[54]

On October 24, Lincoln made the painful decision. He sent the order for "the Pathfinder's" removal to General Curtis at St. Louis. The President charged Curtis to forward it to Frémont by courier. Only if the messenger found the Commander at the conclusion of a successful battle, upon the battleground, or facing the enemy with immediate prospects of battle, should the order be withheld.[55]

By the end of October, Frémont had moved his forces to Springfield. He expected an early engagement between his command and that of Price and McCulloch. Curtis' messenger reached his camp at five o'clock on the morning of November 3. By a ruse he gained admittance to Frémont's tent, where he presented the order. When word spread through the camp of what had happened, the troops evidenced a great deal of discontent; Frémont was generally popular with his men. Some of the officers prevailed upon him to lead an attack the following morning, if Hunter did not arrive before then to assume command. Frémont agreed, but Hunter arrived at ten o'clock that evening. The following morning, Frémont relinquished the command; he issued a farewell address to his troops and departed with his staff for St. Louis. There a large reception, planned principally by his German friends, awaited him.[56]

Thus ended the Missouri career of Major General John Charles Frémont, "the Pathfinder of the West." He had commanded the Department of the West exactly one hundred days. During that time he stirred up one of the great controversies of the war. Much of the bitter factionalism which later plagued

Missouri politically can be traced to the divisions in the Union ranks over the Frémont policies which opposed those of the Provisional Government.

Frémont's relations with the Provisional Government, far from good, ultimately proved one of the causes for his removal. After his failure to arrange a follow-up conference to the Frémont-Gamble interview of September 11, all attempts at cordiality between the civil and military heads of the state ceased. The Provisional Government needed the wholehearted support of the military authority in order to establish firm control over Missouri and to bring peace and tranquility to a divided state. Frémont was sadly lacking in his role. He saw little need for the Provisional Government and considered it in some respects as much a hindrance to the carrying out of military policy as the secessionists.

In this crisis, the Provisional Government was fortunate in having Attorney-General Bates as an ardent spokesman in the Lincoln cabinet and, for one of the few instances in its existence, a common cause with the Blairs. As one commander followed another with regularity during the next few years, the Provisional Government found Bates's presence in Washington an increasingly important tower of strength. Through him, Gamble or Hall could usually get a sympathetic hearing from the President. This closeness helped the Provisional Government hold its critics at bay and allowed it to implement its program to try to bring peace to Missouri.

5

The Partnership Is Cemented

THE STRAINED relations with General Frémont were only one of several problems facing Governor Gamble and the Provisional Government of Missouri in the fall of 1861. The state militia was far from effective in coping with internal dissension. The leaders were handicapped by the small number of men in their command and by the slowness with which arms and money came from the federal government. There also arose the question of how much authority federal officers should have over a state militia. Some local agents had begun drafting and recruiting militiamen into the national service, much to the discontent of the populace. Governor Gamble obtained the promise of General Curtis that this practice would be stopped and that those men already recruited would be released. The need for a more closely coordinated program between state and federal forces was evident.[1]

The state convention had hardly adjourned before Gamble and other leaders began receiving recommendations from throughout the state that the election set for November be postponed. Many questioned the advisability of submitting so important a decision to a populace distraught by physical violence and by emotional involvements. With Price and his army still in possession of, or in a position to menace, large portions of western Missouri, the question arose as to whether effective polling places could be maintained in those areas.[2]

These and other problems caused Governor Gamble to call the state convention once again into special session. That body convened on October 10 at St. Louis. The Governor, in his opening address, enumerated the matters on which he wanted it to act. The convention should, he believed, adopt a military law "more simple and more efficient than that now existing." Gamble revealed that the State Treasury had been reduced to $21,422.73 as of September 24, and much of that amount had probably been absorbed in salaries by the time the convention met. It had become virtually impossible to collect taxes because of the unsettled condition of the state. Some other means would have to be devised to alleviate a pending financial crisis.

Finally, the Governor reported that widespread opinion seemed to favor postponement of the November election. As long as affairs continued in their present unsettled state, it would be extremely difficult to obtain a fair expression of the public will. In this regard Gamble reminded the members that he had been chosen to serve only until November, or until the election of a successor. He offered to retire from office, should they decide to set a later date for the election and wish someone else to serve as governor until that time.[3]

Although absenteeism was quite noticeable at this session, the convention accomplished a great deal in the next nine days to enhance and solidify the authority of the Provisional Government. With only one dissenting vote, it postponed the November election until the first Monday of August, 1862. It continued the incumbent officials in office until that time. To cut down the expenses of government, the convention abolished the Board of Public Works, the offices of state superintendent of common schools, county school commissioner (St. Louis County excepted), state geologist, and assistant state geologist. Salaries of all civil officials in the state were reduced by 20 per cent for the next year. To insure dependable officials who would support the Provisional Government, the convention established a test oath. This oath required the signer to support the constitutions both of Missouri and of the United States, not to take up arms against the government of either, and not to give aid or comfort to their enemies. Each civil officer in Missouri was required to take this oath within the next sixty days or forfeit his office. The

Governor could fill vacated offices by appointment for the remainder of the term.[4]

The convention proposed two schemes to meet the Governor's request for a new fiscal policy. The first called on the Auditor of Public Accounts to prepare warrants in various denominations from five to one thousand dollars, up to a total of one million. These, when signed by the Auditor, countersigned by the Secretary of State, and registered in the offices of both officials, would be redeemable at the State Treasury from funds not otherwise appropriated. The state could use these warrants in payment of any indebtedness it might incur, and it would accept them as payment for taxes. Tax collectors who were found discrediting the warrants would be fined double the amount of those purchased. Since they were designed strictly as a temporary measure, all warrants redeemed by the state were to be destroyed annually.

The second revenue scheme authorized the Governor to issue $1,000,000 of "Union Defence Bonds of Missouri." Redeemable in ten years at 7 per cent interest, these would be issued in denominations of two hundred to five thousand dollars. The interest, payable semiannually, would be secured by having the State Treasurer set aside seventy thousand dollars each year for that purpose. During 1870 and 1871, the Treasurer should establish a "Union Defence Fund" to be raised by levying an additional fifteen cents on every hundred dollars of taxable property. This levy, together with a 25 per cent tax on all tax-gathering licenses issued during those years, would be used to redeem the bonds.[5]

With Price's army in the southwestern part of the state, incessant guerrilla activity elsewhere, and seemingly little prospect of immediate peace in the state, the convention readily agreed with Governor Gamble's plea for a more effective militia. It passed an ordinance providing in detail for a reorganized body of state troops to be known as the Missouri State Militia (M.S.M.). This act declared all physically able white males between the ages of eighteen and forty-five eligible for service by volunteer enlistment once they had taken the test oath. They would receive pay only when on active duty. Any company mustered into state service could enter that of the federal government if it so desired.

As its final order of regular business, the convention adopted a resolution which declared that many of Missouri's citizens who would not serve in the federal forces seemed inclined to participate in a state militia. While many Missourians might disapprove of Northern policy and war in general, they were interested in pacifying their own state. A militia could better suppress "the civil and social war" raging in Missouri than out-of-state troops because of their familiarity with the terrain and with local conditions. In so doing, they would be aiding the federal government. Since the state could not provide for their "arming, maintenance and pay," that should be done by the Administration at Washington. The resolution directed the Governor to proceed to the national capital "to make known to the General Government the condition of the State, its military organization and finances, and to propose to that Government such measures as will enable the State to cooperate efficiently in the prosecution of the present war."[6]

Having fulfilled the Governor's requests, the convention adjourned. It agreed that its existence should terminate at the convening of the legislature which was to be elected in 1862, unless the Governor called it together before that time.[7] Never again was Gamble to find this group so cooperative. Its members recognized that Missouri stood at a crisis. They had no alternative save that of strengthening the Provisional Government to the utmost if the state wished to preserve any independence of action in the months which were to follow.

Governor Gamble soon went to Washington in accordance with the wishes of the convention. In several conferences he outlined the work and directives of that body to President Lincoln. Anticipating large troop needs for the projected military offenses east of the Mississippi River, the President could readily see the value of the proposals for a state militia to relieve federal forces in Missouri. He requested Gamble, on November 4, to draw up specific plans for cooperation between the state of Missouri and the federal government in maintaining the militia. The President made only one proviso: the proposal should be as consistent as possible with the federal laws and regulations for volunteer regiments.

Gamble set to work immediately and was able to submit a memorandum to the President the following day. The Governor was to raise a military force to serve within Missouri which would cooperate with federal forces in repelling any invasion of the state and in putting down rebellion there. This force was "to be armed, equipped, clothed, subsisted, transported, and paid by the United States during such time as they shall be actually engaged as an embodied military force." The Governor was to appoint officers as set forth in the memorandum. To prevent the possibility of any charges of corruption being levied against state officials, Gamble proposed that federal officers handle the disbursement of funds, materials, etc., unless the War Department wished him to designate someone else to do so.

The President promptly endorsed the Gamble plan. On November 6, he sent it to the War Department with the single proviso that the Governor should appoint the commander of the Department of the West as major general commanding the M.S.M. This had been suggested by General McClellan when Montgomery Blair questioned the possibility of divided authority over the troops. General Order Number Ninety-six of the War Department put the memorandum into effect the following day. Governor Gamble, before leaving Washington, appointed Charles Gibson as the state's agent to work with federal authorities in implementing the agreement.[8]

During these negotiations, word arrived that General Frémont had relinquished the military command in Missouri to General Hunter. To the disgust of the latter, the appointment proved temporary. On November 9, the War Department dissolved the departments of the West, Cumberland, and Ohio to form three new commands. These were the Department of New Mexico, assigned to Colonel E. R. S. Canby; the Department of Kansas to be commanded by Hunter (who considered this a demotion); and the Department of the Missouri, whose new commander was Major General Henry Wager Halleck.[9]

Halleck, a native New Yorker and a West Point graduate in the Class of 1839, headed a California law firm when the war began. Through the influence of General Scott, his close personal friend, Halleck received a commission as major general in August, 1861. He was ordered to St. Louis the following November. His new command included Missouri, Minnesota, Wisconsin, Illinois, Arkansas, and that portion of Kentucky west of the Cumberland River. In March of the following year, this was merged into the new Department of the Mississippi, with Halleck continuing in command of the enlarged area.[10]

General Halleck arrived in St. Louis on November 18, 1861, to assume his new post. Before leaving Washington, he held at least two long conversations with Attorney-General Bates. Halleck gave every evidence that he realized the importance of co-operation with the Provisional Government of Missouri in implementing the new militia policy. He urged Bates to write his friends in St. Louis and ask them to call upon him when he arrived there. In complying with Halleck's request, Bates told Glover and Broadhead: "You'll find him accessible & frank, & I think really anxious to do good, & be on the best terms with the true men of the state." Charles Gibson also met Halleck in Washington. He found that the General held views on Missouri which "accord entirely with my own." He reported to Gamble quite optimistically: "I doubt not you will get along with him agreeably."[11]

Thus, the Governor must have had high hopes for the success of his militia operation when he appointed Halleck major general of the M.S.M. under General Order Number One, dated

November 25. The new commander quickly realized that, with the heavy demands of a large department, he did not have the time necessary to oversee the force directly. With Gamble's approval, he named John M. Schofield as brigadier general of the militia with full command of that force within the state. To the latter fell the task of organizing and training the new state troops.

The appointment of Schofield was a wise one. He had a thorough acquaintance with the needs of Missouri. A West Point graduate, he had served as a professor of physics at Washington University in St. Louis prior to the war. He had played an important role in recruiting volunteers for federal service there when the conflict broke out. Following this, he had accompanied Lyon into the field as his adjutant. Of calmer emotions than that martyred hero, Schofield was no less ardent a Unionist. He performed yeoman service with the militia in the months which followed, and eventually he moved into higher posts, including two stints as federal commander in Missouri. In whatever position, Governor Gamble found Schofield one of the most understanding and cooperative of the military men with whom he had to deal.[12]

Charles Gibson had been active in Washington putting other details of the plan into effect. He arrived in St. Louis early in December with a Treasury draft for $250,000 in favor of Gamble for payment of the militia. The Governor deposited the funds to his own account and paid them out on his personal check. It is to his credit that, although his enemies later raised other charges against him, no one ever questioned Gamble's handling of these funds. At the same time the first allotment of arms and equipment arrived. It was enough for 7,000 men. In mid-January, word came that a large supply of clothing and 15,000 additional stand of arms were being shipped. The M.S.M. began to take shape.

The old state militia still existed, but faced with the obvious impracticality of jointly maintaining two different forces, the

Governor now ordered it dissolved. The men were paid off, and those who wished to do so were allowed to join the new force.[13]

It soon became evident that the agreement between the state and federal governments presented difficulties. A technical interpretation by federal officials made it impossible for them to pay and equip less than a full company of eighty-three men. Accordingly, the state was forced to assume responsibility for paying the men forming a new group until enough enlisted to make a complete company. Governor Gamble found it necessary to go again to Washington in January, 1862, to straighten out this difficulty. There he secured a more favorable arrangement whereby men were mustered into the service singly, the federal government paying them from the moment of their enlistment.[14]

By April 15, 1862, some 13,800 men had enrolled in the M.S.M. and had taken the field under General Schofield. These state forces replaced federal troops which were then transferred to the more immediate war areas. Most of the military districts into which the state was divided gradually came under the command of militia officers. In this same period, large numbers of men were being recruited for actual federal service as Missouri Volunteers.[15]

New difficulties arose when Congress, in confirming the agreement between Lincoln and Gamble, provided that the force to be paid from federal funds should not exceed 10,000 men. Consolidation of regiments and the mustering out of some of the troops necessarily resulted. The remaining force served with much credit during its term of enlistment.[16]

Secessionists and guerrillas were not the only menaces to the peace of Missouri. Kansas Jayhawkers, led by Senator James H. Lane and Dr. Charles R. Jennison ("Jim" and "Doc") moved into the western counties under the pretense of protecting government supply trains and other property from the guerrillas. Veterans of the bitter border warfare of the 1850's, Lane and Jennison found it impossible to think of Missourians in any terms other than as slaveholders and natural enemies. They consequently looted and burned indiscriminately wherever they went. By mid-December, Halleck was writing General McClellan at Washington: "The conduct of the forces under Lane and Jennison has done more for the enemy in this State than could have been accomplished by 20,000 of his own army. I receive almost daily complaints of outrages committed by these men in the name of the United States, and the evidence is so conclusive as to leave no doubt of their correctness." In response to a strong protest from Governor Gamble, Halleck advised: "I am doing all in my power to prevent outrages of the kind you refer to, but the want of organization & discipline of the troops, and the inefficiency & bad character of many of the volunteer officers are such that I cannot yet entirely prevent them."[17]

The situation on the border had become so unbearable by the early part of 1862 that Halleck ordered General Pope to drive the Kansans out of Missouri. If they resisted, the Commander directed Pope to disarm them and hold them prisoners. After considerable vacillation, General Hunter, on January 30, forbade any trips by Kansas troops into Missouri unless they had specific authorization from the departmental commander. At the same time he ordered the disbanding of all armed groups not in regular service and threatened to arrest those who violated his orders. General Halleck quickly wrote him: "I am delighted with your recent orders. Keep the Kansas troops out of Missouri and I will keep the Missourians out of Kansas. They can't agree, and make infinite trouble. The only way is to keep them apart."[18]

Meanwhile, George C. Bingham, well-known artist and newly appointed state treasurer, kept up a steady flow of reports from Kansas City to Congressman James S. Rollins in Washington. Bingham urged that action be taken against Jennison from there. Rollins and Congressman Thomas L. Price interceded with the new secretary of war, Edwin M. Stanton, who ordered Assistant Inspector Major A. Baird to investigate and report on the situation. The Inspector did so. He confirmed all previous reports with the observation that the lawlessness could be quelled permanently only by transferring the Kansans to another field of action.

Stanton assured the congressmen "that no effort on the part of the Government will be spared to protect the Union men and loyal citizens of Missouri from all illegal force and lawless violence, come from what quarter it may." General Halleck called out local militia. By April, three companies were stationed along the border to prevent further depredations. Jennison was arrested and relieved of his command that same month, but the political influence of Jim Lane quickly secured his release and ultimate reinstatement. The border area continued to be the scene of great difficulties throughout the war.[19]

Another problem, this of a political nature, faced Governor Gamble by mid-December, 1861. The sixty-day period allowed by the convention for state officials to take the test oath had elapsed. Many had refused to subscribe. Among these were State Treasurer A. W. Morrison, Attorney-General J. Proctor Knott, Register of Lands John F. Houston, and Justices William B. Napton, William Scott, and Ephraim B. Ewing of the Missouri Supreme Court. As a result, their offices were declared vacant. Gamble, charged with finding replacements, appointed able men to fill the vacancies. He named George Caleb Bingham, the noted artist, as state treasurer; Aikman Welch, the vice-president of the convention, attorney-general; and Sample Orr, the Constitutional Union candidate for governor in 1860, register of lands. To fill the Supreme Court vacancies, the Governor chose Barton Bates, the son of the Attorney-General; William V. N. Bay, a former congressman and prominent lawyer of Franklin County; and Benjamin T. Loan. The latter declined because of his desire to continue as commander of the M.S.M. in the Northwest Missouri District. Lieutenant-Governor Hall, acting in Gamble's absence, then named John D. S. Dryden, an eminent attorney from Palmyra.[20] Thus an entirely new set of officials took office under the Provisional Government. Most of them remained at their posts throughout that administration.

On January 10, 1862, the United States Senate expelled Trusten Polk and Waldo P. Johnson, its two members from Missouri, on charges of disloyalty. Neither had taken his seat during the current session of Congress, and both were reported in the South at the time. This action gave Governor Gamble two more appointments to make. He chose John B. Henderson of Louisiana and Robert Wilson of Andrew County. Henderson, a quite prominent Unionist and a popular choice, had played an active role in the state convention and had served as a district commander of the first state militia under the Provisional Government. Wilson, the president of the convention, seemingly owed his selection to Lieutenant-Governor Hall, who announced the appointments in Gamble's absence. Gibson and Frank Blair had wired Gamble urging the appointment of Samuel T. Glover, but their message either reached Missouri too late or the Governor ignored it. Some of the more radical press attacked the Wilson appointment as being too conservative. The *Missouri Statesman* at Columbia deplored these attacks and assured its readers that Wilson would prove an able if not a distinguished senator.[21]

Lieutenant-Governor Hall served as acting governor from January 15 until the latter part of March, 1862, while Gamble lingered in the East. The Governor had gone to Washington to straighten out the difficulties involved in mustering in the state militia. While there he decided to go on to Philadelphia, where he underwent on operation for the excision of a cancer in his face.[22] The need for surgery at this time is but an indication of the ill health which plagued Gamble throughout his administration.

Another concern of the Provisional Government and the military authorities that winter was the question of amnesty for returning secessionists who had become disillusioned with war. Governor Gamble, in his proclamation of August 3, had promised that those wishing to return to the state would be unmolested if they came back peacefully. This rather general pardon raised a variety of problems as many who had gone South began to make their way back to Missouri. Overzealous Home Guards, later to be disbanded by General Halleck, frequently took matters into their own hands. They shot or imprisoned returnees in spite of their assurances of a change of heart. One colonel of an Iowa regiment serving in Missouri attempted to force returning ex-secessionists into the federal army. Some of the Southerners, of course, came back under false pretenses, seeking to use the amnesty policy as a cover for recruiting more men for Price's army.[23]

In an attempt to protect those earnestly desiring to return peacefully, the state convention in October directed that the test oath should be the badge of loyalty. Anyone giving up his allegiance to the Confederacy and subscribing to the oath would not be molested. Governor Gamble reported this action to President Lincoln and sought his support in its application. In doing so, he stressed that "many members of the convention entertained strong confidence that the assurance of forgiveness thus to be offered would induce many misguided men to return peacefully to their allegiance." It would at least be worth the experiment, in the Governor's thinking.[24]

Fortunately Gamble had a military commander willing to accept and implement this policy. A letter from Halleck to the Governor in March, 1862, clearly indicates that the two were following the same course, for the General informed Gamble: "All persons arrested, not for criminal offenses, are released on taking the printed oath of allegiance and giving bonds for future good conduct."[25]

A month later, James O. Broadhead, recently appointed United States district attorney for eastern Missouri, sought instructions from Attorney-General Bates concerning indictments for treason or conspiracy. He believed the amnesty held out by Governor Gamble had induced many to return sincerely to their allegiance. He recommended that these not be criminally prosecuted.

The Attorney-General replied that it was difficult to give a standard formula because "great changes are being made in our military and political relations with the revolted States any minute." Bates did not think it desirable to prosecute treason cases where little chance of success existed. He agreed that Gamble's proclamation should be upheld and confided that he understood "the President is personally pledged to it." As to minor offenses, the Attorney-General told Broadhead to use his own judgment.[26]

Working in conjunction with Governors Gamble and Hall, General Halleck issued a series of orders between December and March designed to strengthen the Provisional Government through an extension of the convention test oath. On December 9, the Commander asked Mayor Daniel G. Taylor of St. Louis to require all city officers to take the oath. He ordered that all state officials who failed to subscribe be arrested by the Provost Marshal General if they attempted to exercise civil authority.

Later orders extended the list of those required to take the oath. Included were the officers of the Mercantile Library Association and the St. Louis Chamber of Commerce; the president, professors, curators, and other officers of the University of Missouri; all licensed attorneys, counselors, and proctors; all jurors serving in the state courts; and the presidents and directors of all railroad companies. The last group was also required to file bonds guaranteeing that they would not employ anyone who had not taken the oath. To climax the issue Halleck directed, at Acting Governor Hall's request, that at all future elections the voters would be required to take the oath.[27]

Halleck's popularity within the state and with the state officials was evidenced by the invitation extended him by Acting Governor Hall, Mayor Taylor, and other prominent citizens to a banquet in his honor. This function was to be held before he left St. Louis to take active command of the spring campaign in Tennessee. Although the General declined the honor because of the uncertainty of his plans, he did accept a sword presented him by the Union ladies of St. Louis as a token of their esteem.[28]

When General Halleck left on April 10, 1862, the temporary command at St. Louis devolved upon General Schofield, who received the brief instruction to "take care of Missouri." The Missouri delegation in Congress soon began urging President Lincoln to give Schofield an independent command in the state during Halleck's absence. Halleck objected that "this is more than his rank entitles him to" and threatened to resign if the move was made. As Halleck became more deeply involved in the campaign beyond the Mississippi, however, the necessity of giving Schofield more independence of action seemed imperative. Consequently, the General yielded. On June 1 he issued an order establishing the Military District of Missouri as a separate command under Schofield. The district included the entire state except the three "bootheel" counties. The new commander promptly divided Missouri into five military districts. Each had its own commander from the ranks of the M.S.M. He reported his total effective force, including both volunteers and militia, at 17,360. As the campaign farther south built up, Schofield sent many of the Union regulars to reinforce Halleck in Tennessee and Curtis in Arkansas, leaving Missouri largely dependent upon the militia for protection.[29]

General Curtis had been assigned to the command in southwest Missouri on Christmas Day of 1861. Determined to make the most of his opportunity to take the field, Curtis whipped his army into shape by rigorous discipline. By February 13 he had routed Sterling Price's forces from Springfield, and early in March he decisively defeated the Confederates at Pea Ridge, Arkansas. A signal triumph, many hoped that this victory would relieve Missouri from further Confederate activity. But Curtis soon moved his army farther south and left the way open for the Confederates to begin sending guerrillas into the state. These men came to enlist and organize reinforcements for Price's army with such success that by early summer armed bands roamed Missouri, creating considerable havoc.[30]

Schofield applied to Curtis for help but failed to receive it. Governor Gamble, expressing full faith in the new commander, urged the Secretary of War to send him Ohio and Wisconsin cavalry then stationed at Fort Scott, Kansas. Stanton hesitated to commit them although they were being held inactive. Gamble wired Bates for help; there was none to be had. Fighting raged on all fronts that summer, so Missouri was forced to wait for help. Indeed, the War Department called upon the Governor for troops to be used in the Eastern theater. Gamble was compelled to write The Adjutant General that it would be impossible to supply any cavalry regiments for use elsewhere because of the urgent need for them at home.[31]

On May 29 General Schofield laid down his program for ridding Missouri of guerrilla warfare. "The time is passed when insurrection and rebellion in Missouri can cloak itself under the guise of honorable warfare," he declared. Marauders "caught in arms" were to be shot down on the spot. Citizens who desired peace should help his men in detecting and punishing outlaws and those who protected them. Those citizens who did not cooperate with the M.S.M. would be considered as no more loyal than those they failed to help apprehend. At the same time Schofield reminded his own officers that they were "not only to abstain from molestation, but to protect from injury all loyal and peaceable citizens."[32]

As the situation worsened, Schofield took more drastic steps. On June 23, he ordered all "rebels and rebel sympathizers" held responsible in their property and persons for damages done by the guerrillas. Five thousand dollars would be collected from these persons for every soldier or Union citizen killed, and from one thousand to five thousand dollars for each one wounded. Full value for all property destroyed would be assessed against and collected from them if they lived in the vicinity of that property. All money collected was to go to the heirs of those killed, to the person wounded, or to the property owners. To carry out these orders Schofield directed the district commanders to appoint county boards of assessment made up of loyal citizens. These boards were to enroll all known rebels and rebel sympathizers and distribute among them any damages reported.[33]

Failing to get reinforcement from outside the state, Schofield decided to call for an all-out enlistment of the state militia. With the consent of Governor Gamble, he issued, on July 22, an order calling upon all those eligible for militia service to enroll in order that the guerrillas infesting the state might be exterminated. Although the Union men responded enthusiastically, many hitherto silent secessionists either hastened to join the nearest guerrilla band or fled the state.

By November of 1862, seventy regiments of this new force had been organized. It became known as the Enrolled Missouri Militia (E.M.M.). The Adjutant General of the state reported, following an inspection trip of the forces in central Missouri, that he was greeted everywhere with but one request: "*Give us arms and the authority,* and our country shall soon be rid of rebels and guerrillas."[34]

This new body of troops supplemented rather than replaced the M.S.M., so that additional means had to be found to pay them. Once again the Provisional Government turned to the federal authorities. Gamble wrote the Secretary of the Treasury on September 17 that all funds appropriated earlier by Congress had been used to pay the excess 3,000 men recruited in the M.S.M. Nothing remained to take care of the pay and subsistence for the 40,000 men of the E.M.M. except that which was taken from disaffected citizens. The Governor asked that money be appropriated by Congress to meet these new demands.

Gamble's agent in the East, Charles Gibson, again busied himself for the Missouri cause. He reported to the Governor on October 3 that Secretary of War Stanton had signed a new requisition for $250,000 to supply the E.M.M. Gamble went to Washington in mid-November to complete the necessary arrangements. Ultimately, departmental headquarters issued an order on January 9, 1863, by which the federal government agreed to forage, subsist, and transport members of the E.M.M. when in actual service on order of the Governor. The state government assumed responsibility for their pay.[35]

The Provisional Government, however, had no funds of its own to take care of the militia. Had it waited for federal authorities to clear all the red tape necessary for appropriations, it would have faced widespread dissension. So it became necessary to look for funds elsewhere until federal support could be obtained. The principal means of securing money during this early period was the levying of arbitrary assessments against disloyal citizens by the various militia commanders. This policy was not new to Missouri. General Halleck had employed it the previous winter to secure funds to aid refugees pouring into St. Louis from southwest Missouri in the wake of Price's army. General Schofield announced the first of the new series of assessments on August 28, 1862. He levied against the "rebels of Saint Louis County" an assessment of $500,000 "to be used in arming, clothing, and subsisting the enrolled militia when in active service and in providing for those families of militiamen and volunteers which might be left destitute." Using his previous pattern, he selected a board of five respected citizens to determine and collect individual assessments. Brigadier General Ben Loan and Colonel Lewis Merrill of the M.S.M. followed his example by levying smaller assessments in various portions of the interior of the state.[36]

While waiting for the funds from this source, Governor Gamble took the more immediate step of requisitioning the St. Louis banks for temporary financial assistance. On September 1, he notified them that the need for $150,000 to buy arms for the militia could not wait. He therefore divided the sum among them in proportion to their capital and promised to repay out of the first money received from the assessments.[37]

While most of the E.M.M. performed notable service in their respective areas, abuses frequently crept into the system. In many local situations, assessments led to confiscations as it became necessary to arrange subsistence for the E.M.M. on duty. At this point some of the militia committed outrages against their "secessionist" neighbors which paralleled in many respects those of out-of-state troops. Local militia officers were usually at fault in these instances. Gamble and the district commanders constantly sought to remedy these violations when they learned of them.[38]

The General Assembly, elected in November, attempted a further solution of the money problem. In March of 1863, it authorized the Governor to issue $1,000,000 in "Union Military Bonds." These were payable in twelve months at 6 per cent interest. The bonds were to be supported by the "monies that may come into the Treasury of the State from appropriations made by Congress . . . for the purpose of paying the military forces thereof." Further backing would come from a two-dollar poll tax on every citizen and a property tax of one-fifth of 1 per cent. The Governor could borrow up to $1,500,000 on these bonds for one to three years and use this money to pay the E.M.M.[39]

When the yield from this measure proved insufficient to cover the revenue demands of the state, Gamble recommended to the General Assembly at its adjourned session the following November the issue of an additional $1,500,000 in "Union Military Bonds." To help overcome the depreciation of the previous issue, he asked that the March bonds be made receivable for a part of the general state tax. The legislature complied. It authorized the State Treasurer to accept the bonds for all state taxes up to 50 per cent for the years 1863 and 1864 and for delinquent payments. At the same time it ordered the Treasurer to deposit all monies in the "Union Military Fund" in the Missouri State Bank of St. Louis, to be used in redeeming the bonds when they came due.[40]

General Schofield had announced originally that exemption from service in the E.M.M. might be purchased for a rather small sum, in the hope that this money might be used to help pay militia subsistence. Quickly realizing the inequity of this policy, he revoked it a week later and ordered all loyal men to report for duty. "Disloyal men and those who have at any time sympathized with the rebellion" should report to the nearest headquarters, be enrolled as such, and surrender their arms. They could then return to their homes "where they will be permitted to remain so long as they shall continue quietly attending to their ordinary and legitimate business and in no way give aid or comfort to the enemy."[41]

The decision to rely on the enrollment of local militia did not prove popular with some of the more ardent Unionists, especially in St. Louis. They still tended to look upon the residents of the interior as pro-Southern at heart. They doubted the reliability of local militia as opposed to federal troops when it came to a showdown in defending Missouri. The new order emphatically stated that disloyalists should not be organized into companies "nor required nor permitted to do duty in the Missouri Militia." Yet some careless officials did mistakenly enroll registered secession sympathizers into the E.M.M. Others no doubt joined under false pretenses to escape possible assessment. Whatever the cause, reports began to spread that the E.M.M. could not be relied upon. Inevitably much of the blame fell on Governor Gamble.[42]

A delegation of St. Louis Unionists, led by Henry T. Blow, journeyed to Washington early in August, 1862. They sought the removal of Schofield from his command and the diminution of Gamble's influence in military affairs. To add strength to their proposals they claimed to have the authorization of Frank Blair, but Blair denied this. He desired a military commander in Missouri—whether Schofield or some other mattered little—who would be "authorized to act without respect to Governor Gamble." He told General Halleck that none of the Union men had any confidence in Gamble; consequently, he should be ignored. Blair also recommended the disbanding of the state military organization as far as practicable.[43]

Frank Blair had written in this vein to his brother Montgomery a few days earlier. In this more confidential letter, he revealed his prejudice against the state militia by asserting that they should be mustered into federal service even as the German Home Guards had been. He cited the great dissatisfaction among the German radicals in St. Louis because of this action. The Home Guards had been promised at the time of their original enrollment that they would not see service outside the state. Now, having lost their irregular status, many of them served farther south. As to Gamble, Frank confided: "I believe that he is now disposed to do what is right, but our people will not give him credit for it and will not accept the right thing at his hands for fear of some lurking sinister design." He disagreed with those who wished Gamble replaced by a military governor, although he reiterated his feeling that the Governor should be ignored in military matters.[44]

Gamble was not unaware of this criticism. In an open letter directed at his critics, the Governor defended the militia and praised the service they had rendered. He declared it unfair to criticize them or him when "the need for the militia is plain." Writing to General Halleck, who had just become general-in-chief of all United States forces, the Governor again defended "my pet State Militia." He reported: they "fight well." Anticipating continued trouble from the guerrillas, Gamble asked if some of the Missouri volunteer regiments might not be sent home to protect their state. He also informed Halleck that he had written President Lincoln to see if the military draft might not be suspended in Missouri. Again he argued that many would serve in the militia who would flee the state before consenting to draft service in federal forces. Significantly, Gamble closed by referring to the "disposition to criticise General Schofield and to have him removed from the command." These critics were radicals "incapable of judging correctly" the measures necessary to put down rebellion. To answer them, Gamble testified simply: "General Schofield is doing well, according to my judgment."[45]

Charles Gibson wrote Gamble from St. Louis that "many evil disposed persons for their own selfish & ambitious ends are

General Lyon

Frank Blair, Jr.

Governor Jackson

General Price

Rival Leaders at Outset of War

Plate 1

Governor Gamble

Willard P. Hall

Edward Bates

John B. Henderson

They Kept Missouri in the Union

Plate 2

General Frémont

General Halleck

General Curtis

General Rosecrans

General Schofield

Union Military Commanders of Missouri

Charles D. Drake

B. Gratz Brown

Thomas C. Fletcher

Missouri's Radical Leaders

Plate 4

busy circulating & fabricating various rumors & conjectures to the effect that the President is about to displace you & appoint a military Governor for this State." As a result, seeds of discord and misunderstanding were being planted in the minds of many Union men to weaken the hand of the Provisional Government. Gibson urged Gamble to issue a second proclamation branding the rumors as scurrilous so that there might be no misapprehension as to the cordiality of federal-state relations. At the same time he recommended arresting those responsible for the rumors.[46] The Governor took no such action. He doubtless realized that to do so would simply accentuate the charges and give them wider currency.

General Halleck had kept Schofield informed of the activities of his enemies in Washington. Now he received a reply: "As to the charge of inefficiency, I believe it comes solely from the men who would have me adopt an extreme policy, not sanctioned by yourself or by the President. If I thought otherwise I would ask to be relieved at once; and if, upon examination, you think the good of the service will be promoted thereby, I will cheerfully accept a less responsible command."

In an unofficial letter to Halleck the same day, August 12, Schofield expressed the fear that some might use the current discontent to attempt dividing his command. This would be an extremely unwise move, he thought. It was "not only important but absolutely necessary" to have Missouri and Arkansas under the same department because of projected military operations and their common dependence upon St. Louis as a base of supplies. He recommended strongly that Kansas be placed in the same department with Missouri in order to secure harmonious relations between the forces of the two. This much-needed cooperation seemed impossible to accomplish as long as two separate commands existed.[47]

While official Washington pondered charge and countercharge, forces along the western border operated to indicate the wisdom and urgency of Schofield's latest recommendation. That area had been plagued throughout the spring and summer of 1862 by the guerrilla activities of William Quantrill and his gang. These Confederate partisans had been goaded into action originally by the Lane-Jennison raids of the previous winter. Once begun, their retaliatory measures increased in tempo as the spring progressed. They harassed Union communications and supply trains and generally disrupted the entire command in that area. They were familiar with the country and received support from many of the citizens who had suffered at the hands of the Kansans. They could strike quickly and vanish almost into thin air. Orders to the militia to kill them on sight only increased their zeal.

The climax of all this activity came on August 11. Quantrill and his men attacked and captured the Union garrison at Independence, a major post on the border. Schofield now undertook a concerted effort to rid the area of guerrillas. To do this, he sought the cooperation of Brigadier General James B. Blunt, commanding the Military District of Kansas. The campaign which followed turned out miserably, due in large measure to the dilatory movement of Kansas troops sent by Blunt.

Early on the morning of September 6, the will-o'-the-wisp Quantrill appeared at the small town of Olathe, Kansas. He captured its garrison and thoroughly looted it, killing three civilians. This galvanized the Kansans into action. A fruitless ten-day chase followed across three western Missouri counties.[48]

To add to the tumult, Lane and Jennison began sending irregular raiding parties into Missouri to take advantage of the general disruption. One of the primary purposes of these marauders was to steal or entice Missouri slaves away from their masters to serve in Lane's "nigger regiment." The Kansas senator prided himself on his Negro "recruits." He taught them that Missourians were traitors and had no rights which they were bound to respect. He armed them without any federal authority and then sent them back into Missouri to seek more recruits from among their fellows.

By early September the people of Clay and Jackson counties became so alarmed that they sent a delegation to Governor Gamble seeking some sort of relief. Late in August the E.M.M. had captured eight of Jennison's irregulars in Clay County. The raiders had twenty-five Negroes and forty horses which they had stolen indiscriminately from the farmers in the area. When the local officials refused "Doc's" demand for the prisoners' release, he threatened retaliation by making a grand recruitment raid into Missouri. He boastfully estimated that some 5,000 or 6,000 Negroes would flock to his banner. The entire force would "forage on the enemy." Any who did not follow him would be hanged from the first tree.

Alarmed, Gamble forwarded the delegation's bill of particulars to the President. With it, he dispatched a strong note seeking Lincoln's intervention. "If such an invasion is made I will resist it with all the force I can command," he warned, with a promise to give the Kansans "a taste of the evils of war in their own territory."[49]

Although rumors of an invasion by Jennison continued to trouble the Missouri air throughout October, none materialized. The border settled down. Quantrill and his men moved south for the winter. Then, late in November, the "invasion" occurred. A detachment of the Twelfth Kansas Cavalry, under Colonel Charles W. Adams, a brother-in-law of Jim Lane, marched into Jackson County. The cavalry came ostensibly to look for bushwhackers. Failing to find any, they turned to indiscriminate plunder. Soon they had forty slaves, mostly children, better than one hundred horses, and miscellaneous wagons, mules, cattle, and household goods as booty.

Before the raiders could recross the state line, a troop of M.S.M. under Brigadier General Richard C. Vaughn intercepted them. Vaughn had already ascertained from Generals Curtis and Loan that the Kansans had no authority to be in Missouri. As the Kansans drew themselves up in battle formation to confront the Missourians, Vaughn sent a messenger forward to ask under what orders they were operating. Adams transmitted one from General Blunt. Dated October 9, it directed the Twelfth Kansas Cavalry to keep order along the border. It specifically forbade them to plunder.

An interview between the commanding officers followed. Vaughn demanded the return of all the property taken and the release of the slaves. Adams demurred on the latter, but when Vaughn insisted forcefully, the Kansan gave in rather than risk a fight with fellow Unionists. Vaughn thereupon arrested Adams for violating his orders and directed him to report to St. Louis on December 15 for trial. With nightfall coming on, he decided to wait until morning to transfer the stolen property. During the night, however, the Kansans attempted to escape. Vaughn pursued and overtook them. He arrested Adams' subordinate, Lieutenant Colonel Josiah E. Hayes, who had engineered the flight. Vaughn now directed the immediate release of the Negroes and the return of the stolen property to its rightful owners. He ordered Hayes to report to St. Louis with Adams. Then he provided an escort for the Kansans, to ensure their return whence they had come without further incident.

Adams and Hayes reported to departmental headquarters at St. Louis at the designated time. Major General Samuel R. Curtis, now commanding the department, sifted the evidence on both sides. This indicated strongly that the Kansans did nothing to advance the interest of the department in crossing the state line. Obviously, they had violated military etiquette in refusing to cooperate with the officer in whose district they were operating. Yet Curtis released them and ordered them restored to active duty.[50] This wrist-slapping exercise did little to assuage the irritated feelings of Missouri officials who had already begun agitating for Curtis' removal. But this story remains to be told.

6

Difficulties Mount Under Curtis

INCREASINGLY, the reports from the border had brought the War Department and General Halleck to the realization that tighter unifying action along organizational lines needed to be accomplished. It will be recalled that in March, 1862, the then departments of Kansas and of the Missouri had been consolidated with everything west of Knoxville, Tennessee, to form the Department of the Mississippi. This in turn had been divided into military districts. Since Halleck's move to Washington in July as general-in-chief, the Department of the Mississippi had been largely a paper entity. Now came a decision to divide it into its original component parts, with one major exception. The newly created Department of the Missouri, established on September 19, included Kansas and the Indian Territory in addition to Missouri and Arkansas. According to Halleck, Schofield's recommendation of August 12 was a major factor in the Administration's decision.

The President appointed Major General Curtis to command the new department, with headquarters at St. Louis. In writing Schofield, Halleck explained this appointment as "the only way of cutting the knot" of political demands upon the President. With Western politicians, including the Blairs, "pulling all kinds of political wires to cut up the West into departments for the benefit of each," the appointment of Curtis could be defended on the ground that he was the ranking officer in the area.[1]

Samuel R. Curtis was no stranger to St. Louis and Missouri. A native of New York, he had graduated from West Point in 1831. The outbreak of the Civil War found him practicing law in Keokuk, Iowa, and serving his district in Congress. He resigned his seat there in August, 1861, to accept appointment as brigadier general. The following month, he arrived in St. Louis to begin his war career. His service under Frémont and his command of the army in southwest Missouri and in Arkansas have already been noted. His decisive victory at Pea Ridge won him promotion to major general and paved the way for his new command.[2] Curtis had proven himself in the field, yet he never ceased being a politician-general. This duality ultimately brought his downfall in Missouri.

General Schofield was at Springfield when he learned of the new arrangement. He was undoubtedly disappointed at not being promoted to the position Curtis now assumed. He promptly wrote Governor Gamble asking to be relieved from the command of the District of Missouri and the state militia. Under the new setup, he preferred command in the field army in southwest Missouri then engaged in an attempt to drive the guerrillas out of the state. Curtis complied with his request two days later. He abolished the District of Missouri and gave Schofield temporary command of the forces in the field. This responsibility the latter continued to hold until November 20 when he relinquished the post temporarily because of ill health.[3]

There now arose, at Gamble's instigation, a question which boded ill for the future relationship of the Governor and the new commander. On September 22, three days after Curtis assumed command of the department and technically the command of the M.S.M., Gamble wrote General Halleck. An officer of volunteers in St. Louis had claimed the right to command the E.M.M. and to order them into service. The Governor raised the question of whether the M.S.M. and the E.M.M. were state or federal troops and asked who had authority to command them.[4]

Halleck replied on September 27 in a cold, detailed letter which completely missed the point of Gamble's inquiry. Most of the message was a citation of procedure for mustering state militia into federal service. This concerned the Governor not at all. Only in a brief final paragraph did the General even touch the question at hand. There he stated that he agreed with Gamble that federal officers had no authority over the E.M.M. until the units were brought into actual United States service.[5]

This constituted a somewhat evasive answer, but Gamble did not pursue the matter until other circumstances forced the question into sharper focus. Upon the recommendation of an examining board, the Governor had dismissed Colonel Albert Jackson of the M.S.M. for incompetence. The Colonel appealed his case to the Secretary of War, seeking reinstatement on the ground that the Governor had no legal authority to dismiss him. The points raised entailed a lengthy conference of Lincoln, Halleck, and Stanton to determine who commanded the militia, the President or the Governor. Gibson wrote Gamble that the trio considered the command of the Missouri militia a most important issue. On it hinged the President's control of the militia of the other states.[6]

The upshot of the White House conference was a decision that Colonel Jackson's discharge was illegal. Halleck wrote Gamble accordingly on October 3. The grounds used to arrive at this conclusion indicate that the War Department considered the Missouri militia as actual United States troops.[7]

Gamble protested in a long, bitter letter. Reiterating his question of September 22, he informed Halleck that it still lacked an answer. The Governor denied that the militia in any way constituted United States troops. He asked Halleck to re-examine the original agreement setting up the militia. Colonel Jackson had never been mustered into federal service. Indeed, Jackson had served as the muster officer in bringing his men into the service of the state. Consequently, the Governor asserted that he had full authority to dismiss him. He cited other cases in which he had dismissed men from the state service under similar circumstances. He had also accepted resignations for various causes.

All of this had been done because state troops were involved. Gamble had no objection to the militia being mustered into federal service—if it was done with their consent. These troops had served gallantly in the past; they would continue to do so in the future whatever their status.[8]

This whole proceeding puzzled Gamble. During Halleck's stay in Missouri, the two men had worked closely together in organizing the militia. The Governor thought a feeling of mutual trust and respect had developed between them. His misapprehensions ended when Halleck wrote him unofficially that his two previous communiqués had come at the direction of the Secretary of War. The first, designed for general consumption, had been published to serve as an answer to claims raised by other governors. As to the second, it appeared to Halleck that the original agreement between Gamble and the President had been left deliberately vague. All could interpret it to suit themselves. "I don't think it will make much difference anyway, so far as you and I are concerned," he confided. "I am very certain that it will not, for I know that we can cordially co-operate. If left to me, your action will in all cases be confirmed, for I know that you will do nothing which is not right and just."

To this, the Governor replied promptly and heartily. He concurred readily in the sentiments expressed by Halleck and asserted: "Would to God it were possible for those in power to conceive of a man acting from perfectly unselfish patriotism." Gamble contemplated starting for Washington on business shortly, and he expressed the hope of personal consultation then.[9]

Gamble arrived in the capital in mid-November to solicit additional federal support for the E.M.M. During his consultations at the War Department, the topic of authority over the militia naturally came into the conversation. Halleck undoubtedly had been working on Stanton. The latter now agreed to ratify all past actions by the Governor with regard to removals and resignations. At the same time the Secretary asked the right to approve all future ones. This the Governor considered a restriction upon his authority. He feared its undermining influence at home. He unwisely wrote President Lincoln before leaving the capital to ask that the question be settled by him. "I have been about to consolidate the regiments," he reported. "I have no such power if they are not a state force."

When he failed to receive an answer toward the end of his stay in the East, the Governor wrote Bates from Philadelphia. He asked him to bring pressure upon the President to make a decision in the matter. Lincoln was vexed at this continued agitation of what seemed to him a relatively minor problem. He had difficulty in hiding his annoyance while discussing the situation with the Attorney-General. The President could not understand that Gamble sought political support to show his constituency. Lincoln feared that a specific statement would bring in a raft of new problems. Better, he thought, to settle each difference as it arose, on the basis of its own merits. Stanton's proposal seemed quite liberal and logical. Another month elapsed, however, before he decided in favor of the Secretary's arrangement.[10]

By mid-December the campaign to open the Mississippi River had begun. Troops were badly needed in that theater. President Lincoln wired both Gamble and Curtis asking if the E.M.M. could maintain law and order north of the Missouri River. Their control of the area would release regular troops for service farther south.

The Governor responded immediately: "I can maintain law and order north of the Missouri River with the enrolled militia alone if they can be certainly provided for with subsistence, clothing, and pay for the time they may be in actual service. . . . Taking other troops would help rather than hinder me. I would keep the smallest number in service that could protect the country." This dispatch is interesting. It seems to indicate Gamble's assumption that he alone controlled the E.M.M. and his desire to show what he could do with them if given the chance. When Gamble received no further word, he wired Lincoln to ask the President's intentions. He requested that immediate orders be given so that arrangements could be made.[11]

The President replied that he did not wish to institute the arrangement without the "concurrent judgment" of both Curtis and Gamble. The former's had not been received. He suggested the two men confer and reach agreement.

Curtis had answered Lincoln's original query promptly enough, but in the negative. He asked that the matter be left to his discretion. He promised to pull the regular troops out of the region soon. Such a move would be unwise at present, however, because the area had just been cleared of guerrillas. Even now they might be filtering through the lines. Curtis hinted vaguely that the E.M.M. was not always reliable. Many of its officers were proslavery men, and the General advanced the opinion that some secessionists had entered its ranks.

Curtis also broached the subject of conflicting authority. Gamble seemed to "desire the sole control" of the E.M.M. The Governor had so worded the commission making him major general of the M.S.M. as to seem to exclude him from any control over the other militia. Curtis considered himself commander of all troops in the state but, he confided, he had been careful not to press the issue. He and Gamble got along pretty well. As the use of the E.M.M. increased, however, a definite statement of the "paramount sovereignty" of the United States would have to be made and enforced in such a way as to "avoid eternal discord and strife."[12]

Perhaps one reason Curtis did not care to press the issue of authority with Gamble came from his awareness that efforts had been made already to have him removed from command of the department. Whether Curtis knew the source of these efforts is not clear. Certainly Gamble wasted no time in seeking to make his appointment as short as possible. To aid him, the Governor chose a strange partner: Montgomery Blair. Five days after Curtis assumed the command, Gamble queried the Postmaster-General: "How on earth did he [Curtis] come to be appointed to this Department?" He claimed that the General was more a politician and a cotton speculator than a military man, and decried having such an individual in command at such a crucial time. "Help us to get clear of Curtis," he pleaded.

Gamble found Blair a willing ally, although had he known the reason he might have been wary. The Postmaster-General had been boosting his brother Frank for departmental commander and was quite disappointed when Lincoln bypassed him. Now he wrote the Governor that Halleck had been responsible for the Curtis appointment. He promised to do what he could to help Gamble "get clear" of him. Blair asked for evidence of Curtis' cotton speculations—information which might be used to further the project. This evidence the Governor provided. Blair laid the Curtis case before Halleck and Lincoln. The President, seemingly impressed with Curtis throughout, informed the General that charges had been preferred against him and asked for a reply.

Curtis responded quickly. Although he did not know his accusers or their charges, he could guess at their identity. He had heard rumors that the matter concerned his policy of licensing cotton speculators during the time he commanded the forces in Arkansas. Curtis explained his policy. He charged those ("secessionists") whom he had excluded from cotton dealing as being the source of the present trouble. He denied any personal involvement in speculation and apologized to Lincoln for causing him concern in the matter. The President apparently accepted his explanation, for the matter ended here.[13]

The most serious disputes during the Curtis regime concerned the issues of confiscating the property of and collecting assessments against pro-Southern men. These levies became so great that eventually they led to an open break between Gamble and Curtis. This time, Gamble's objections to Curtis resulted in the latter's removal from his command.

On September 5, Secretary of War Stanton had sent General Schofield a communiqué. As he understood many persons within the Missouri Military District were subject to the Confiscation Act passed by Congress, he asked Schofield to enforce its provisions. This act, passed the previous July, provided for the confiscation of the property of those known to be supporters of the "rebel cause." Slaves whose masters were known "rebels" would be freed whenever the opportunity presented. Upon receipt of Stanton's request, Schofield issued an order to this effect but made no attempt to carry out its enforcement.[14]

General Curtis, however, quickly succumbed to the radicals who demanded the rigid enforcement of the order. He established an unrelenting policy with regard to secessionist sympathizers. To carry out this policy, Curtis expanded and solidified the provost marshal system. This system served as the cornerstone for the administration of martial law in Missouri. Henceforth each military district was to have a provost marshal with as many deputies as he might need. All would be subject to the Provost Marshal General at St. Louis. This military police force had broad authority. If necessary to ensure the peace in their district, they could "cause the arrest and confinement of disloyal persons," and cases of a minor nature might be tried locally. This provision gave these officials tremendous power. Serious offenders were to be sent to St. Louis with sworn charges and evidence in writing. While this system was not new in Missouri, General Curtis made it much more effective and gave its officials new responsibilities. Soon hundreds of arrests were being made. Union stockades and prisons bulged with individuals incarcerated for a variety of reasons.[15]

One of the major problems connected with the rigid enforcement of the Confiscation Act in Missouri concerned the question of runaway slaves. General Halleck had established the policy of excluding these unfortunates from the various military posts and camps throughout the state. He contended that the military could not be responsible for determining whether runaways belonged to a loyal or rebel master and should or should not be returned.[16] The Confiscation Act provided that all fugitive slaves entering Union lines should be given shelter. Under no circumstances should they be returned to their masters. When Curtis sought to implement this policy, trouble quickly followed. Reports began coming in that some of his more ardently radical troops were deliberately enticing Negroes away from their masters and then setting them free when they got into camp. Governor Gamble refused to allow the militia to carry out this policy. When one of the militia commanders, claiming to carry out federal policy, brought some fugitive slaves to St. Louis, contrary to orders that he send them back to their masters, the state Adjutant General suspended him for insubordination.[17]

Curtis issued supplementary orders in an effort to clarify the policy. The new orders specifically forbade the soldiery to entice the slaves of loyal masters. Curtis wrote Brigadier General Ben Loan in northwest Missouri: "The Negroes of loyal Union men should be encouraged to stay at home and mind their business. It is only the Negroes of men in rebellion or giving encouragement to rebellion that are free. Some overt act is implied, and here in Missouri, where a large majority of the State is loyal, we should be quite certain that the occasion for free papers justifies it."[18] The extent to which the district commanders heeded this admonition varied with their political views. The problem of fugitive slaves plagued federal-state relations throughout the rest of the war. Slaves became aware that escape to Union military lines meant automatic freedom. Since there were few who did not take advantage of this avenue to freedom, the Confiscation Act, as much as anything, brought practical emancipation to Missouri.

The idea of martial law had always been repugnant to Gamble. Curtis' increased use of it certainly did not improve the Governor's feelings toward him. There is no evidence that Gamble protested the situation at this time, but Lincoln, apparently alarmed at the increased tension and arrests, wired Curtis on December 17: "Could the civil authority be introduced into Missouri in lieu of the military to any extent with advantage and safety?" The General shot back a message the same day: "The peace of this State rests on military power. To relinquish this power would be dangerous." This exchange closed the matter temporarily, although the Secretary of War did curtail somewhat the provost marshal system in Missouri in mid-January, 1863.[19]

It had been the practice to send people suspected of Southern loyalties to prison or to exile them to some Northern state. Curtis stepped up these banishments. He began to send many of these persons south to join their Confederate friends. Many were wives and families of Missourians who had joined the Southern forces. Those sent in this manner were allowed to take $1,000 with them if they had families, $300 if they were single. The remainder of their property was confiscated for the Union cause.[20]

In carrying out banishments Curtis relied heavily upon the provost marshal system under Franklin A. Dick, his Provost Marshal General, who used so little discretion that much dissatisfaction arose. One case in particular deserves attention. It involved one of St. Louis' more distinguished conservative ministers, the Reverend Mr. Samuel B. McPheeters, pastor of the Pine Street Presbyterian Church. This minister's difficulties had begun the previous June when, in a public ceremony, he baptized Sterling Price Robbins, an infant whose parents belonged to his church. He later claimed that he knew nothing of the baby's name until the parents announced it in the midst of the ceremony. He could not then deny the child the rites of the church. Some of the more radical members of his congregation became incensed and began to examine his public prayers more closely. Their examination led them to decide that he was not vocal enough in upholding those in authority before the Almighty.

Thirty members, led by George K. Strong, a prominent attorney, addressed a communication to McPheeters. They sought to test his loyalty with a series of minute questions to which they wanted explicit answers. The minister replied in general terms to their charges and reminded them that he had taken the test oath as required by the state convention. This failed to satisfy the radicals. A running correspondence continued through the fall. McPheeters refused, as a matter of principle, to allow himself to be interrogated. So heated became the dispute that part of the correspondence took place through the pages of the *Missouri Democrat,* as the Strong faction sought public support.

Most of the members of the Pine Street Church stood behind McPheeters in the controversy. Strong and his supporters never approached a congregational meeting with their charges but contended that the church was filled with "secessionists" and that the pastor aided and abetted their sentiments.

The climax came on December 19. The Provost Marshal General, at the instigation of Strong, issued an order banishing McPheeters and his family from Missouri. He turned over control of the Pine Street Church to a three-man committee of the radical faction. No hearing was held. The order caught the minister completely by surprise. It allowed him ten days to settle his affairs and take up residence somewhere "North of Indianapolis and West of Pennsylvania" for the remainder of the war.[21]

The Session of the church met the following evening. Reluctantly the members agreed to abide by the order, although ecclesiastically they had charge of the congregation in the absence of the pastor. They expressed their deep regret at the fate of their minister while implicitly protesting the order in its entirety.

McPheeters was not content to accept banishment without protest. He packed his suitcase, but not for exile. He knew

Edward Bates quite well, and Governor Gamble's brother was a member of his congregation. The minister decided to take his case to the highest authority in the land. He set out for Washington with the express purpose of securing an interview with Lincoln through Bates's auspices. The Governor offered to write him a letter of commendation to take with him, but McPheeters declined. He feared this would bring him automatic pardon in Washington. Rather, he wished to secure redress at the hands of the President on the merits of his contention that no pastor should be harassed on political questions by a faction of his congregation.

Granted a White House interview through Bates, McPheeters made a convincing presentation of his case before Lincoln. The President wired Curtis on December 27 to suspend the order of banishment. The General fired back a strong protest the same day, defending the action taken and asking for a free hand in the matter. Both Curtis and Dick apparently feared that an upset in this case, which had gained great notoriety, might jeopardize their entire policy.

Curtis sent Strong to Washington. The attorney did not impress Lincoln with his case against McPheeters. The President wrote Curtis that the entire case seemed to rest on circumstantial evidence; no proof had been offered to show that McPheeters had violated the test oath. Undoubtedly the minister had Southern sympathies, but Lincoln could discern no overt evidence of disloyalty. He was willing to leave the matter in Curtis' hands, however, and agreed to rescind his suspension of the order if the Commander so desired.

On one point Lincoln made himself emphatically clear: "The U. S. government must not, as by this order, undertake to run the church. When an individual, in a church or out of it, becomes dangerous to the public interest, he must be checked; but let the churches, as such take care of themselves. It will not do for the U. S. to appoint trustees, supervisors, or other agents for the church."[22]

Curtis complied with this portion of the President's judgment and returned the Pine Street Church to the control of its ruling Session. Further, he allowed McPheeters to remain in St. Louis, but suspended him from the active ministry; he knew that his case against the minister was shallow. He had gained his main point, however, when Lincoln agreed to leave the case in his hands. Perhaps Curtis felt that moderation might impress the President and assuage the feelings of McPheeters' influential conservative friends who already had a number of scores against him.

When it became apparent that McPheeters would be allowed to remain in St. Louis permanently, some of his friends applied to Curtis at the end of March for his reinstatement. Before agreeing to this, the General demanded of the minister specific answers to certain questions designed to elicit the extent of his loyalty. These McPheeters refused to give on the grounds that he had refused them earlier to Strong's committee. Principle would not now permit him to change his course. As a result of this stand, he remained under suspension throughout the Curtis regime. After a change of commanders had occurred late in 1863, the minister's friends, including Governor Gamble, began agitation in Washington for restoration of his full ecclesiastical rights. The campaign proved successful. On December 22, 1863, all restrictions on the Reverend Mr. McPheeters were removed, and the Pine Street Church promptly invited him to resume his pastorate.[23] The perseverance of one man against the military brought final vindication. Many others, however, were not so fortunate.

The assessment against St. Louis secessionists by General Schofield also presented difficulties. The board established to handle the work had barely begun its task before General Curtis assumed command. Since the purpose of the levy was to raise funds for the support of the E.M.M., Curtis concluded that Schofield had acted in his capacity as militia commander. He expressed genuine surprise therefore, when he received a communiqué from Gamble which seemed to indicate differently.

On December 1, Dr. William G. Eliot had written the Governor that the assessment was doing more harm than good in St. Louis. To make it effective would require "patient investigation," as there were many differing shades of opinion among the city's residents. While the existing board had made every attempt to perform its duties impartially, "a general impression of inequality in the rule of assessment and its application prevails." Such a situation might have been expected. No two tribunals would arrive at the same conclusion regarding persons and amounts. The eminent president of Washington University maintained that only unqualified proof of disloyalty should warrant assessment. In such cases those found guilty deserved a far worse punishment.

Governor Gamble endorsed Eliot's letter and sent it to Curtis, asking that he give it his careful consideration. As the assessment had been directed and enforced by the military, this seemed but the logical procedure to the Governor. It was his endorsement of the letter which surprised Curtis. The Commander believed the matter entirely within the state's jurisdiction. He forwarded the letter to General Halleck for clarification. Could the federal government levy such a tax for a state purpose, Curtis asked. Did it conflict with the Confiscation Act? Did it conflict with the federal constitution in its mode and object of taxation?

Dr. Eliot wrote a letter of clarification to Halleck on December 13. He apologized for the furor he had touched off. He shared General Curtis' opinion regarding the origin of the authority for the assessment order and had not intended that his remarks should go beyond the Governor's desk. Eliot reiterated his views, with the added information that circumstances had so changed that the original purpose for the assessments no longer prevailed. Money for the state forces was now available from other sources.[24]

General Schofield was in St. Louis at the time, recuperating from an illness. In reply to a letter of inquiry from the president of the St. Louis assessment board, he asserted that he had issued the order under his authority as commander of the Military District of Missouri. While Gamble had approved the measure before its announcement, it had not been issued under the Governor's authority. Schofield further revealed that the order had never received either the approval or the disapproval of the War Department.[25]

Gamble now placed the matter in the President's hands with the statement that he could get no answer from Curtis as to whether this was a state or federal concern. He reported citizens daily applying to him for relief which he did not believe himself empowered to give. No need now existed in the E.M.M. for the money thus raised. Therefore Gamble recommended suspension of the board's activities. He assured the President that such action would add to the groundswell of Union feeling already existing in the state.[26]

Lincoln took direct action on December 10. He ordered Curtis to suspend for a time all proceedings of the assessment board and to send him a statement of the pertinent facts on the question with his opinion on it. An order from General Halleck five days later made permanent the suspension of assessments. It gave as the grounds for such action the opinion that "no present military necessity" demanded the enforcement of assessments. The General-in-chief left the door open for possible resumption by warning: "Should new insurrections occur in Missouri, and the people of St. Louis again afford aid and comfort to the enemy, they may expect to suffer the legitimate consequences of such acts of treason."[27]

Governor Gamble now decided that the assessment policy should be abolished throughout the state. He wired the President on December 31 that he had stopped the practice by the militia and requested Lincoln to bring an end to federal levies. For his reason Gamble used one terse sentence: "Great distress is produced." Six days later, the Missouri Congressional delegation (with one exception) presented the President with a memorandum to the same effect.

Lincoln thereupon wrote Curtis suggesting that he confer with Governor Gamble on this and other controversial matters in Missouri. Obviously tired of being bothered with Missouri's problems, the President concluded: "I could at once safely do (or you could safely do without me) whatever you and he agree upon. There is absolutely no reason why you should not agree."[28] Lincoln little realized that he had asked the seemingly impossible. Gamble and Curtis stood on opposite sides of practically every question which confronted them.

The conference Lincoln wanted was quickly arranged. Curtis reported its results to the President on January 15. It was obvious from his letter that he and the Governor had agreed on very little. Instead of reporting any joint decisions, Curtis outlined his own views on assessments, banishments, troop deployment, etc. He reiterated his previous view that conflict of authority must ultimately come out into the open, but expressed the hope that it could be handled adroitly. Curtis informed the President that "our Union men" opposed the lifting of the assessments in the interior, for they felt that these had deterred the secessionists from lawlessness. The Commander had had innumerable petitions and letters urging him to allow the policy to proceed. The county commanders who made the levies claimed to know the situation better than he did. Consequently, Curtis moved "cautiously and quietly" in this regard "so as to avoid any new inspiration of rebel outrage."[29]

Lincoln and the War Department had also received numerous petitions. Most of these disagreed with the Curtis viewpoint on assessments and urged their cessation. On January 20, the Secretary of War wired that the previous suspension of the levies had been intended to apply to all Missouri; he requested that it be so interpreted until further notice. This order in no way affected the confiscation system which Curtis had been employing so readily. It continued in effect until Schofield resumed command of the department in May.[30]

As Curtis maintained his reluctance to give Gamble and the E.M.M. free rein in north Missouri, the Governor wrote Lincoln once again on February 4. He mentioned the January conference with Curtis and outlined a plan of action which he had presented to the General at that time. Curtis rejected the scheme as too costly. Gamble had heard no more since then. The Governor, nevertheless, had begun to put his plan into operation without Curtis who maintained only one regiment of volunteers in north Missouri. Gamble asked the President for his approval.

The plan involved the use of four especially chosen militia regiments. These would rotate regularly from one established base to another in the region "to present the appearance of overwhelming military strength." Time was of the essence in Gamble's view. He warned: "To establish order in this State requires that you Mr. President shall manifest publicly whatever confidence you may have in me."[31] There is no record of a Presidential reply to this message. Curtis continued to maintain some regular troops in north Missouri throughout his regime.

Until this time the relations between Curtis and Gamble had been amicable, at least on the surface, but after the January conference, cordial cooperation ceased. It became increasingly obvious that Curtis was either consciously or unconsciously in league with the Radicals who were just beginning their agitations against the Provisional Government. The Conservatives charged that Curtis permitted and encouraged his officers to slander Governor Gamble and the militia and to interfere with the internal and social affairs of the state. Bates wrote from Washington that he had had to talk down a whispering campaign against Gamble by warning Halleck and Stanton, among others, that failure to support the Governor would mean anarchy in Missouri. Gamble meanwhile urged Curtis to suppress the *Neue Zeit,* a German paper in St. Louis which had begun writing highly inflammatory editorials against the Provisional Government. But the General took no action.[32]

Early in February Gamble received a letter from Schofield at Springfield. It reported a movement under way, instigated by Jim Lane and General Blunt, to get the Department of the Missouri under Kansas control with the latter at its head. Curtis reportedly knew of the plan and was agreeable to retirement or transfer to another command. Schofield enclosed a letter from Blunt which he offered as evidence, but which has not been found.

How reliable this rumor may have been is not known. Schofield had been carrying on a feud with Curtis for some time. While on sick leave in St. Louis that winter, Schofield had suggested that Blunt not be given a field command with his army in the southwest. He recommended that Blunt be returned to the Kansas district instead. Curtis rebuked Schofield and informed Jim Lane of that officer's recommendation, thereby betraying Schofield's confidence. Lane became so angered at what he considered a reversal for Blunt that he blocked Schofield's confirmation as major general in the Senate while Blunt's promotion to the same rank went through without trouble.

In the meantime, Curtis ordered Schofield back to his command in the field, although the latter had indicated that he had no desire to return to that post. His troops had successfully engaged the Confederates at Prairie Grove, Arkansas, during his absence. Blunt had played a prominent role in this victory and was now appointed to command the Military District of Kansas. Schofield did not wish to reimpose himself at the head of his forces under these circumstances, so he requested a transfer to Grant's army before Vicksburg. Curtis refused.

When Schofield reached his command, he found no enemy facing him. Much to his disgust, he spent an idle winter at Springfield. In such circumstances, he did not hesitate to write Halleck at Washington. He explained his situation and requested a transfer with his men to the Mississippi theater of operations. Without waiting for a reply, he wrote the General-in-chief a second letter complaining that Curtis hindered his every movement. He renewed his appeal for transfer, and it was eventually forthcoming.[33]

Efforts to secure the removal of Curtis were fully under way by early 1863. Gibson, Bates, Rollins, and other Missouri leaders in the capital repeatedly urged the matter. It was no easy task, for Gamble also had his antagonists in the capital. Hamilton Gamble, Jr., visiting Washington that winter, informed his father that he had had no idea there were so many persons plotting against the Governor until he arrived there. He reported that Gamble's loyalty was not only doubted but actually denied by committees and petitions seeking his removal.[34]

The movement against Curtis gained ground late in February when Senator John B. Henderson enlisted in the cause. His major purpose in heading the campaign was to increase his political influence in Missouri where the legislature was in the process of electing someone to fill the two Senate seats which he and Robert Wilson held by appointment. He shortly secured election. Whether this was due to his activities in the Curtis affair is uncertain. Regardless of motive, Henderson proved an able ally for the anti-Curtis forces. By February 24, he had secured Lincoln's assurance that Curtis would be removed, once a successor was selected. When the President hesitated too long to suit him, Henderson, accompanied by Gibson and Rollins, visited the White House on March 5. He threatened Lincoln with political opposition if the order for Curtis' removal was not forthcoming. The President again promised action. Finally, on March 10, he issued the order replacing Curtis with Major General Edwin V. Sumner.[35]

Attorney-General Bates and the other Missouri conservatives in the capital considered Sumner's a good appointment. Indeed, Bates wrote Gamble that it marked the turning point in Missouri affairs. Sumner called on the Attorney-General several times before leaving Washington. Bates posted him on the situation he would find in St. Louis and urged him to cooperate with the Provisional Government. The high hopes held for his command were rudely dashed when Sumner died suddenly in Syracuse, New York, en route to his new post. Halleck immediately telegraphed Curtis to retain the command until further notice.[36]

Lincoln now found himself in a cross-fire. Numerous petitions arrived from the Radical element seeking Curtis' permanent reinstatement; the agitation against Curtis also resumed. Senator Henderson had returned to Missouri with the adjournment of Congress. When he heard of Sumner's death, he immediately wired Lincoln and followed the wire with a letter seeking a quick replacement for Sumner to obviate the necessity of retaining Curtis. He informed Gamble of his action and assured him that he felt certain the President would act favorably.[37]

At the same time General Curtis sent the President a despairing letter in which he asked not to be retained in command. Feigning innocence as to the cause of his removal, he asserted that reinstatement would render his situation untenable because of the already implied lack of trust. He now realized that he had apparently failed to satisfy a number of influential people, including the Governor. He maintained that he had not been aware of it at the time. In his characteristic self-righteous style, Curtis concluded that he had outserved his usefulness.[38]

Lincoln hesitated to make another change in the command. April passed into May with Curtis still at his post. Interpreting his retention as a vindication, the General moved increasingly into the Radical camp. By the first of May the situation had become almost unbearable for the Conservatives. Gamble wrote Lincoln: "The disorders in this Military department are frightful. Crime in almost every form is committed with impunity." The Governor blamed what he considered Curtis' mismanagement. He especially denounced his placing the western tier of Missouri counties south of the Missouri River in the Kansas district—an action which had aroused the old animosities along the border.

A number of prominent St. Louis citizens, including Samuel T. Glover and James O. Broadhead, also emphasized Curtis' mismanagement. They blamed Missouri's difficulties on Curtis' support of Radical policies. In particular the situation surrounding slavery had become bad. Negroes were being encouraged to leave their masters and come into the army camps, bringing with them "horses, mules, and other property as their inclinations may fancy."[39]

Although he still failed to find anything personally wrong with Curtis, the President decided that he could postpone action no longer. Accordingly, he informed the Secretary of War on May 11 that he had decided to relieve Curtis once again. He suggested Schofield as his successor, subject to the approval of Stanton and Halleck. No doubt Lincoln made this last recommendation in the hope that Schofield would be able to re-establish a cordial working relationship with Governor Gamble and thereby end the almost ceaseless flow of argument from Missouri.[40]

The War Department readily gave its approval to the change. Halleck notified Schofield on May 13. That officer had finally been promoted brevet major general in April and transferred to Tennessee. Now he returned to St. Louis on May 24 to assume a difficult and arduous role, but one for which he was well suited. The move came as a great relief to most of the Conservatives. Attorney-General Bates confided to his diary:

> It was the only course that could save Mo. from Social war and utter anarchy. The Radicals seemed to have come to the conclusion that Mr. Lincoln's plan of emancipation was all wrong, too slow and cost too much money; and that the best way to abolitionize Mo. was by violence and fraud—And if the state were thrown into anarchy, all the better. It would depopulate the State, by death and banishment. And they could settle it anew, getting improved lands, for nothing![41]

Missouri had been secured for the Union, but the emancipation issue, which rose to fever pitch during the Curtis administration, split the old Union party asunder. The Conservative and Radical parties emerged as chief contenders for control of the state. Their struggle for power was just as bitter as had been the fight over secession. The Radicals would accept no neutral ground on any issue they deemed essential to the successful prosecution of the war. Increasingly, emancipation became the foremost item on their agenda. They became the leading antagonists of the Provisional Government throughout the remainder of its existence.

The Radicals sought military support by which they might harass as Southern sympathizers anyone who did not agree with their viewpoint. General Curtis in no small way contributed to the encouragement of their excesses by his opposition, right or wrong, to Governor Gamble. Eventually the Radicals gained sufficient strength to carry the state politically. By that time they had made intolerance their watchword, and name-calling had become an everyday pastime with them. The effects of these developments will be seen in the chapters which follow.

7

Missouri Confronts Emancipation

IN HIS proclamation of August 3, 1861, Governor Gamble made clear the stand which his administration would take with regard to slavery when he declared: "No countenance will be afforded to any scheme or to any conduct calculated in any degree to interfere with the institution of Slavery existing in the State. To the very utmost extent of Executive power, that institution will be protected."[1]

The Governor took this stand not from any great love of slavery but because the Missouri constitution recognized its legal existence. As chief executive of the state under that document, he felt obligated to uphold its provisions in this as in other matters. Most citizens felt relieved at his assurances. Slavery did not have the hold numerically and economically in Missouri that it had in most other Southern states, yet the people generally considered it as a part of their way of life. A prevalent statement of the times claimed that "every decent Missouri family had at least one, and usually from two to four, as house servants."[2]

When General John C. Frémont issued his emancipation proclamation in late August, 1861, Gamble ardently opposed it. The Governor, in Washington at the time, doubtless had ample opportunity to make known his views on the matter to President Lincoln. He found the President more than sympathetic at this stage of the war. Lincoln soon rescinded Frémont's order. Although Frémont's German supporters expressed disappointment at the President's action, the issue died down during the winter as other concerns came to the fore. Fortunately for Gamble, the question of emancipation did not become a major issue in Missouri until the second quarter of 1862. By that time, the Provisional Government was firmly established and could keep the matter fairly well under control.

Renewed antislavery agitation on a large scale emerged, however, following President Lincoln's message to Congress on March 6, 1862. The President recommended the adoption of a joint resolution placing the federal government on record as willing to "cooperate with any State which may adopt gradual abolishment of slavery." Lincoln suggested that Congress might even grant monetary aid to a state to help in compensating its slaveowners. The President made his own position clear:

> Such a proposition on the part of the General Government sets up no claim of a right of Federal authority to interfere with slavery within State limits, referring, as it does, the absolute control of the subject in each case to the State and its people immediately interested. It is proposed as a matter of perfectly free choice with them. . . . While it is true that the adoption of the proposed resolution would be merely initiatory, and not within itself a practical measure, it is recommended in the hope that it would soon lead to important practical results.[3]

This statement served as an answer to those in the abolitionist ranks who were beginning to cry for a stand on slavery.

A meeting of the border state representatives in Congress on March 10 gave Lincoln little encouragement of support in this issue. Still, the joint resolution passed the House on March 11 by a vote of 89 to 31 and the Senate on April 2, 32 to 10. In the balloting most of Missouri's delegation in the House abstained, although Frank Blair supported the measure and Elijah H. Norton opposed it. Missouri's two senators split on the issue, Henderson favoring it and Wilson opposing.[4]

Missouri's fall election campaign had gotten under way by this time. Almost immediately the question of slavery became an issue. Its leading antagonist was Charles D. Drake of St. Louis, a recent convert to emancipation. Drake had studied law with Governor Gamble and had practiced in St. Louis since

1834. He had been successively a Whig, a Know-Nothing, and a Democrat in the 1850's and had supported Douglas and Claiborne Jackson in the 1860 canvass. As late as July, 1861, he denounced antislavery agitation.

During the following winter, Drake underwent a thorough conversion. As the Radical movement emerged in 1862, he became its most ardent and fluent spokesman. His speech at Union, Missouri, on April 7, set the theme for the campaign against slavery:

> As it has, for many years, been generally conceded by cool-headed and sagacious men, slaveholders among us, that Slavery is not essential to our prosperity . . . as it is known to retard immigration to our State; as it is, beyond doubt, the origin and life of this horrible rebellion; as it is undeniably true that, but for its existence among us, we should have been almost wholly exempt from the immediate presence of this war within our boundaries; and as, judging from the past and the present, it may be expected to be a fruitful source of trouble in the future; it appears to me . . . that, to provide, in some well-considered, equitable, and gradual way, for its eventual removal from our soil, would do more than all other things, to lift Missouri speedily out of her present unhappy condition, and start her forward in a fresh and higher career of prosperity.[5]

Although Drake had no detailed plan to propose at this time, he sounded the clarion call. Others quickly joined him.

Governor Gamble returned to Missouri in mid-March, 1862, after a lengthy stay in the East, to find his popularity running high. Under Halleck, military operations within the state had been encouraging to Union sympathizers. With the extension of the test oath, secession sentiment seemed on the wane. Two other men had announced their candidacies for the governorship, but Gamble's return brought a strong current of opinion urging him to be the Union candidate. Letters and petitions came to him from all parts of the state. The *Missouri Republican* predicted that should he so decide he would find no opposition; all Union men would unite behind him.

With some reluctance the Governor finally responded on May 12. While he preferred private life and would not seek public office openly, he would render his services to the state if the people demanded them. The public generally took this as an indication of Gamble's willingness to be a candidate for the governorship. Shortly thereafter one of his opponents withdrew from the race, stating that he feared the campaign would be one of bitter feelings and strife in which he had no desire to participate. The other avowed candidate ran into trouble with the provost marshal at Rolla who arrested him for making a "secessionist" speech, although he had done nothing more than criticize certain Administration policies. The candidate was soon released to attend the state convention to which he was a delegate, but the incident effectively ended his campaign.[6]

As the approaching election raised certain problems, Governor Gamble deemed it necessary to call another session of the state convention to deal with them. Speculation immediately began as to whether that body would take any stand on the emancipation issue. Emancipation societies formed throughout the state; newspaper comment became manifest. The *Missouri Democrat,* the leader of the Radical papers, came out in favor of some scheme of gradual compensated emancipation. Conservative opinion, as voiced by the *Missouri Republican,* definitely opposed such a move for the present. The *Republican* favored waiting until after the war to decide the matter unless it became obvious through the August ballot that the people wished an earlier decision.[7]

The members of the convention gathered in Jefferson City on the first Monday in June. The Governor explained that he had called them together because no other body existed to which he could turn for legislative assistance upon matters necessary to the continued well-being of Missouri. Gamble reviewed events in the state since the first meeting of the convention, with special emphasis on the actions he had taken as governor to carry out their directives. Then he began to enumerate the current problems. Most of these centered around the approaching election. Missouri had gained the right to send two additional congressmen to Washington as a result of the 1860 census. This increase in representation necessitated a redistricting of the state to assure a fair selection.

The Governor called attention to objections to the early August date set for state and Congressional elections in Missouri's constitution but made no suggestions regarding a change. He did recommend annulment of the provision of the July, 1861, session for submitting the work of the convention to the people. More than 30,000 Missouri servicemen outside the state would not be able to vote. Certainly their voices should be heard on such a vital question. Then, too, such an election would make a choice between the Provisional Government and no government. The state would be without a functioning administration should the people annul the work of the convention. Furthermore, after a year's existence the maintenance of the Provisional Government should not be open to question.[8]

While the convention waited for its committees to begin reporting, it debated a resolution declaring the seats of eight members vacant because their holders had gone over to the Confederacy. The special committee dealing with the matter recommended the expulsion of five of the men, including Sterling Price and Uriel Wright, who had definitely espoused the Southern cause. The other three seats should simply be vacated because their owners had left the state for reasons unknown. Three attempts to have certain names stricken from the resolutions failed. The convention then accepted the recommendation unanimously.[9]

Once the other committees began to report, the convention went quickly to work grinding out the legislative program requested by the Governor. It also added some ideas of its own. The convention encountered surprisingly little difficulty in passing an ordinance redistricting the state, to the general satisfaction of all concerned. In an endorsement of General Halleck's policies, it extended the provisions of the test oath ordinance to include all voters, candidates for office, jurymen, attorneys, bank officers, teachers, ministers, and the officers and faculty of the state university. Election judges and clerks were required to take yet another oath that they would not record the vote or permit it to be recorded for any person who had not previously taken the test oath. Violation of this ordinance could result in trial for perjury. Provision was made for voting by Missouri volunteer troops outside the state in subsequent elections. And the convention amended the state constitution to permit the holding of all general elections, state and national, in November.[10]

Perhaps the most lively topic of the convention was what should be included in the fall election. The committee on elections and elective franchise presented an ordinance which it deemed was in accord with the Governor's message. This ordinance provided for the continuation of the Provisional Government in office until the regular fall election of 1864, at which time the term of the administration elected in 1860 would normally expire. An amendment was proposed from the floor, calling for dispensing with the 1862 election for all offices except members of Congress, continuing present county officials in office, and the filling of any vacancies by appointment by the Governor. Another amendment was proposed which would give the Governor the power to call a special election before 1864 to choose members of the General Assembly if he thought such an election necessary. Debate on these amendments consumed most of the next day. When the vote came, the convention defeated the amended amendment, 29 to 40, and then killed the ordinance, 31 to 35.[11]

Most of those who voted against the ordinance did not intend it as a criticism of the Provisional Government, but that evening word reached the members that Gamble and Hall looked upon the vote as a censure of their administration. The members, who had wished merely to give the people a chance to name their own officers in the 1862 election, were puzzled by

Gamble's and Hall's reaction. Their vote was based on the assumption that the provisional officers would stand for election and be chosen without difficulty. The next morning the convention, out of consideration for the feelings of Gamble and Hall, voted 43 to 15 to reconsider the ordinance. It then passed, 45 to 21, after an unsuccessful attempt to have it referred back to committee. Most of the members who voted against the ordinance the second time later joined the yet unformed Radical party which was to contend bitterly with Gamble and Hall during the next two years.

As a result of the vote on the ordinance, the convention continued the Provisional Government in office through 1864. To show their unqualified confidence in Governor Gamble, the members unanimously adopted the following resolution:

> *Resolved,* That this Convention has undiminished confidence in the ability, integrity and patriotism of Governor Gamble and the other officers of the Provisional Government elected by this Convention at a former session, and now continued in office by an ordinance adopted at the present session.

Several members reiterated these sentiments in speeches on the floor of the convention.[12]

The reasons for Governor Gamble's attitude in this matter remains one of the mysteries of his administration. The question is not discussed in any of his extant personal correspondence. To what extent Lieutenant-Governor Hall may have influenced him at this time is not known. Certainly the view Gamble took must have seemed to many members of the convention at the time as a reversal of his previously known feelings. He had been reluctant to accept the governorship when first offered it; he had indicated a willingness to relinquish it the previous October should the convention so desire; further, his announcement in May had seemed to make him a candidate, albeit a reluctant one, in the forthcoming election.

An examination of his message to this session of the convention may throw some light on the subject. Here Governor Gamble stated that he did not think the existence of the Provisional Government should be brought into question at a time when it had existed successfully for almost a year. If rejected, anarchy would result. While the election of officials would not necessarily be a test of the popularity of the Provisional Government, the defeat of the incumbents might seem to imply disfavor. The extent to which Gamble feared possible defeat should he stand as a candidate before the people is not known. On the eve of the convention his elder brother, Archibald, whom he greatly respected, wrote in questioning terms of the vote he might expect to receive from the unvocal majority.[13]

If Gamble had such a feeling he made a serious mistake in allowing himself to fall prey to it. The popularity of the Provisional Government was at its height in the summer of 1862; the *Missouri Republican* estimated that the secessionists could muster no more than 20,000 votes against Gamble in the fall election.[14] Even this number is probably an overstatement of the opposition to Gamble. Most of that group had been disfranchised by the test oath ordinance. While a split appeared in the ranks of the Unionists that fall over emancipation and the use of the militia, it did not assume large enough proportions to hurt Gamble until after the convening of the newly elected legislature. Had Gamble and Hall then had the power of a legal election behind them, they would have had a much easier time facing the problems which confronted them during the next two years. Following the adjournment of this session of the convention, those problems mounted steadily, and the popularity of the Provisional Government waned. No doubt its failure to stand before the people for election was a factor.

To the surprise of many, the conservative Governor made no mention of slavery or emancipation in his opening message to the convention. Nevertheless, Samuel M. Breckinridge of

St. Louis, a Conservative, introduced an emancipation ordinance on June 6 which called for an end to the importation of slaves into Missouri; all slaves born after January 1, 1865, were to be freed at the age of twenty-five; the General Assembly should provide some means of compensation for the owners of the freed slaves by taking advantage of the offer of Congress embodied in its resolution of April 2; if adopted, the ordinance should secure the approval of the voters at the 1864 election before going into effect.

Breckinridge set forth his position in a long speech. He insisted that the war had doomed slavery in Missouri as elsewhere. Recognition of this fact would secure more quickly the necessary Eastern capital which the state needed for her economic development after the war. He pointedly asked the Conservatives to vote for his measure in order that more radical demands might be curbed. Breckinridge warned them that should they fail to do so a bitter conflict would develop over this question to the great harm of the state.

Most of the Conservatives paid little heed to this plea. As soon as Breckinridge had finished, Congressman William A. Hall, the brother of the Lieutenant-Governor, moved that the ordinance be laid on the table—a move to kill the measure as far as this session was concerned. In the vote which followed, Hall's motion passed, 52 to 19.[15]

The moderate proposal of Breckinridge had been the work of several St. Louis Conservatives who realized that if they faced the issue squarely they might control it better. They did not expect the measure to pass, but wished the issue joined. Samuel T. Glover wrote Broadhead suggesting that if the convention voted down the ordinance an attempt should be made to secure a resolution to the simple effect that "Slavery ought not to be perpetual in Missouri."[16]

The Conservatives took no further action on the floor of the convention. They may, however, have placed pressure on Gamble to make some kind of stand, for the Governor sent a special message to the convention on June 13, the eve of adjournment, asking it to adopt a resolution in response to the offer made by Congress. He reminded the members of the aid which the state had received from the federal government in the past. Gamble feared their action on the Breckinridge ordinance without an explanation might be interpreted as hostility to the Congressional offer. He did not ask them to reconsider the ordinance but did request that through a resolution they make clear their action on the question of emancipation.[17]

The convention referred the Governor's message to a special committee of five, all of whom had opposed the ordinance except Breckinridge, who was named chairman. The committee reported a resolution which acknowledged the Congressional offer and declared it worthy of "deliberate and respectful consideration." Although the majority did not feel authorized "to take action with respect to the grave and delicate questions of private right and public policy presented by said resolution, yet this body desires to recognize the liberality therein displayed . . . and to express its profound appreciation thereof." Considerable debate followed before the convention adopted the resolution, 37 to 23. Most of the opposition came from the more extreme Conservatives.[18]

Senator Henderson wrote Gamble to commend his action in securing the resolution. He had approved Lincoln's proposals the previous March. Now he considered it important that the President receive some approbation from the border states for whom he was trying to do a great deal. Looking to the future, Henderson warned: "We cannot secure interest in slave property by closing our mouths or our ears in Missouri whilst events here are daily demonstrating to all who take the time or pains to think at all that if this war continues (and I think it will continue long enough to accomplish this end) slavery will be forever destroyed in the United States."[19]

Two days after the adjournment of the state convention, another group met in Jefferson City. Called by B. Gratz Brown, Thomas C. Fletcher, and other budding Radicals to consider the emancipation question, it attracted 195 delegates from twenty-five counties. There were many speeches before the group adopted a platform drawn up by Brown. This document called for a plan of gradual compensated emancipation and asked the legislature to avail itself of the offer of assistance by Congress and the President in carrying this out.[20]

The *Missouri Democrat* praised the work of the meeting with the observation that the organization of an emancipation party was a welcome event. The conservative *Missouri Statesman,* on the other hand, condemned the group. If slavery were doomed, as Breckinridge and Brown proclaimed, it should be allowed to die a natural death. The paper accused the emancipationists of delaying the day of that death by their action rather than hastening it. Another critic, albeit on different grounds, was Charles D. Drake, later a leader of the Radical party which grew out of this meeting. He did not participate in the proceedings and indeed, denounced the members at a later date as not being as "emancipationistic" as they claimed to be.[21]

Events were happening in Washington which were to have a profound effect on the situation in Missouri. The Radicals in Congress had been pushing for more daring action than simply an offer to help border states compensate their slaveowners. To take care of their own back yard, they passed a bill providing for compensated emancipation in the District of Columbia. Debate followed on a measure to abolish slavery in the territories. There was considerable denunciation of those generals in the field who returned fugitive slaves to their masters. Finally, toward the close of the session, the Radicals managed to pass the Confiscation Act discussed previously.[22]

As the Radical movement gained momentum in Congress, the President called the border state congressmen together on July

12. He urged them to use their influence in bringing about emancipation in their states under the April 2 resolution. Kentucky and Maryland had ignored this completely, and Missouri's response had been far from satisfactory in Lincoln's eyes. Again, the President met with a lack of enthusiasm. Twenty of his listeners, including Senator Wilson and Representatives Hall, Phelps, Price, and Rollins of Missouri, issued a joint reply two days later. They assured Lincoln of their loyalty but declined to comply with his wishes. They denied the right of the federal government to interfere with a problem which they considered strictly within the province of the states. They pointed out that adequate compensation would add a tremendous amount to the national debt and impose a tax burden on the people which they did not feel could be justified. Seven others, including Representative John W. Noell of Missouri, wrote collectively that they would endeavor to carry out the President's proposals, and Senator Henderson wrote a separate reply promising his cooperation. [23]

The President's thinking on emancipation had advanced one step further by this time. He had come to the realization that emancipation could not begin in the border states, yet he felt that slavery was a millstone around the neck of the United States. The President determined to free the slaves farther south, even though it might be done only on a technical basis at this time. He began broaching the matter to members of his cabinet on the ground that the base on which the war was being fought needed broadening. At a full-scale Cabinet meeting on July 22, he found the group divided. Interestingly enough, Montgomery Blair seemed more concerned about the sensitivity of the border states than Edward Bates, who endorsed Lincoln's plan enthusiastically. The entire Cabinet agreed with Secretary of State Seward, however, that this was not an opportune time for such a move, inasmuch as Union arms were meeting reverses everywhere. Consequently, the President shelved his proposal until a more propitious moment—after the battle of Antietam. On September 23, Lincoln announced that all slaves in those states still in rebellion at the first of the year would be free.[24]

At the time of Lincoln's proclamation, the governors of most of the Northern states were meeting at Altoona, Pennsylvania, to consult on measures they might undertake to aid the war cause. Governor Gamble had declined to attend, largely on the advice of Bates who wired: "GO NOT. WHATEVER THE DESIGN, THE END IS REVOLUTIONARY." A letter followed, explaining that the conference owed its origins "to the leaders of the extreme wing of the Republican party," namely, the abolitionists. When this same conference drafted a resolution approving the President's proclamation, Governor John A. Andrew of Massachusetts sent Gamble a copy seeking his endorsement. The Missouri governor declined on constitutional grounds. He declared his belief that this constituted an unwarranted interference by the federal authority with a state problem.[25]

While the Emancipation Proclamation did not apply to Missouri directly, it appeared in time to have a profound effect on the state's fall election. Coming as it did in the final stages of the campaign, Lincoln's proclamation had the effect of moving many Missourians one step further left from the position they had held earlier in the summer. B. Gratz Brown and his supporters from the Jefferson City emancipation convention joined Charles D. Drake at the extreme left and began demanding more immediate freedom for Missouri's slaves. Many of these men had belonged to the fledgling Republican party prior to the war. They had been called "Black Republicans" derisively at the time by the Democratic opposition; now it took no effort to apply the name "Charcoal" to them.

The Breckinridge Conservatives now attracted a larger number, including Governor Gamble, into their ranks. Lincoln's proclamation made these men realize that some form of emancipation was inevitable. As the Charcoals considered this middle ground colorless, they came to apply the sobriquet, "Claybanks," to these gradual emancipationists. That minority of Conservatives who still stood adamantly against emancipation were termed "Snowflakes" by the *Missouri Statesman* because they were "more concerned about the white man than about the nigger."[26]

Most Missourians manifested little interest in the election of 1862 for several reasons. Foremost was the disfranchisement of many citizens because of their refusal to take the test oath required by the state convention. Much unrest still existed in the western half of the state, making that area unreceptive to a full-fledged campaign. Emancipation was the only major issue. Party lines tended to disappear. Most candidates ran on an individual platform which either supported or opposed the concept of immediate emancipation as embraced by Lincoln's proclamation.

When the votes had been counted, only one thing was clear: Missourians generally favored emancipation in some form. Five of Missouri's nine congressmen had been elected as Republicans or outright Emancipationists. Frank Blair wired Lincoln: "The Legislature is emancipation in both branches on your plan & secures two Senators to support the administration." This proved to be an overstatement. The Charcoals swept St. Louis, where they elected five state senators and eleven of twelve representatives. The interior of the state tended to be more conservative. The forthcoming session of the General Assembly presented a body sharply divided both on the form of emancipation and the election of senators.[27]

The Twenty-second General Assembly convened at Jefferson City on December 29, 1862. It received the Governor's message the following day. This document dealt with three topics primarily: finances, railroad legislation, and emancipation. On the last subject, Gamble suggested a plan for gradual compensated freedom. He gave three reasons for his position: (1) the substitution of free labor for slave labor would encourage immigration from the other states into Missouri; (2) emancipation would discourage the efforts of the Confederacy to gain the state; and (3) there had been a diminishing number of slaves since war broke out, and that type of property was no longer secure. Gamble reminded the members that, under the state constitution, they could pass no emancipation law which failed to compensate the owners for the loss of slave property unless the legislature secured the prior consent of the masters to such a scheme.

To overcome this difficulty and to gain the aid of the federal government, the Governor recommended that the legislature provide that all children of slaves born after the adoption of the act should be free. They should, however, remain under the custody of their mother's owner until reaching a certain age. In this way the only compensation needed would be that required to pay for the diminished value of the female slaves, who could no longer bear slave children. Such an amount could readily be gained through the Congressional resolution. Under this scheme those Negroes already in servitude would remain slaves the rest of their lives.[28]

After a month of debate, the General Assembly passed concurrent resolutions declaring that $25,000,000 in Congressional aid would be needed to carry out emancipation in Missouri. Agreement ended here. In the weeks which followed the members wrangled long and loud over the method of emancipation. The Claybanks wanted the old state convention to handle the problem, while the Charcoals wished a new convention called to deal specifically with this question. Neither group could gain a majority in both houses, so the matter lagged.[29]

By February 6, the *Missouri Republican* became thoroughly disgusted with the prolonged proceedings. They had consumed six weeks and produced nothing. The *Republican* recommended that the General Assembly forget emancipation and concentrate on getting sorely needed revenue into the State Treasury. Ten days later, State Treasurer George C. Bingham wrote Congressman James S. Rollins that he believed the Charcoals were stalling on the emancipation question. They would oppose any scheme which would secure justice for the slaveholder. In their demands for immediate emancipation he feared they might drive many Conservatives from the state. Then they could take over from want of opposition.[30]

While the Missouri General Assembly remained deadlocked over the means of carrying out emancipation, Congress considered the question of providing the state with funds to compensate the slaveowners for their anticipated losses. Representative John W. Noell and Senator John B. Henderson introduced bills in their respective houses. The two measures differed considerably. Noell's allowed only $10,000,000 compensation and stipulated that, in order to qualify, Missouri must endorse immediate emancipation by January 1, 1864. The Henderson bill set aside $20,000,000 for Missouri's use, with gradual emancipation the anticipated goal. The Noell bill passed the House early in January with only the author and Rollins voting for it from the Missouri delegation. In the Senate, Henderson undertook a thorough revision of the measure to make it conform more nearly to his own. This completely altered bill passed the Senate on February 12, but the necessity of its returning to the House killed it, as Noell and his Radical allies refused to accept the changes.[31]

The significance of this matter lies in its indication of the willingness of Congress to help Missouri in some way; the tragedy rests in the inability of Noell and Henderson to agree on a joint bill which could readily have been pushed through both houses, and in the determined opposition of Hall, Norton, and Price in the House and of Wilson in the Senate. These four

Conservatives from Missouri opposed any form of compensation as government interference with states' rights. They sought to block the bill's path at every turn.

The General Assembly adjourned late in March without perfecting an act of emancipation. Governor Gamble now decided to call the state convention into session once again to deal with the matter. In issuing his call on April 15, he made it explicit that he did so primarily for this one purpose.[32]

Eight vacancies existed in the convention, necessitating a special election to fill them. A lively contest ensued between the Charcoals and the Claybanks. The most important test of strength came in St. Louis, which had just elected a Charcoal mayor. There someone had to be chosen to replace Uriel Wright. Charles D. Drake became the Charcoal candidate when that group's original choice, B. Gratz Brown, failed to return from an eastern trip to file the required oath for candidates in time.

The *Missouri Republican* had repudiated Drake earlier. Now it came to the support of his Claybank opponent, James E. Yeatman, the head of the St. Louis Sanitary Commission. Drake received the support of the *Missouri Democrat* which forced a somewhat reluctant German press into line. The Germans remembered Drake's diatribes against them in the prewar era. They could never believe that the lawyer had had a change of heart from his Know-Nothing days. To them he seemed a mere political opportunist, and their distrust of him lasted far into the Reconstruction period.

Little difference existed in the actual statements of the two candidates. Drake demanded immediate emancipation "in the most speedy manner consistent with good order" while Yeatman desired slavery "abolished in the shortest possible time consistent with true humanity and common justice." But Drake attacked the Gamble government and gave the impression that he stood on an unqualified Radical platform. His flair for dramatic oratory, perhaps as much as anything, carried the day for him.

In all, the Charcoals elected five delegates to the convention, each of whom was pledged to a platform of swift emancipation.[33]

In the period between the election and the meeting of the convention, the radical *Democrat* delivered a bitter denunciation of Governor Gamble. It is typical of the abuse which the Radicals heaped on those who failed to stand with them in the years which followed:

> Governor Gamble never thoroughly enjoyed the confidence of the truly loyal people of Missouri. He was not raised to office by their votes. He had entered the Convention not without grave suspicions resting upon his loyalty, and his elevation to the responsible position of Governor of the State did not dispell all doubts. Nevertheless, the Union men of Missouri were disposed to acquiesce in his selection, give him a fair trial, and if he honestly carried out their views, render him a hearty support. In this, after a trial of nearly two years, he has signally failed. At the end of that period . . . we see him trembling with apprehension in his chair of state, and his public organs sending out piteous notes of alarm lest an indignant people may rise up to hurl him from his place.

The *Democrat* listed seven causes for Gamble's failure as governor. These were (1) extraordinary selfishness; (2) nepotism; (3) narrowmindedness; (4) desire for preservation of his own power; (5) seeking support from the President more than from the people; (6) interference with and material thwarting of the operations of all federal military commanders, procuring their removal and appointment in such quick succession as to allow no settled state policy; and (7) high partiality for friends and political sympathizers in militia appointments.[34]

The next day the *Republican* called the attack "a pitiful performance." It voiced the opinion that the *Democrat's* charges would be funny if they were not so disgusting.[35] Although the accusations made by the *Democrat* obviously had malicious intent and overlooked or misconstrued a number of facts, they represented the views of a growing number of Radicals.

Governor Gamble addressed the New York delegation to the Chicago Ship Canal Convention when it visited St. Louis a few days later. He ignored the abuse flung at him by the Radicals and assured the visitors that emancipation was imminent in Missouri. Emancipation would cut a link binding the state to the South and make it more attractive to the introduction of Eastern capital. Even on this occasion the Radicals sought to goad him. The new Radical mayor, Chauncey I. Filley, followed Gamble to the platform. He expressed his delight to learn that the Governor now favored "immediate emancipation as St. Louis does."[36]

The state convention met for the fifth time on June 15, 1863, in the Capitol at Jefferson City. The highly partisan *Democrat* classified the members as follows: 35 Conservatives, 28 Copperheads, 18 Radicals, and 11 Rebels.[37] It failed to mention how it arrived at the criteria for these categories. No other paper made any attempt at such a classification.

In his opening message to the convention, Governor Gamble concerned himself largely with emancipation and military affairs within the state.[38] Regarding the former, he reminded the members that the General Assembly had not acted upon the question. He added that its urgency was increasing. Unlike his stand with the Assembly the previous December, Gamble did not undertake to lay down a definite plan of emancipation in his message to the convention. He wisely recognized the divergent views held by the members, although he sagely admonished them:

> This, however, I may be allowed to say, that if a body of intelligent and patriotic men will approach the subject with a deep conviction that it is of the highest importance to the State that the subject be disposed of, they will be able to dispose of it by agreeing upon some measure, although it may not, in all its details, be the exact expression of the will of any individual who sustains it.

In concluding, the Governor made it clear that he would not remain aloof from the proceedings of this session as he had from the past two. He announced in rather an emphatic manner: "I propose, gentlemen, to take my seat in your body, (of which I am still a member), in order that I may render any assistance in my power in maturing and adopting such measures as you may attempt for the good of the State."[39] With this statement, Gamble once again became the leading figure of the convention.

Although the *Democrat's* classification may not have been entirely accurate, it soon became evident that at least three distinct groups existed in the convention. These were the Claybanks, led by Governor Gamble; the Charcoals, whose chief spokesman was Charles D. Drake; and the Snowflakes, led by James H. Birch. The first two groups both favored some type of emancipation though differing as to how and when it should be carried out; the third thought the question of emancipation entirely outside the scope of the powers delegated to the convention.

This last group made its move early. When someone moved to have the Governor's message printed, Birch took the floor to state their case. He revealed by his remarks that this group was still living in the past; they failed to see that conditions and sentiment had been changed by the wartime disruption of the state. Birch denounced Gamble for calling the convention to consider a matter outside its jurisdiction. He maintained that retention of slavery and loyalty to the Union were not incompatible and denied that destruction of the institution would bring peace to Missouri. Realizing the hopelessness of his cause, but unwilling to go down without a struggle, Birch closed by crying that he could not stand idly by and see a policy such as Gamble proposed brought about contrary to established law.[40]

With such speeches the proslavery group unerringly played into the hands of the Charcoals. The latter had maintained throughout the preconvention period of 1863 that this body was out of tune with the times. They contended that a new convention should be called which would more nearly express the will of all the people with regard to emancipation.

The Charcoals lost little time in presenting their proposals. When Birch had finished his speech, Drake stood ready with a resolution calling upon the convention to pass an ordinance providing for the emancipation of all slaves by January 1, 1864. Slavery should be perpetually prohibited from Missouri after that date.

Drake hesitated at this early stage to propose outright immediate emancipation with no safeguards, so he included in his resolution a clause providing for a system of apprenticeship to follow the granting of freedom. This system would be maintained "for such period as may be sufficient to avoid any serious inconvenience to those interests with which slave labor is now connected, and to prepare emancipated blacks for complete freedom." Drake's resolution also included a proposal to submit such an ordinance, if passed, to a vote of the people on the first Monday of August, 1863. The Charcoal leader asked that his resolution be considered the following day, but Sample Orr moved that it be referred to a committee of nine. Pending consideration of this motion, the convention adjourned for the day.[41]

An amended version of Orr's motion was adopted the following day. It provided for a nine-man committee on emancipation with one member from each Congressional district. The convention elected the following to serve: Governor Gamble, Isidor Bush of St. Louis, Joseph Bogy of Ste. Genevieve County, M. H. Ritchey of Newton County, John F. Phillips of Pettis County, Abram Comingo of Jackson County, Lieutenant-Governor Hall, his brother Congressman William A. Hall, and Senator John B. Henderson. Of these, Bush was the only Charcoal.

Judge Breckinridge now repeated his performance of the previous session. His new proposal differed from Drake's in that the system of apprenticeship would end definitely on July 4, 1876. During the interim, slaveowners would not be required to pay taxes on their human property. Breckinridge made no provision in his ordinance for ratification by the electorate.

Drake wished to have his resolution acted on directly by the convention, but it, with that of Breckinridge, was referred to the committee of nine. While these were not the only ordinances proposed, they represented the considered opinion of the majority of the respective groups which backed them. All proposals were referred to the committee.[42]

After a delay occasioned by the necessity of Gamble's being absent part of the time, the Governor reported as chairman of the committee on June 23. Debate began the following day on his proposed ordinance which called for an end to slavery, except as punishment for crime, on July 4, 1876. All slaves brought into the state who did not at the time belong to citizens of Missouri and all slaves brought in from seceded states should be free. To prevent this plan's being upset by some future legislature of a more radical stripe, the ordinance would forbid the General Assembly to pass any emancipation act without the consent of the slaveowners. The committee report made no provision for ratification by the people. Isidor Bush submitted a minority report which embraced the Breckinridge proposal in form, although it would end apprenticeship on July 4, 1870.[43]

It may seem strange that Gamble and the majority should submit what appears on the surface to have been an extremely conservative proposal. Yet it differed from the Breckinridge plan mainly in that slavery would continue through July 4, 1876, rather than granting the slave his technical freedom first and then tying him to a long period of apprenticeship. The Claybanks, of course, realized that, regardless of the package which surrounded it, the date was far too distant for Charcoal acceptance. Undoubtedly anticipating an eventual compromise solution, the

Gamble group probably thought that by starting from an extreme position the final arrangement would be more to their liking.

The Charcoal element lost no time in proposing amendments. Drake immediately sought to have the date of emancipation advanced to January 1, 1864. This motion went down to defeat, 18 to 65. Amendments and debate then followed in rapid succession. J. J. Gravelly of Cedar County proposed immediate emancipation, owners being compensated $300 for each slave. This, too, was defeated decisively, whereupon Drake made another attempt to get the date of emancipation advanced. This time he proposed November 1, 1866, and declared it the latest date he would accept. He modified his position only to the extent of being willing to have an apprenticeship period of seven years beyond the date of emancipation. Breckinridge rose to rebuke Drake for his adamant stand. He reminded the Charcoal leader that he should be willing to compromise in order to secure the best method possible.[44]

Governor Gamble now took the floor, as it appeared that little was being gained and that all might be lost through wrangling. He proposed informally July 4, 1867,[45] as the date for emancipation. All slaves freed were to remain with their owners for the following periods: (1) those over forty years of age for the remainder of their lives; (2) those over twelve years of age until they reached twenty-three; and (3) all others until July 4, 1874.

Drake declared this proposal acceptable if Gamble would add that these slaves could not be sold in the interim. This the Governor did. In addition, he moved the date of his amendment up to November 1, 1866, to make it more palatable to the Drake Radicals. Before Gamble's proposal could be acted upon, Senator Henderson, convinced that November 1, 1866, was too early a date for the majority to accept, moved that emancipation be effected November 1, 1868. This motion carried, 51 to 32. A bitter debate followed between Henderson and Drake over the question of forbidding the sale of slaves in the amendment.[46]

Controversy still raged when Major General John M. Schofield, the newly appointed commander of the Department of the Missouri, visited the hall and was seated as a special guest. The General, who held the balance of power within the state, was no neutral observer. On June 23, three days before his visit to Jefferson City, Schofield had written William G. Eliot that he had no doubt the convention would pass an emancipation ordinance. It would not perhaps be as speedy in its operation as some, themselves included, might like. The General believed, however, that once the ordinance passed, Missouri would be virtually a free state. Social and economic interests would adjust themselves accordingly. Schofield strongly expressed his hope that once the convention had taken action it would receive the wholehearted support of all citizens.[47] The General had conveyed similar views in an earlier letter to John E. Williams of New York. He favored a plan which would be acceptable to both sides: compensated, gradual, but "speedy" emancipation. Schofield noted later in his memoirs that he used his personal influence with members of the convention, including the Governor, to this same end.[48]

General Schofield did not content himself with simply exerting his own influence to secure a satisfactory ordinance. He believed that positive assurance of support from the Administration would aid the cause of emancipation in the convention. He therefore wired President Lincoln on June 20, asking for authority to pledge in some manner, directly or indirectly, that the federal government would back any ordinance passed and would protect slavery under it.[49]

The President replied two days later. He agreed that such a pledge might be given if the period between the enactment of the ordinance and the final abolition of slavery was to be relatively short and if provision were made that no slave should be sold during that period.[50] Schofield undoubtedly made this information known to his friends in Jefferson City during his visit there on June 26, but it apparently had little effect on the Conservatives. The final version of the ordinance contained neither of Lincoln's two conditions.

On June 29, James O. Broadhead moved the substitution of July 4, 1870, for the date in Henderson's amendment. After that date the provisions of Governor Gamble's amendment regarding periods of servitude should be applied. The convention accepted this substitution, 54 to 30. Then began another series of attempts to amend the ordinance. One of the more important amendments accepted came from Abram Comingo. It provided that slave-owners should be exempt from all taxation on their slave property after the passage of the ordinance.[51]

An important consideration before the final vote was whether the handiwork of the convention should be submitted to the electorate for approval. Alexander M. Woolfolk of Livingston County proposed that a ballot marked simply "For Emancipation" and "Against Emancipation" be placed before the people in the November, 1864, election. Drake did not like this proposal. He thought it failed to test the power of the convention over the issue. He therefore moved to amend Woolfolk's proposal to make the ballot read "For the Emancipation Ordinance" and "Against the Emancipation Ordinance."

Gamble objected to Drake's motion on the grounds that such action might bring defeat to the work of the convention. Some people might oppose only portions of the ordinance, yet for that reason be forced to vote against all of it. Then too, he argued, submission to the electorate in some sections of the state would be a farce because of unsettled conditions. In the end, the convention agreed and voted down the question of submission.[52]

Drake made one last effort to have his way in the convention. He proposed a substitute for the entire ordinance calling a new convention, to be elected in November, 1863, to deal with the question. Again he met defeat, 19 to 61.[53]

Debate completed, the convention proceeded on July 1 to a final decision on the ordinance as amended. Adoption came by a vote of 51 to 30. With few exceptions, this represented a split along partisan lines, Claybanks versus Charcoals and Snowflakes. The latter two groups, however, opposed the ordinance for entirely different reasons.[54]

The press of Missouri lined up characteristically in taking a stand on the ordinance, each paper acting according to its past policy. The *Missouri Statesman* quoted an article from the *St. Louis Union* which showed nineteen outstate papers favoring the ordinance and only eight opposed. Adding the St. Louis papers to the list, one found the *Union* and the *Republican* strongly endorsing the ordinance while the radical *Democrat* just as vehemently opposed it.[55]

Although emancipation had been effected by the state convention, the Radicals did not cease their agitation to change the situation. Indeed, the convention's failure to provide immediate emancipation launched the Radicals on a full-fledged campaign to overthrow the Conservatives and rescind the convention's action. In this they finally proved successful when Missourians, in the election of 1864, approved a Radical proposal to call a new constitutional convention.

8

The Radicals Mount Their Offensive

GENERAL SCHOFIELD had been at his new post but a few days when he received a letter from President Lincoln which revealed the Chief Executive's personal thoughts on Missouri. The President wrote:

> Having relieved General Curtis and assigned you to the command of the Department of the Missouri, I think it may be of some advantage for me to state to you why I did it. I did not relieve General Curtis because of any full conviction that he had done wrong by commission or omission. I did it because of a conviction in my mind that the Union men of Missouri, constituting, when united, a vast majority of the whole people, have entered into a pestilent factional quarrel among themselves, General Curtis, perhaps not of choice, being the head of one faction, and Governor Gamble that of the other. After months of labor to reconcile the difficulty, it seemed to grow worse and worse, until I felt it my duty to break it up somehow, and as I could not remove Governor Gamble, I had to remove General Curtis.
>
> Now that you are in the position, I wish you to undo nothing merely because General Curtis or Governor Gamble did it, but to exercise your own judgment, and do right for the public interest. Let your military measures be strong enough to repel the invader and keep the peace, and not so strong as to unnecessarily harass and persecute the people. It is a difficult role, and so much greater will be the honor if you perform it well. If both factions, or neither, shall abuse you, you will probably be about right. Beware of being assailed by one and praised by the other.[1]

The choice of Schofield to head the department at this time was undoubtedly wise. He was thoroughly familiar with affairs in the state and had utmost confidence in Governor Gamble.

That official returned his regard. Thus the two could work together with great benefit to Missouri. This very situation, however, made Schofield anathema to the Radicals from the outset. Through the German press and the *Missouri Democrat* they bitterly denounced those responsible for the removal of General Curtis. Only someone with no previous Missouri connections might have hoped to escape Radical abuse. Schofield certainly could not.[2]

The new commander began to encounter problems with the Radicals shortly after he reached his post. A copy of Lincoln's letter, cited above, somehow fell into Radical hands. They proceeded to make political capital of it. Drake quoted part of it during a debate in the state convention on June 25; two days later the *Missouri Democrat* printed it in full. This last move greatly angered Schofield, who was attending the convention in Jefferson City at the time. Inasmuch as he considered the letter official and confidential, Schofield feared its publication might be construed by Lincoln as a breach of confidence on his part.

Upon his return to St. Louis, the General sent for George W. Fishback, one of the proprietors of the paper. He demanded to know how the *Democrat* had obtained the letter. Fishback replied that his partner, William McKee, was responsible for it. Schofield asked McKee on two occasions to call at his headquarters to explain how he had come into possession of the letter, but the newspaperman ignored both requests. Failing to secure satisfaction, the General arrested McKee and demanded to know the paper's source of information. Although McKee declined to divulge it, Schofield released him on an oral parole and gave him ten days to formulate a reply.[3]

Schofield's arrest of McKee stirred the Radicals into action. They appealed directly to the President, charging Schofield with violating his instructions in the letter in question by arresting McKee. Without determining which letter had been published, Lincoln wired Schofield of the Radical complaint. He requested that the matter be dropped. Obviously wishing to avoid further controversy, the President pleaded significantly: "Please spare me the trouble this is likely to bring."[4]

In his reply, Schofield explained and defended his action. He believed McKee had "obtained the letter for publication through some friend of General Curtis, to whom, I presume, you sent a copy of it, and not through the infidelity of some person in my command." At the same time he expressed his willingness to comply with the President's request to avoid further controversy.

Lincoln had sent a copy of the letter to Curtis, but that officer hastened to assure the President, through an aide, that he was not responsible for its publication. Lincoln, while sympathizing with Schofield's motives, had no desire to prolong the issue. So he closed the door on it with this message to his commander: "While I admit that there is an apparent impropriety in the publication of the letter mentioned without my consent or yours, it is still a case where no evil could result, and which I am entirely willing to overlook."[5]

The "evil" had been done, however, for the incident caused a tremendous stir. So far as the Radicals were concerned, they now felt confident that had Lincoln been able to remove Gamble, he would have done so. They agitated this theme continually. The publication of the letter, in reality, added more fuel to the fire which the Radicals had already begun building under the Provisional Government.

Governor Gamble did not hesitate to express his views in the affair. He had known nothing about the letter prior to its publication but, upon seeing it in print, he sent Lincoln a stinging defense. He rebuked the President for attacking him in a manner "unbecoming your position," and called the publication of the Lincoln message a "most wanton and unmerited insult." Gamble denied that he had ever acted as a factionalist. He assured the President that his every action was molded by a desire to do his duty by his state and country. He reminded

Lincoln that, although he had disapproved of Administration acts in the past, he had never attacked the President or his advisers personally because of the possibility that it might damage the national cause. Gamble implied that Lincoln, in doing this very thing to him, had weakened the Governor's position in the eyes of the people of Missouri.[6]

Lincoln replied ten days later. He had declined to read what his secretary called a "very cross" letter "as I am trying to preserve my own temper, by avoiding irritants, so far as practicable." He assured Gamble: "I was totally unconscious of any malice, or disrespect towards you, or of using any expression which should offend you, if seen by you."[7] This soothed the Governor temporarily.

The letter to Schofield had come to public light just two days after the state convention returned to the Governor the resignation which he had submitted at the opening of the June session. Gamble had called the convention, as noted in the preceding chapter, to deal with the question of emancipation. This issue took up most of his opening message. He dropped a bombshell in their midst toward the close of his remarks, however, by announcing that he felt this a suitable time to tender his resignation, to take effect on the last day of the present session. He explained that he had long contemplated the move; he now believed the task for which he had been called to the governorship had been fulfilled.[8]

Drake and the Radicals tried to secure resolutions accepting the resignation and calling for a state election in the fall. Their efforts met rebuff. The convention passed a substitute motion on June 23 returning Gamble's resignation to him. With it went the request that he continue in office until the 1864 election.

When he arrived in Jefferson City, General Schofield also urged Gamble to reconsider his resignation. Schofield reasoned that there would be no improvement secured in such a move. The conservative nature of the convention would not allow it to elect anyone who would greatly alter Gamble's policy. Indeed, the whole result might be "confusion worse confounded."[9]

Gamble hesitated to change his resolve. Before doing so, he sought to reach an understanding with Schofield as to the policy they might mutually pursue should he retain his office. He assured the General that he did not doubt his loyalty, yet he was tired of the attacks being made upon him; his health was suffering under the strain. With regard to cooperation between the civil and military authorities, Gamble enumerated the following measures which he thought Schofield should adopt as department commander: (1) make it known that the Provisional Government is recognized and will be supported, with military power if necessary, by the federal government; (2) allow no interference by the military in civil and criminal procedures carried on through state courts in federal military posts; (3) prohibit recruiting of Negroes without the written consent of the Governor and punish those so doing; (4) carry out confiscations only under directions from the War Department. Concluding, Gamble assured Schofield:

> When we arrive at a perfect understanding between ourselves I am willing to put myself in the same boat with you, and we will sink or swim together. If you should be censured or removed from this command because of what is done to carry these propositions into effect, I will abandon office immediately.

All of this would obviously have forced Schofield from the middle path down which Lincoln had directed him. Consequently, the General replied that he could not enter into any such agreement. Rather, he must be free to act according to circumstances or to carry out any orders from the President.[10]

In spite of Schofield's refusal and the Lincoln letter, which had been published by this time, Gamble officially withdrew his resignation on the last day of the session. He did so, he reported, although he knew that more criticism would be his portion. He pleaded with the members once again to cooperate with him in suppressing the enemies of the state and suggested that they put partisan politics aside until this had been accomplished.[11]

The *Missouri Democrat* had claimed a Radical victory when Gamble resigned. It crowed that his resignation resulted from popular demand and not from the Governor's own free will. Another article in the same issue, however, reported that some observers thought the Governor's resignation simply a scheme to get convention backing. They suspected that Gamble would eventually withdraw his resignation upon the solicitous request of that body.[12]

Although this ultimately happened, there is no evidence to indicate that Gamble's resignation was other than sincere. His health had never been good. Criticism had been heaped increasingly upon him. Yet he recognized that if he resigned, the Conservative cause would be left virtually leaderless at a critical moment. Deeply interested in seeing the new emancipation policy carried out, Gamble seemed to believe that the times demanded his sacrifice. To this end, he somewhat reluctantly withdrew his resignation.

Gamble was not without his supporters. The *Missouri Republican* asserted, in urging the convention to reject his resignation, that the Governor held the confidence of the "real people" of the state. After the convention's adjournment, the *Republican* enthusiastically praised Gamble. It announced that the whole state, except the "Jacobins" and "Revolutionists," rejoiced that he had agreed to withdraw his resignation.[13] The Conservative organ failed to mention how many people in the state belonged to the two groups named. The rest of the Missouri press seemed more concerned with the emancipation ordinance which the convention had adopted than with Gamble's resignation.

The probability of closer cooperation between the military command at St. Louis and the Provisional Government was further enhanced, shortly after Schofield's arrival, by the selection of James O. Broadhead as provost marshal general of the department. This close friend of the Governor had received the post largely through the efforts of Senator Henderson and Representative Rollins, both staunch Gamble men. Charged with supervising martial law in the state, the position carried tremendous power.

Broadhead's predecessor, Franklin A. Dick, had not always seen eye to eye with the Governor. Dick was a Curtis man who had irritated Gamble in the McPheeters case and others. He had also irked the Governor by refusing to arrest the editor of the *Kansas City Journal of Commerce*. That journalist had written a scurrilous article the previous March, blaming Gamble for the guerrilla warfare along the border. When Schofield succeeded Curtis, Gamble refused Dick the necessary commission to allow him to remain in office. The *Democrat* roundly denounced the move, but it evoked slight comment from the rest of the state's press. A change usually occurred when a new commander took over.[14]

One of the first demands confronting Schofield was the need for troops to aid General Grant in his campaign against Vicksburg. Even before he reached St. Louis, Schofield received a message from General Halleck asking that he send all the volunteer troops he could spare from Missouri and Kansas into the field. Schofield complied and thereafter relied entirely upon the state militia to maintain order within Missouri. Commenting on the difference between himself and General Curtis in this regard, Schofield later wrote: "For my part, I could see neither necessity nor excuse for quarreling with the governor of Missouri, and thus depriving myself and the nation of his legitimate aid."[15]

Troubles on the Kansas border soon increased. Unfortunately, Schofield continued Curtis' policy of attaching western Missouri counties to Kansas in forming military districts. On June 9, the new commander created two such districts to replace the old Military District of Kansas. The District of the Frontier, comprising this area south of the thirty-eighth parallel, remained under the command of Major General Blunt; the District of the Border stretched north from parallel thirty-eight to the Missouri River and encompassed the remainder of Kansas.[16] Here the influential Jim Lane virtually dictated the choice of Brigadier General Thomas Ewing, Jr., one of his political sycophants and a brother-in-law of William T. Sherman, as commander. Urged on by Lane, Ewing began a ruthless suppression of the border population, which had spawned a considerable guerrilla force to combat the Kansas Jayhawkers earlier in the war. Not trusting the Missouri militia to maintain order in this area, Ewing relied on Kansas troops whose "loyalty was unquestioned." By August 3, as guerrilla activity continued unabated, Ewing in desperation wrote Schofield. He proposed a mass evacuation from the border of those families known to harbor the desperadoes.

General Schofield hesitated to approve such a sweeping policy. Yet he realized that, regardless of cause, the situation was becoming increasingly difficult. Consequently, he approved the general plan on August 14. In so doing, he instructed Ewing that the group affected should be limited to the smallest number possible because of the expense involved and "the suffering it may cause to children and other comparatively innocent persons."[17]

On that same day, another of Ewing's policies reached a tragic climax. One of his innovations had been the incarceration of the mothers, wives, and sisters of those suspected of guerrilla activity. Disaster came on August 14 when one of the makeshift prisons in which they were housed collapsed. Five women were killed, and several others were seriously injured. When word of this accident reached the guerrillas hiding out in the vicinity, it carried with it the rumor that Ewing had planned the tragedy deliberately. No evidence exists to support this story, but these desperate men needed none.

The border commander soon issued the order putting into effect the plan which Schofield had just approved. The guerrillas were spurred into action. Led by the young William Quantrill, a large force of them moved out of Johnson County, Missouri, headed for Lawrence, Kansas. Their leader had long since chosen Lawrence as a target. After an all-day and all-night ride, the Quantrill gang swooped into the Kansas town early on Friday morning, August 21, 1863. There followed one of the bloodiest massacres in the history of irregular warfare. Some 150 men and boys of Lawrence were gunned down, leaving 80 widows and 250 orphans. Property damage totaled more than $2,000,000. Only one guerrilla lost his life; he had stayed behind in a drunken stupor and was shot by an Indian. A vengeful mob, finding his body, tore it to pieces.[18]

By the evening of August 22 the guerrillas were back in Missouri. They disbanded but were pursued by most of the Union troops along the border. Those caught were promptly executed. Kansas, emerging from the bloody disaster, thirsted for revenge. Governor Thomas Carney warned Schofield in a terse message: "I must hold Missouri responsible for this fearful, fiendish raid." He called for a court of inquiry. And in the same breath, he reported that he had requested arms from the Secretary of War. His requisition had been promptly approved. Jim Lane organized a meeting in Leavenworth which resolved to raise a large force of Kansas men by September 8. It was their purpose to enter Missouri and retaliate against its citizens.

The Radical press of Missouri joined the cry being raised by the Kansans. The *Democrat* went so far as to accuse Governor Gamble of supporting Quantrill. Indeed, it held him personally responsible for the outrages perpetrated by the guerrilla leader.[19]

Lane and A. C. Wilder wired Lincoln on the 26th: "The imbecility and incapacity of Schofield is most deplorable. Our people unanimously demand the removal of Schofield, whose policy has opened Kansas to invasion and butchery." The President promptly forwarded the message to the General, seeking an explanation for the entire Lawrence affair. In his reply, Schofield hedged. He sought to pin the blame on Curtis and the Radicals and their policies. He promised action, however, and assured Lincoln that he had taken measures to strengthen the force along the border to prevent future raids.[20]

Under these conditions, General Schofield left St. Louis for the border. He arrived at Leavenworth on September 2. There he conferred with Governor Carney, Jim Lane, and other Kansas leaders. Lane wished to make "a large portion of Western Missouri a desert waste, in order that Kansas might be secure against future invasion." He tried to persuade Schofield to lead personally the force he proposed to send into Missouri. He assured the General that they would abstain entirely from unlawful acts.

Schofield declined. He had already issued an order forbidding any armed men not in military service to cross the border from one state to the other. He immediately proceeded to station sufficient troops in the region to enforce this order. On September 4, he wired Acting Governor Hall: "There will be no invasion of Missouri by the people of Kansas. The Governor and the people of Missouri may be perfectly at ease on that subject."[21]

Schofield did prevent the Kansans from seeking indiscriminate revenge, but he failed to save the Missouri border from devastation. Urged on by Jim Lane, General Ewing decided that circumstances necessitated the implementation of the program he had instituted only partially before the Lawrence raid. Without waiting to secure Schofield's consent, he issued General Order Number Eleven on August 25—a document forever infamous in Missouri history. General Order Number Eleven required all persons in Jackson, Cass, Bates, and the northern half of Vernon County, living more than a mile from Union military posts, to abandon their homes within fifteen days.

Those who could prove their loyalty might remain at some post in the area; all others would have to move completely outside the military district.

To make matters worse, Ewing brought in the Fifteenth Kansas Cavalry under the intensely despised Doc Jennison to help carry out the order. This outfit performed an already brutal assignment so vengefully that the area lay in ruin within two weeks. It was known for years as the "Burnt District." In Cass County, which had had a population of 10,000 before the war, only 600 remained; Bates County was reduced to an even greater degree.[22]

Acting Governor Hall strongly protested the order and asked Schofield to rescind it. The Commander hesitated, then reluctantly approved it as the only possible remedy for a hopeless situation. His explanation to the War Department is a good summary:

> The evil which exists upon the border of Kansas and Missouri is somewhat different in kind and far greater in degree than in other parts of Missouri. It is the old border hatred intensified by the rebellion and by the murders, robberies, and arson which have characterized the irregular warfare carried on during the early period of the rebellion, not only by the rebels, but by our own troops and people. The effect of this has been to render it impossible for any man who openly avowed and maintained his loyalty to the Government to live in the border counties of Missouri outside of military posts. A large majority of the people remaining were open rebels, while the remainder were compelled to abstain from any word or acts in opposition to the rebellion at the peril of their lives. All were practically enemies of the Government and friends of the rebel guerrillas. The latter found no difficulty in supplying their commissariat wherever they went, and, what was of vastly greater importance to them, they obtained prompt and accurate information of every movement of our troops, while no citizen was so bold as to give us information in regard to the guerrillas. In a country remarkably well adapted by nature for guerrilla warfare, with all the inhabitants practically the friends of guerrillas, it has been found impossible to rid the country of such enemies. At

> no time during the war have these counties been free of them. No remedy short of destroying the source of their great advantage over our troops could cure the evil.[23]

All of these events occurred while Governor Gamble was absent from Missouri on another eastern trip. He and his family left St. Louis on July 21 to go to Philadelphia where they hoped to obtain surgical aid for his wife, whose eyesight was failing. While there, the Governor received a letter from Attorney-General Bates urging him to come to Washington. The President wished to see him, and Bates thought that much good could come of such a visit.[24]

Gamble went to Washington. Undoubtedly he hoped to straighten out the difficulties he had had with Lincoln and to enlist the President's full support in the struggle against the Radicals. The conference proved instead a decisive failure. According to Gamble, former Governor William Dennison of Ohio, "accidentally or purposely," walked by in the corridor just as the discussion turned to the "graver aspects" of the Missouri political situation. The President hailed Dennison to join the conversation, which finally took such a turn that Gamble deemed it proper for him to leave. He had accomplished nothing except an intensification of his already bitter feeling against Lincoln. When the President remarked that he hoped Gamble would not release his "cross" letter to the press, the Governor shot back that he intended to publish it whenever expedient. Gamble never published the letter, but in relating the interview to Bates later, he quite revealingly summed up his feelings: "I express to you my profound conviction that the President is a mere intriguing, pettifogging, piddling politician."[25]

On the return trip to Philadelphia, the Governor suffered an accident which delayed his departure for Missouri more than a month. He had been resting his elbow on the window ledge of the train. Timbers of a narrow bridge his train was crossing struck his arm, and a fracture resulted. He went on to Philadelphia where it was necessary for him to remain some time for treatment. Gamble made a slow recovery from his injury. The *Missouri Republican* reported on August 31 that he was still confined to his room and faced the prospect of being unable to travel for another two weeks. As a matter of fact, Gamble did not return to St. Louis until September 20. It was reported then that his arm was still lame and its condition would prevent him from immediately assuming his active duties.[26]

While General Schofield was en route to investigate the Kansas border situation early in September, the Radicals were gathering at Jefferson City for a mass emancipation convention. Four grievances had been set forth by the ten Radical leaders who called the meeting: (1) the insecurity of the lives and property of Union men; (2) the emancipation ordinance; (3) the Provisional Government's extension of life; and (4) the return of secessionists without restraint by the authorities.[27]

The convention organized and designated its resolutions committee. Then it settled down to listen to a lengthy harangue by Charles D. Drake in favor of immediate emancipation during which he roundly denounced the Gamble administration for its stand on that issue. The convention formally endorsed "every word and sentence" of Drake's address.

After more speeches, the convention heard from its resolutions committee. The committee reported a sweeping series of statements for the group's consideration. In addition to the resolutions praising Frémont's emancipation proclamation and calling for the immediate abolition of slavery in Missouri, four of these stood out above the rest. They called for (1) Gamble and Hall to vacate their offices, as the Provisional Government had been untrue to the loyal people of Missouri; (2) President Lincoln to remove General Schofield from the command of the Department of the Missouri; (3) the appointment of a committee of seventy (one from each county represented at the convention) to go to Washington and lay before the President a petition containing their grievances (they also extended an invitation to the Union men of Kansas to send a codelegation); and (4) the appointment of a committee of public safety to confer with the loyal men of the state in order to organize and arm them for the protection of their homes.[28] This last resolution seemed to give substance to the long-held contention of the Conservatives that the Radicals intended to use violence to overthrow the Provisional Government.

The convention chose Drake as chairman of the committee of seventy. It charged him with the task of preparing the address which that group was to present to the President upon its arrival in Washington. Stirred by the Missourians' action, the Kansas Radicals held a similar meeting at Leavenworth. They adopted resolutions which, among other things, denounced the "Gamble-Schofield policy" as one designed to keep Missouri a slave state and Kansas a captive province of that state. They also appointed a committee headed by Senator Jim Lane to accompany the Missouri group to the national capital.[29]

After numerous stops en route for speechmaking, the two committees reached Washington on September 27. They were forced to wait three days for an interview with the President.

Things were fast getting out of hand in Missouri during September. The trouble on the Kansas border and the action of the Radical emancipation convention in denouncing Gamble, Schofield, and the militia greatly encouraged the Radical and German press in their outcries. Their incendiary editorials incited at least one E.M.M. regiment to mutiny. The regiment was being sent from St. Louis to New Madrid to relieve the Twenty-fifth Missouri Volunteers for duty in Arkansas. In response to an editorial protesting their enrollment, this group brought their steamboat to shore. There they abandoned it and returned home by land.

About the same time, General Schofield discovered a plot by some Radicals to kidnap Governor Gamble and himself in an attempt to take over operations in Missouri. The plotters had tried to take the guard at Schofield's residence into their confidence, but he reported the plot to Schofield, and it was nipped in the bud.

All these evidences of disaffection alarmed the General. On September 17, he issued a directive threatening fines and punishment for those who endeavored to create dissatisfaction among the troops or who tried to incite the people to violence. He announced that those newspapers violating the order would be suppressed.[30] In explanation of his order, Schofield enclosed seventeen articles of an incendiary nature from the Radical Missouri press in a letter to General Halleck three days later. Describing their effect, the General minced few words:

> The revolutionary faction which has so long been striving to gain the ascendancy in Missouri, particularly in St. Louis, to overthrow the present State government and change the policy of the national administration has at length succeeded, so far as to produce open mutiny of one of the militia regiments and serious difficulties in others.
>
> . . . I am thoroughly convinced of the necessity for prompt and decided measures to put down this revolutionary scheme, and my sense of duty will not permit me to delay it longer. It is barely possible that I may not have to enforce the order against the public press. They may yield without the application of force; but I do not expect it. The tone of some of their articles since the publication of the order indicates a determination to wage the war which they have begun to the bitter end. This determination is based upon the belief that the President will not sustain me in any such measures as those contemplated in the order. A distinct approval of the President of my proposed action, and a knowledge of the fact here, would end the whole matter at once. . . . It is difficult, I am aware, for any one at a distance to believe that such measures can be necessary against men and papers who claim to be "radically loyal." The fact is, they are "loyal" only to their "radical" theories, and are so radical that they cannot possibly be loyal to the Government.[31]

This last comment hit home with Lincoln. He had witnessed the same tendency in the Radical leaders. Consequently, the President did not hesitate to approve Schofield's order, although he did admonish, through Halleck, "the exercise of great caution and discretion" in its enforcement.

As a result, the *Missouri Democrat* was led to comment that there could be little hope of any results from the visit of the Radical committees to Washington. It blamed the entrenchment there of the moneyed, unscrupulous Missouri Conservatives.[32]

Certainly, the Conservatives had not been idle. James S. Rollins wrote both Montgomery Blair and Edward Bates urging them to use their influence to protect Schofield. He sent the Attorney-General a letter vehemently setting forth the Conservatives' complaints against the Radicals, for transmission to the President. Bates saw Lincoln on September 26. He delivered both the Rollins letter and a similar one from James O. Broadhead and received assurances from the President that Schofield would be sustained unless something new and unexpected should be revealed against him. Blair had written Rollins earlier to the same effect. It would seem that Lincoln had determined his course of action even before the Radicals left St. Louis.

Apparently one of the letters which most influenced Lincoln at this time was that from Joseph A. Hay, the uncle of one of the President's secretaries. Hay wrote that he had heard Drake in a speech at LaGrange, Missouri, recently. The Radical leader had denounced Lincoln as "a Tyrant and a Dictator" because of his recent attempt, through Schofield, at interference with the state convention on the emancipation issue. Joseph Hay informed the President that he wished Lincoln to know who his "friends" and his "opposers" were in Missouri.[33]

Lincoln received the two Radical delegations at nine o'clock on the morning of September 30, in the East Room of the White House. With the doors locked and reporters barred, Drake proceeded to read his lengthy address of grievances. He demanded the removal of Schofield and his replacement with Major General Benjamin F. Butler of New Orleans fame. He called for the disbanding of the E.M.M. and the substitution of federal forces for it. And he requested action by federal authorities to see that persons not entitled by law to vote did not do so. The President heard the complaints and discussed the demands with the Radicals in detail. He gave them no immediate answer except to refuse to consider their demand to remove Schofield. Indeed, he warmly defended that officer's actions.[34]

Drake later wrote that he felt it a mistake to have the informal discussion after his address. During this time various members of both delegations made statements, mostly of a backbiting nature, against General Schofield. Lincoln took advantage of the meanness of the delegates' charges in his reply. The President's attitude is evident from John Hay's transcribed notes of the conversation which took place. The Radicals made it clear that they opposed Schofield because his policies ran counter to their plans for destroying the Provisional Government, and Lincoln was quick to observe their motives.[35]

Ignorant of events in Washington, Schofield sent the President a letter of defense which arrived the day after the audience. He reported conditions in Missouri better than at any previous time. He pointed out with obvious pride that he had accomplished this favorable situation with 20,000 fewer men than Curtis had had earlier. Surplus troops had been sent to reinforce Grant and Rosecrans. The Commander asserted that while he cooperated with the Provisional Government he did not allow Governor Gamble to dominate him. He had used his whole influence to secure emancipation, although the results had not quite been what he and Lincoln wanted. Trying to set the political picture straight in Missouri, Schofield warned the President that his support came from the Conservatives, not the Radicals.[36]

Lincoln undoubtedly realized the source of his support. He confided to John Hay that, while he approved the Radical program over that of the Conservative Provisional Government, he could not condone the methods whereby the Radicals sought to achieve it. He predicted though: "I believe, after all, those Radicals will carry the State & I do not object to it. They are nearer to me than the other side in thought and sentiment, though bitterly hostile personally. They are utterly lawless—the unhandiest devils in the world to deal with—but after all their faces are set Zionwards."[37]

The President drafted his formal reply to the Radicals on October 5, although he did not send it to Drake until the 14th. He reiterated his refusal to remove Schofield, with the declaration that no definite proof had been presented to show that that officer was responsible for Missouri's ills. He was not thoroughly familiar with the E.M.M. Yet, by their own application for its replacement with federal troops, the delegation admitted that the militia served a definite purpose. Nothing had so gratified Lincoln the previous June as Schofield's being able to send reinforcements to General Grant at Vicksburg. He reminded them that this had been possible largely because the E.M.M. was capable of policing Missouri. He promised to look into the matter, however, and determine the "exact value" of the E.M.M. Lincoln agreed that something should be done regarding the Radicals' demand concerning voters. He had directed Schofield to take care of this matter.[38]

The President's reply was so damaging to the Radical cause that Drake withheld its publication until October 23. By that time he had formulated a reply to be published with it. Publication followed by two days the demand of the *Missouri Republican* that the President's message be released to the public.[39]

On October 1, Lincoln reminded General Schofield that although no organized military force existed in Missouri at present to oppose the federal government, should such reappear the Commander's duty would be only too plain. He considered it Schofield's immediate obligation "to advance the efficiency" of his force and "to so use it, as far as practicable, to compel the excited people there to leave one another alone." The President did not wish to interfere with any of the policies which Schofield had adopted recently to ensure peace. Still, he did enjoin him to (1) prevent the return of fugitive slaves by the military or their enticement of slaves away from their homes; (2) allow no enlistment of colored troops without specific orders either from himself or the War Department; (3) stop confiscation until further notice; (4) see that only qualified voters exercised that right; and (5) rid the state of marauders by military means. In this last regard, Lincoln asked Schofield to report on the value of the E.M.M.

In his report of October 20, Schofield cited instances in which the E.M.M. had proved a valuable military adjunct during the past year and a half. He did note that some of them had become increasingly partisan as political tension mounted, a tendency which negated much of the benefit derived. Consequently, the General recommended that the militia's place could and should eventually be taken by federal volunteers and conscripts raised within the state.[40]

Schofield was not the only one to be disturbed by conditions in Missouri. Shortly after his return from the East, Governor Gamble wrote the President that his patience was exhausted by the accusations of disloyalty brought against him by the Radicals. He reminded Lincoln that he had never shirked in using the resources of the state to support the federal government. He asked that the department's military commander be given authority to maintain the Provisional Government with all the forces at his control.[41]

A few days later, Gamble received a letter from his brother Archibald, berating him for maintaining public silence in the face of his enemies. "You have allowed a licentious press to pervert all your acts and to misrepresent you as a Traitor," he wrote disgustedly. He urged Gamble to rise up and defend himself. "Your friends stand in need of arguments and statements by which to sustain you," Archibald remonstrated, "and by withholding them you are delivered over bound into the hands of your enemies."

When the Governor failed to hear from Lincoln within ten days, he decided to take this more drastic step. On October 12, he issued the following proclamation to the people of Missouri:

> Many evil disposed persons are now engaged in endeavoring to produce disaffection towards the State Government with the avowed purpose of overthrowing it by violence if they shall be unable to accomplish their end by other means. They endeavor to attract other citizens to their support by the circulation of most unfounded Statements and misrepresentations. Among this class of persons are to be found men who bear about with them commissions from the State Government and many who have obtained notoriety only by the favor of that Government; while others of them have been removed from office and still others have been refused office by that Government.
>
> So far as the end which they seek can be effected by means conforming to the constitution, and the laws, through the expression of the popular will, no objection can be made to any change in the Government which the people may desire to make, but the proclaimed purpose of effecting it by violence, demands that the people should be put upon their guard against a scheme which may result in the complete ruin of the State.

The Governor enumerated point by point the things which he had done since taking office to promote the safety and well-being of the state. Then he outlined the lies which had been rendered against these actions. He ended his message with a plea for unity and deliberative thought.[42]

President Lincoln finally replied to Gamble on October 19; he had delayed answering because of the press of official duties. Lincoln believed the Governor overestimated the seriousness of the situation in Missouri. The President informed Gamble that General Schofield had full authority to put down any violence which might threaten the state, and he assured the Governor that he stood just as ready to protect the Provisional Government as any other state administration which might have been more regularly chosen. The President specifically approved that part of Gamble's proclamation upholding constitutional change and denouncing violent overthrow of government. But, he asked, does the Radical party itself threaten to overturn the Provisional Government or are only some of its more outspoken members advocating such a course?[43] Gamble had no choice but to accept the President's assurances and carry on the affairs of the state as best he could.

General Schofield's report to the President on October 25 gave evidence that conditions had quieted down by the late fall of 1863. The General thanked Lincoln for his generous support and asserted that he believed the crisis past in Missouri. All the loyal people were coming gradually to the realization that they must cooperate if lawlessness were to be put down. They had become aware that they must sustain the Commander's military directives in order that law might be enforced. Schofield enclosed a letter from Lieutenant-Governor Hall which reported that conditions in northwest Missouri, one of the trouble spots throughout the war, were quieter now than at any previous time.[44]

The Radicals did not agree with this opinion concerning conditions in the state. They complained that many disloyal men and former rebel sympathizers had enlisted in the militia. These now threatened the loyal Union men who resided in that area; Ben Loan sent Secretary of War Stanton a large sheaf of affidavits to this effect.

The President forwarded the affidavits to Schofield on October 28. The General confirmed the statement that a large number of "returned Missouri rebels" had enlisted both in the militia and in the Kansas volunteers. These enlistments were effected at his direction during his recent tour of that area. While they had caused commotion in the militia for a time, the use of the returned "rebels" had proved a cure for many of the region's ills. The men who enlisted had repented of their disloyalty; they had taken the oath and given their bond. Schofield found them most reliable in keeping order because of their desire to prevent any more damage to what property remained to them. "If I can make a repentent rebel of more service to the government than a man who never had any political sins to repent of," the General asserted, "I see no reason for not doing so." He agreed with Lincoln, who had noted that Loan's affidavits anticipated future difficulties but had not cited actual harm done. Schofield had yet to hear the first report of a murder, robbery, or arson in that entire region since the new organization had been effected. He assured the President that he was keeping the area under careful surveillance. "The prospects of future peace in the state are highly encouraging."[45]

Conditions became so quiet militarily within the state by December that Gamble wrote Schofield proposing that those in the state militia who wished to re-enlist in the federal forces as veterans be allowed to do so. His suggestion was well taken. Schofield issued an official order to that effect on December 22—an obvious admission on the part of both the state and federal authorities that they felt it safe to reduce the state forces, as conditions were becoming more settled. The order carried out in part Schofield's promise to Lincoln of the previous October.[46]

In the political arena, the fall of 1863 saw the Radical-Conservative rivalry center on a contest for control of the Missouri Supreme Court. The recent session of the state convention had ordered an election for November to fill the three seats on the Court vacated in January, 1862. Both groups had a slate of candidates in the field. The Radicals at their emancipation convention in September nominated Henry A. Clover of St. Louis, Arnold Krekel of St. Charles, and David Wagner of Lewis County. The Conservatives did not hold a convention but declared their intention to support the three incumbents, Barton Bates, William V. N. Bay, and John D. S. Dryden. All had been appointed by Governor Gamble the previous year.[47]

Both parties considered the election of vital importance to their future. The Radicals carried on an extensive campaign, some of them declaring the need for a change in order that the new judges might unseat the Provisional Government on constitutional grounds.

The Conservatives contented themselves with issuing occasional replies to Radical charges. They were the party in power, and it appeared that they had the backing of the federal government because of the close cooperation between Gamble and Schofield. The Conservatives also controlled the patronage, a decided factor in their favor. Governor Gamble's proclamation of October 12 was probably their most effective weapon in the campaign. Its clear appeal caused many voters to think twice before succumbing to Radical propaganda. The Conservatives followed Gamble's proclamation a few days later with an article signed by Lieutenant-Governor Hall and others, belaboring the Radicals for their revolutionary tenets. The Conservatives were not without concern over the outcome of the election. Attorney-General Bates wrote Broadhead as late as October 24 that the party would have to carry the election or future elections might be jeopardized.[48]

The election was close—so close that at first it appeared that the Radicals had won. The *Missouri Democrat* so claimed as early as November 9. It soon became evident, however, that a great deal of fraud had been perpetrated in the returns for the various military units, and this had accounted for the Radical margin. The *Missouri Republican* cited one instance—the returns for the Fifth Cavalry—in which the Radicals received 1,084 votes to 5 for the Conservatives. Curiously, only 726 men in the unit were eligible to vote. When the official returns were announced, the Conservative ticket emerged victorious 43,180 to 40,744. General Schofield had issued orders in accordance with Lincoln's instructions, restricting the vote to those who could meet the suffrage requirements, which included taking the test oath. He reported to the President that the election passed off quietly and in good order. Most of the outstate press confirmed this opinion, although the *Republican* and the *Democrat* made partisan charges that the party of the other had permitted ineligible persons to vote.[49]

The judicial election setback had a temporary sobering effect on the Radicals. Certainly it made them realize that their strength did not approach the claims they had been making so extravagantly. They soon had consolation, however, in the election of B. Gratz Brown to the United States Senate to fill the seat held by the Conservative Senator Wilson. This victory indicated a definite consolidation of party ranks in the legislature. At its regular session earlier in the year, the General Assembly had deadlocked. A three-way (Charcoal, Claybank, Snowflake) race had failed to produce a senator for the term ending 1867. Now, at the adjourned session, party lines emerged sufficiently to reduce the race to a two-man contest and give Brown a nine-vote margin over James O. Broadhead.

Brown had been a Radical leader from the outset. He had a long antislavery record going back to the 1850's when he edited the *Missouri Democrat*. Following his election to the Senate, Brown made the dramatic announcement that he would go to Washington as a representative of the state and not of his party.[50] He promptly forgot this statement when he arrived at the national capital. There he began working ardently to undermine Schofield, Gamble, and the Provisional Government.

The General Assembly which met in November, 1863, also faced the necessity of filling Missouri's other Senate seat for the term ending in 1869. The legislature had elected John B. Henderson at its earlier session to serve out the term until March 4, 1863. He immediately announced that he would seek re-election. Apparently sensing the rising Radical strength in Missouri, Henderson by August began to edge away from his previously forthright conservatism and became more critical of the Provisional Government. The *Missouri Democrat* accused him of straddling the fence to secure the votes of both Radicals and Conservatives when the legislature met. Henderson denied privately that he had courted the Radicals with any deal. Yet he outpolled his opposition by a handsome margin, which indicated that he had found some favor in certain Radical eyes.[51]

Even though Henderson filled one of the seats, the *Democrat* was greatly elated about the Senate election. It reported that rumors were circulating in Jefferson City that Governor Gamble would resign because of the results. The *Missouri Statesman* replied that the rumor of Gamble's resignation resulted from the Governor's ill health. Should Gamble resign, Lieutenant-Governor Hall would complete his term.[52] The resignation never came.

During that same fall, some of Missouri's leading Radicals became attracted to the Union League of America. This group had been organized a year earlier to help arouse enthusiasm for the Union cause. No state-wide organization existed in Missouri, but a number of local chapters sprang up under affiliation with the Kansas, Iowa, or Illinois state councils. When the League held its annual meeting at Washington in December, five Missouri Radicals appeared as delegates. They sought to use the council sessions as a national forum to air their grievances against Gamble and Schofield. The council rejected a plea to send a special committee to the President on the Kansas-Missouri situation. Rather, it appointed a three-man group to see Lincoln about securing better protection for Union men throughout the country and to make special mention "that the complaints of our truly loyal brethren of Kansas and Missouri have produced the conviction in our minds that something should be done for their better protection and relief."[53]

Lincoln received the committee but made no promises. He confided to John Hay: "I know these Radical men have in them the stuff which must save the State [Missouri] and on which we must rely. They are absolutely uncorrosive by the virus of secession. . . . The Conservatives, in casting about for votes to carry through their plans, are tempted to affiliate with those whose record is not clear. If one side *must* be crushed out & the other cherished there could be no doubt which side we would choose as fuller of hope for the future. We would have to side with the Radicals." The President, nevertheless, deplored as "simply monstrous" the Radical distrust of Gamble and his associates, for even Drake and many of his friends had been antiabolitionist before the war.[54]

Lincoln found it more difficult to overlook other reports which reached him. B. Gratz Brown and Congressman Elihu B. Washburne of Illinois accused Schofield of taking sides in the internal politics of Missouri. Washburne, a close personal friend of the President, had asked the General to use his influence to secure the election of both Brown and Henderson. This would ensure each party a senatorial seat and prevent a repetition of the earlier deadlocked legislature. Schofield reportedly answered that he could not consent to Brown's election. After securing office, Brown made a proposal to Schofield through an intermediary: If Schofield would throw his political weight behind the measure before the General Assembly to call a new state convention, Brown would not oppose Schofield's permanent promotion to major general by the Senate. According to Brown, this proposal received a similarly unfavorable answer from Schofield.[55]

The President called Schofield to Washington for personal consultation. The General denied the accusations. Lincoln assured him: "I believe you, Schofield; those fellows have been lying to me again." Nevertheless, the new situation was complicated by Lincoln's realization that however Schofield might answer the charges, a dilemma would result. Either Schofield's integrity or that of Washburne and Brown must suffer. Therefore, the President decided to act in the matter before such a climax was reached.[56]

Another situation arising at the same time helped Lincoln solve his problem. Major General William S. Rosecrans had become *persona non grata* to Generals Grant and Sherman because of his behavior in the action around Chattanooga. The two commanders were favorably disposed toward Schofield. The President secured the approval of Senators Henderson and Brown for the appointment of Rosecrans as commander of the Department of the Missouri. He also received their assurances that they would support his nomination of Schofield for the permanent rank of major general with a command in the field. In this way two troublesome problems could be solved, and both men receive a promotion.

Lincoln sought the approval of Secretary of War Stanton and General Halleck for this arrangement on December 18. Apparently one of these men suggested that General Pope might be a better choice for the command at St. Louis if Schofield were to be relieved. Lincoln replied that the two Missouri senators thought there might be too much prejudice against him because of his previous service in the state. Halleck and Stanton acquiesced.

Once this routine procedure had been discharged, the nomination of Schofield was sent to the Senate. The Commander remained at the capital for several weeks during this process and looked forward eagerly to a field command, as it meant an escape from the political intrigues which had plagued him in Missouri.

Meanwhile Lincoln encountered new obstacles in the Senate. Senator Brown attempted to undermine the President's action. Although he did not personally oppose Schofield's confirmation, Brown urged certain of his colleagues to do so. A private conference with certain leading senators was required before Lincoln was able to carry out his plan regarding both Schofield and Rosecrans. This delay prevented the latter from assuming his new command until January 30, 1864.[57]

General Halleck, writing to William G. Eliot the following day, summed up quite accurately the situation in Missouri which brought about Schofield's transfer:

> I knew what his [Schofield's] instructions were, and I believe that he was honestly and faithfully carrying them out. . . . Missouri is a very difficult Dept. to command, and I know of very few officers fitted for the place. The President does not understand the condition of affairs there. . . . I sincerely hope that he [Rosecrans] may give satisfaction. He may do so if he will keep clear of the political factions which will attempt to use him for their own purposes.[58]

It was impossible for General Schofield to weather the Radical storm indefinitely. He simply cooperated too closely with Governor Gamble. Although he had not always pleased the Provisional Government with his policies,[59] he had the confidence of its officials. Far more often than not he supported them openly against Radical attacks. For any commander to remain long in Missouri, it was absolutely necessary for him to stay neutral so far as the state political scene was concerned. This, in reality, was impossible to do in a situation in which the political picture tied so closely to the military. Neither party was content to see the other gain the advantage which the military could give. Thus, throughout the war, Lincoln found himself constantly assailed with demands from one side or the other that a new commander be appointed. To a certain extent the President was responsible for bringing this condition on himself. As Halleck noted, he did not always understand the situation within Missouri. He saw the strife there as a party struggle for power, yet he failed to appreciate its intensity and the basic issues underlying it in their local context.

Lincoln's attitude toward the whole Missouri situation is best summed up in a letter he wrote a group of St. Louis Radicals in May, 1863, when contemplating the removal of General Curtis: "It is very painful to me that you in Missouri cannot or will not settle your factional quarrel among yourselves. I have been tormented with it beyond endurance for months by both sides. Neither side pays the least respect to my appeals to your reason."[60]

As long as the Provisional Government remained in power, this condition continued. General Rosecrans proved no more a match for it than did any of his predecessors. Perhaps General Halleck himself came closer to winning the respect of both sides than any of the others who served in the department. His early removal to a command in the field took him out of the active Missouri picture before he had a chance to become too involved in state politics.

9

The Radicals Triumph

THE ARRIVAL of General William S. Rosecrans at the end of January, 1864, to take command of the Department of the Missouri coincided with another event of great significance, the death of Governor Gamble. The Governor had been in ill health since his last eastern trip in the late summer of 1863. Nevertheless, he had taken an active role in the judicial election campaign and in preparing for the adjourned session of the General Assembly. Rumors began circulating as early as November that he would resign because of his health and allow Lieutenant-Governor Hall to finish the remainder of his term. Few paid serious attention to these rumors, for the Governor continued at his duties in Jefferson City where the legislature was meeting. That he took an active interest in the work of that body is evidenced by the three veto messages and the several special communiqués he sent it.[1]

On December 17, Governor Gamble slipped and fell on the ice while descending the steps of the State Capitol and severely injured his yet unmended elbow. Gamble returned to St. Louis to recuperate but, his strength weakened and his resistance low, he contracted pneumonia. On January 15, the *Missouri Republican* reported that the Governor had been confined to his bed since the 9th but, it continued optimistically, he was now improving. No serious symptoms were evident.

Three days later the paper changed its tone. It now informed its readers that Gamble's illness had taken a turn for the worse. No one was certain how long his confinement would last. No more appeared in the papers until February 1, when the *Republican* announced that the Governor's condition had become critical, and the family had sent for his son, Hamilton,

Jr., in the East. The younger Gamble did not arrive in time to find his father alive. The same issue of the paper carried a later item reporting the Governor's death as having occurred just before noon on Sunday, January 31, 1864.[2]

Lieutenant-Governor Hall immediately assumed the gubernatorial office. He announced Gamble's passing to the General Assembly on Monday, February 1. The new governor paid a fitting tribute to his predecessor, which history has since borne out:

> Surrounded by difficulties, such as never before beset a Governor of this State, it is not strange that his administration of affairs should have failed to satisfy all. His official career is now a part of history, and it is confidently believed that when the animosities of the present shall have yielded to the decision of cooler judgment, all will admit that he discharged his difficult and arduous duties with an eye single to the best interests of the country.[3]

In this respect, it is interesting to note also the comment of Attorney-General Bates, Gamble's brother-in-law and long-time partner and friend. He wrote in his diary:

> To the Public, his death, especially now, is a calamity; for he stood, like a lighthouse on a rock in the edge of a stormy sea, not only to give warning of the danger, but to resist its violence. . . .
>
> And now perhaps, in the article of death, he serves his country as effectually as in the best actions of his life. Death has fixed a seal not only upon the man, but his acts and policies also; and so, desperate factionists, seeing small hope of success in their schemes, will, I hope, in a good degree, cease from troubling.[4]

Such would not be the case. The *Missouri Democrat* had continued to criticize Gamble almost to the day of his death. Now it paid him brief tribute: "His private character and personal reputation are unblemished. His public and official course has been freely canvassed and heavily censured, but the shield of death is over it now."[5] The year 1864 was *the* election year. The Radicals, many of them political opportunists, could hardly be expected to cease their agitation for long.

The State of Missouri owes a great debt of gratitude to Hamilton Rowan Gamble for his services during this crucial time in its history. He gave unselfishly of himself to help Missouri weather the internal storms which threatened to wreck it. Although he came to the governorship in one of the most unusual extralegal actions any state ever witnessed, his conservatism and moderation were important staying factors in the whole drama of Missouri during the Civil War. His policies kept many loyal to the Union who would otherwise have gone over permanently to the Confederacy. Through the militia he made it possible for many to enlist in the Union cause who would have had little inclination to do so had Missouri pursued a radical course from the beginning.

In time, Gamble's conservatism began to displease many of the "stauncher" Union men. A lawyer and a jurist, he found it difficult to circumvent Missouri's increasingly outmoded codes. Being of Southern background, Gamble tended to tread carefully in thinking of emancipation. This caution alienated him from those who sought quick freedom for Missouri's slaves. The inevitable result was a split in the Union ranks and the emergence of the Radical party.

In wartime, men are prone to do many things they would not contemplate under ordinary circumstances. Charles D. Drake is a good example of this response to unusual pressures. Drake had been strongly proslavery before the war, yet he came to see slavery as the sole cause of the conflict and was determined to wipe it out in his own state. The Radical party had its beginnings with men who followed sincere convictions; it soon attracted the political opportunists. Gamble probably could not have stemmed this Radical tide even had he joined it. When he indicated his willingness to compromise in the convention over the emancipation ordinance, his own Conservative group refused to go along with him. Gamble's dependence upon their support thus hindered him while giving him added strength. In his death, the Conservatives lost a powerful leader.

In his first message to the General Assembly, Governor Willard P. Hall made it quite evident that his policies would differ little from those of his predecessor:

> I am aware of the embarrassments I must encounter in succeeding so good a man and officer, and I solicit your kind support whenever I shall deserve it. My chief and constant effort shall be to co-operate with the Federal Government in its effort to suppress the existing rebellion. In doing this, I shall not be solicitous to find fault with the President, with Congress or our Generals in the field. I shall rather defer my objections to whatever I may consider blameworthy in the acts of either to a more propitious period, and trust, by a cordial support of the Government of the United States, to contribute something to the restoration of peace. In this course I shall expect to receive the approbation of yourselves and of the people of Missouri.[6]

One of the first acts passed by the General Assembly after Hall became governor called for a new state convention to reconsider the emancipation question and to look into the possibility of revising the Missouri constitution in view of changed conditions. The call for the convention needed to be ratified by a popular referendum at the fall election. The selection of delegates (two from each senatorial district) would be held at the same time so that the convention could meet in January, 1865, if approved by the voters.

The previous December, Hall had cast a tie-breaking vote to lay the measure on the table in the Senate where he presided. The Radicals, who had been gaining strength steadily as the session progressed, resurrected the measure. When it passed by large majorities, the Governor signed it. He reported confidently to Rollins that the Conservatives would defeat the scheme at the polls that fall.[7]

This new issue gave additional importance to an already

crucial election. November of 1864 would offer the people of Missouri their first opportunity to choose a full slate of state officials since 1860. Both Radicals and Conservatives were determined to have their men elected. Then too, this was a presidential election year, although in this issue the political lines were not so distinctly drawn in Missouri.

Both Radicals and Conservatives began preparations for 1864 early. The former group found itself divided in its loyalties where the Presidency was concerned. Many, particularly those from the German element, were dissatisfied with Lincoln's policies in Missouri. They hoped for a national Radical convention which might support Secretary of the Treasury Chase or some other candidate of like stripe. They signed a call for a Slave-State Freedom Convention to meet at Louisville on February 22, in the hope that it might serve such a purpose. When they attempted to move the Louisville convention in the direction of Chase's nomination, however, they met the decided opposition of Charles D. Drake. A member of the Missouri delegation, Drake believed such a move premature. He favored Radical participation in the regular Republican (National Union) convention in the hope, presumably, of averting Lincoln's renomination. Drake carried the day at Louisville. The Freedom Convention confined itself to pressing for more immediate emancipation in the border states.[8]

Undaunted by the events at Louisville, B. Gratz Brown and certain Missouri Radicals joined others from ten states in an invitation to those of like faith to gather at Cleveland on May 31. There they would nominate a "true" Union ticket. This convention attracted a motley crew from sixteen states. They represented a variety of interest groups, all of them Radical. General John Charles Frémont received their nomination. He had been the darling of the German Radicals since his days in Missouri in 1861. The convention adopted a decidedly Radical platform.[9]

The Missouri Conservatives meanwhile had been laying their plans for the campaign. Thomas H. Allen, a prominent Conservative Unionist, wrote James O. Broadhead as early as November 16, 1863, asking if he would consider heading the Conservative ticket in Missouri the following year. He reported that many desired a mixed slate of Conservatives and Democrats. A month later, Alexander J. Reid, the editor of the *Louisiana Journal,* informed Broadhead that he felt the people in that area inclined toward the Conservatives. The party needed a paper the size of the *Democrat* to influence the people more strongly; many persons heeded a paper "according to its size and the boldness of its tone." He urged that the *St. Louis Union* be expanded to fill this need.[10]

Steps were taken in this direction. R. J. Howard wrote Montgomery Blair on December 28 that "our friends," including Broadhead and Glover, had met to consider placing Lincoln's name at the masthead of the *Union* as that paper's candidate for the Presidency. Although there was some opposition to such a move this early in the campaign, it was apparently overcome. The *Union* came out for the President's re-election the first week in January, 1864.[11]

During January and February, the Conservatives began forming Lincoln clubs throughout Missouri. The one in St. Louis sent out a call on April 11 for the first of three state political conventions to be held in 1864. It met at St. Louis on May 18 under the banner of the Unconditional Union (Conservative) party for the express purpose of choosing delegates to the National Union (Republican) convention at Baltimore. The *Missouri Democrat* bitterly denounced the meeting as "bogus Unionism." It accused the group of trying to split the Radical party, which it called the true Union force in Missouri.

Undeterred, the Conservatives chose twenty-two delegates to go to the Baltimore convention and instructed them to vote for the nomination of Lincoln. Governor Hall headed the delegation, which included James O. Broadhead; William F. Switzler, the editor of the *Missouri Statesman;* Samuel M. Breckinridge; and James B. Eads, the noted St. Louis engineer. The convention strongly endorsed Lincoln's war policies. It called for cooperation with him while condemning those unwilling to unite behind the decision of the national convention. While it favored a constitutional amendment abolishing slavery, the convention went on record as approving the segregation of the Negro to the point of granting him a special territory for settlement. Lacking a concrete organization, the Conservatives established a state central committee which was instructed to call a convention following that at Baltimore to nominate a state and electoral ticket.[12]

The Radicals held their state convention at Jefferson City a week later. The call simply stated that the meeting would be held for the purpose of nominating state candidates and conducting "other business." The Radical Union Executive Committee in St. Louis carefully avoided mentioning the Baltimore convention for fear of alienating their more extreme adherents.[13]

When the convention met, a bitter floor fight developed over a resolution to send delegates to the National Union conclave. For a time it appeared that a split might occur in the state meeting. The more extreme Radicals feared that the Baltimore convention would give an automatic endorsement to Lincoln, whose policies they distrusted. They had already called the meeting at Cleveland to nominate Frémont and wished to avoid placing the Missouri party in an ambiguous position on the Presidency. The majority of the Radical leadership realized that unless they tied their party to the National Union movement in place of the Conservatives, they could have little hope for the fall campaign. A vote on the resolution resulted in its adoption, 341 to 99, with the delegates from St. Louis voting against it, 59 to 34. Some of the Germans walked out of the convention in protest. They soon returned as they saw that the mood of the meeting continued along an anti-Administration trend. Thereupon, the convention chose twenty-two uncommitted delegates to go to Baltimore. These included Charles D. Drake; John F. Hume, the editor of the *Missouri Democrat;* and the three Radical congressmen, Ben Loan, Joseph W. McClurg, and Henry T. Blow.

The resolutions adopted by the convention sustained the federal government in a vigorous prosecution of the war. They protested the authority given the Provisional Government by the Lincoln administration, however, and rejoiced at the prospect of the imminent deliverance of Missouri from its control. Realizing that part of their difficulties lay in the make-up of the Lincoln cabinet, the Radicals called for the ousting of those (Bates, Blair, Seward) not in sympathy with their program. They denounced what they considered the unfair rejection of parts of the soldier vote in the previous fall election. Finally, they reiterated their major theme, immediate emancipation in Missouri, and went on record as favoring a national constitutional amendment to end slavery.

Proceeding to the nomination of state candidates, the Radicals chose Thomas C. Fletcher for governor. A compromise choice, Fletcher had been in the regular army since 1862 and had attained the rank of colonel. He currently commanded a brigade in Sherman's Army of the Tennessee. He had been a delegate to the Republican national convention in 1860, where he voted for Lincoln. Fletcher had not been active in recent Missouri politics because of his army career, so he had made few enemies. Charles D. Drake had wanted the nomination. Certainly the Radicals' best spokesman and seemingly their logical choice, he proved unacceptable to the Germans because of earlier disagreements. Many members of the party feared his extreme utterances would cost them votes.[14]

The rival factions of the old Union group in Missouri thus chose two delegations to vie for representation at the National Union convention at Baltimore. One of these had definitely been instructed to vote for Lincoln. The other went uninstructed but bound by a resolution which declared that a President should serve only one term. Both groups stopped off at Washington en route to Baltimore to see Lincoln. He remained officially uncommitted as to which delegation he favored.[15]

The Baltimore conclave opened on June 7. After a short floor debate, the convention approved a report from its committee on credentials seating the Radical delegation from Missouri by a vote of 440 to 4. This would seem strange inasmuch as the Radical delegates were definitely known to oppose the renomination of Lincoln. Certainly it proved somewhat embarrassing to the convention managers. When the roll call to nominate a candidate for the Presidency occurred, the entire convention voted for Lincoln with the exception of the Missourians. They cast their ballots for General Grant, but when the end of the roll call showed Missouri alone in the opposition column, its delegation chairman moved that the President's nomination be made unanimous.[16]

A brief examination of events on the national scene during the winter and spring of 1864 can offer a satisfactory explanation for the Baltimore convention's seating of the Radicals. Secretary of the Treasury Chase had been flirting with the Radicals in Missouri and elsewhere in the hope of securing the Presidential nomination. Chase's was a futile dream from the beginning. Nevertheless, he developed a bitter antagonism against Montgomery Blair who staunchly supported the President and promoted his renomination. Chase's machinations with the Missouri Radicals caused some of the more liberal Conservatives there to seek help from Frank Blair, about to resume his seat in Congress after serving with Sherman's army in Tennessee. This the hot-tempered Blair rendered only too willingly. The heated feud culminated in two bitter tirades on the floor of the House. Frank castigated Chase and the Missouri Radicals for their opposition to the President, while openly accusing the Secretary of the Treasury of using his office to the personal profit of his friends.

The Radicals in Congress thwarted an investigation of Blair's charges. Then they deprived him of his seat, on the ground that his army commission made him ineligible. Unable to stop the popular groundswell for Lincoln's renomination, which the Blairs were doing all in their power to promote, the Radicals struck back through the convention credentials committee. They played up the Missouri Radical delegation as truly Republican while insinuating that the Conservatives were a bunch of "johnny-come-latelys." Secretary of the Navy Gideon Welles noted: "There was much intrigue and much misconception in this thing." So the delegates later discovered, when the vote of the Missouri delegation set off a tumult of disapproval in the convention chamber.[17]

The Unconditional Union party of Missouri, whose delegates had been denied seats, went out of existence as an active political body. Its executive committee, set up to call a state nominating convention, never fulfilled that function. Most of its members either supported Lincoln quietly or went over to the Democratic party.

This latter group, which consisted of the remaining Conservatives in Missouri, met in their state convention at St. Louis on June 15. They had been called together by several hundred signers for the express purposes of choosing delegates to the national Democratic convention at Chicago and of selecting a state central committee. When they met, the delegates confined their activities to those two specific functions. They declared that they would nominate state candidates and electors after the national convention. Among those chosen to go to Chicago were John S. Phelps, Sample Orr, Thomas L. Price, William A. Hall, and former Senator Robert Wilson, all leading Conservatives. They were instructed to vote for General George B. McClellan, the eventual nominee of the party.

Upon the delegation's return, General Thomas L. Price was chosen as the party's nominee for governor. Price had earned his military commission in the state militia in 1847. He had been a staunch Benton supporter in the 1850's and had served briefly both in the Missouri General Assembly and in Congress.[18]

The *Missouri Republican* and the *Missouri Statesman* immediately hoisted the Democratic ticket to their mastheads and actively supported that party's candidates throughout the campaign. Most of the Radical press, led by the *Missouri Democrat*, had long since announced its support of Lincoln and Fletcher. The latter, however, hedged in supporting the President for reelection through fear of alienating the Germans. He made no open statement of his feelings regarding the Presidency until the end of October, a month after Frémont had withdrawn from the race.[19]

All of this political activity operated against a background of increasing unrest and military action in Missouri. After comparative quiet during the winter, widespread guerrilla warfare had broken out again late in the spring of 1864. During June and July, it increased to hitherto unknown proportions. The state of Kansas had been reconstituted as a separate military department under General Curtis shortly before Rosecrans became commander at St. Louis. The District of the Border had been abolished. Its Missouri counties had been transferred to Brigadier General Egbert Brown's District of Central Missouri; Tom Ewing was brought to the District of St. Louis. The Kansas troops who had kept the border in a state of terror were replaced by the tough Second Colorado Cavalry, an outfit which had no special hatred for Missourians.[20]

General Brown soon reported bitterly to headquarters that some Kansans were again raiding the border counties indiscriminately. In view of these forays, some renewal of guerrilla warfare was only natural. Rosecrans now sought to coordinate state and federal military efforts more closely to meet this menace. The E.M.M. had been placed under his control in February. He promptly ordered a new enrollment taken in every county by May 1. Early in May, Rosecrans recommended to the War Department that certain regiments of the E.M.M. be mustered into the permanent service of the federal government. When no action had been taken on this a month later, he wrote Governor Hall, in Washington en route to the Baltimore convention, asking him to approve the move and recommend it to the War Department.

The General pointed out that these regiments had been serving the United States recently without provision for pay. Only if they were mustered into actual federal service could they receive compensation. Rosecrans also recommended to the Governor that he get the approval of the War Department to convert the M.S.M. into United States Volunteers in so far as practicable. Too, their change in status would allow them to be better equipped and provided for. The General further requested Hall to obtain authority to raise an additional two regiments of infantry and four regiments of cavalry to serve for at least six months. These forces would be needed, Rosecrans reported, if the farms of Missouri were to be protected against invasion.

Governor Hall endorsed the letter upon receiving it on June 9. He promptly sent it to the War Department, which authorized Rosecrans the next day to accept M.S.M. re-enlistments and muster them into federal service for a period of three years or for the duration of the war. Another order issued the same day approved the mustering in of the special regiments Rosecrans wanted. They were to be taken for a twenty-month period, retroactive to November 1, 1863.[21] Although this seems a definite reversal of previous policy, it marked but the natural culmination of the transition already begun by Gamble and Schofield the previous December. By these moves the state and federal forces were more closely integrated than at any time since 1861.

As conditions continued to worsen in June and July, it became necessary to resort to drastic measures to put down the guerrilla uprisings and to thwart the invasion of Missouri by Confederate forces from Arkansas which was expected momentarily.

General Rosecrans followed up his military reorganization with a proclamation to the people of Missouri on June 28. Daily appeals for protection came to him from all quarters. These were accompanied by assurances that the people were ready and willing to unite to preserve the peace. In the light of these declarations, Rosecrans called upon the citizenry to adopt the following measures in the various localities: (1) hold public meetings in each township and county to set up committees of public safety (these would work with the local district commanders and through them with Rosecrans to gain advice and information which might be useful in keeping the peace); (2) by agreement with the Governor choose and organize one or two companies of one hundred men from the E.M.M. in the locality to protect their county. These men were to be paid by the state when on active duty with the approval of Hall. In conclusion, Rosecrans appealed: "I confidently rely upon all good men in the State to unite in this movement in behalf of humanity, and for the protection of life and property. I am fully persuaded, if you do so unite, with zeal, energy, and in good faith, a short time will restore a state of profound quiet within your now distracted borders."[22]

Conditions were especially bad in north Missouri where Brigadier General Clinton B. Fisk commanded the Union forces and the militia. On July 12, Fisk wrote Rosecrans that there had been a general "rebel uprising" in the region. Guerrillas under a leader named Thurston threatened St. Joseph. Reinforcements were needed, and Fisk was hastening to St. Louis to see Governor Hall about securing them. "Every loyal man in Missouri will have to shoulder his gun for war, and that, too, without delay," he remonstrated. "The very atmosphere is rank with treason."[23]

Both Rosecrans and Governor Hall backed Fisk strongly. Rosecrans issued a special proclamation to the people of north Missouri on July 16. He charged that they had no one to blame but themselves for the outrages being committed there. The

General reminded them that he could not keep order so long as they refused to cooperate and protected the enemy. He called upon them for help in putting down bushwhackers.

Governor Hall, upon the receipt of a complaint from that vicinity, forwarded it to General Fisk and assured that officer of his cordial cooperation. To his correspondent Hall wrote that he was prepared to help Rosecrans and his subordinate commanders because he had confidence in them. When Fisk appeared in St. Louis in mid-July seeking help, he received the men he needed from Hall. These troops saved the day.[24]

Not all his fellow Conservatives shared Hall's views. James O. Broadhead wrote Attorney-General Bates on July 24 that conditions in Missouri were now worse than they had been at any previous time. He had grave doubts about the wisdom of Rosecrans' appointment to command the department. He feared that the Administration had sent Rosecrans to Missouri "either as a punishment to him or to us, or else out of utter indifference to our fate." Broadhead also thought Fisk a poor choice for the post in north Missouri and criticized his recent moves there.

Bates replied that he shared Broadhead's views. He promised to do all he could to remedy conditions, but he cautioned that he had had several conflicts with the military lately and would have to proceed slowly. The Attorney-General confided to his diary that he could see no reason why Rosecrans should have so much trouble with guerrillas when, just nine months before, Missouri had been so quiet.[25]

John G. Nicolay, Lincoln's private secretary, had visited St. Joseph a month earlier en route to a vacation in the Rocky Mountains and observed similar chaos. Nicolay blamed much of the difficulty on the division of authority. He praised Fisk, whom he considered a conscientious commander. That officer was handicapped, however, by the Provost Marshal General's agents and by the Governor. Both exercised independent commands within his district. The President's secretary particularly criticized the Provost Marshal General's agents. They had hired one Truman to make independent investigations in the area. His purpose was to "ferret out a great conspiracy which had for its object the capture of Hannibal, Quincy, and other points by guerrillas." The man had turned out to be a scoundrel. He killed indiscriminately and stole from those he murdered. At the time of Nicolay's writing, Fisk had arrested him, and he was awaiting trial.[26]

The provost marshal system had always been a bone of contention in Missouri. It continued until war's end, causing much distress. Broadhead had also complained of the Truman episode in his letter to Bates. It had been part of a major scare which seized Rosecrans and his provost marshal general, Colonel John P. Sanderson, that spring. Sometime in that period, Rosecrans uncovered in St. Louis a master plot of the Order of American Knights, a secret organization cosponsored by General Sterling Price and Clement L. Vallandigham, the Copperhead ex-congressman from Ohio. The order's major purpose was supposedly the establishment of a great northwestern Confederacy through spontaneous uprisings. Its alliance with the South would end the war. Rosecrans greatly exaggerated the strength of the movement, yet he aroused the fears of Governor Richard Yates of Illinois and others who aggravated Lincoln with their cries for help just when the campaigns of Grant and Sherman needed every available man. The order was infiltrated by Sanderson's detectives. Eventually, they broke it up by one mass arrest in St. Louis, but much trouble resulted from the methods used to accomplish this end.[27]

Reports had been circulating generally that Governor Hall had hindered General Rosecrans in his efforts to pacify the state. These disturbed Hall in the light of the cooperation he had given. He wrote the Commander on July 22, asking him to refute the charges. This Rosecrans did the next day with the statement that he had received only the most cheerful cooperation from the Governor in all matters. The *Missouri*

Republican came quickly to the support of Hall. It praised him for his efforts and reported that he and Rosecrans worked hand in hand.[28]

Rosecrans finally received authority from the War Department to muster into federal service as many six-month Missouri volunteers as he thought necessary. He called for ten regiments. On July 28, Governor Hall issued a proclamation asking the people to respond quickly and willingly to this call. He reminded them of the conditions which beset the state and of their prompt response to similiar crises in the past. Indeed, his message gave them little choice. Should an insufficient number of volunteers be raised, he would have to call out the militia. In serving as volunteers they would be paid and provided for by the federal government; as militia they would serve without pay since the Provisional Government had no funds at present for paying the troops.[29]

Guerrilla warfare had now been reinstituted actively for five months. Apparently it was but a preparation of the state for invasion. Confederate forces under Sterling Price moved into Missouri from Arkansas in the latter part of September. Price hoped that by this time the state would be in such chaos that thousands of former secessionists would flock to his banner. To his dismay he found such was not the case.

Price's army marched in three columns, with plans to effect a junction near Fredericktown. On September 26, General Rosecrans called out most of the E.M.M. to meet the emergency. Business was suspended in St. Louis for forty-eight hours to allow the local citizenry to prepare for the defense of the city and to permit the active forces in the city to take the field against Price. All shipments of goods to the interior of the state were banned. An order was issued that all traitors and spies attempting to pass through Union lines to the guerrillas or the invading rebels would be shot.[30]

Letters taken from the Confederate dead near Springfield indicated that Price had 12,000 men. He planned to head for

Jefferson City through Rolla, once his columns formed their juncture. Rosecrans still feared that he might try to move on St. Louis first. A force of Union troops under General Tom Ewing intercepted the Confederates at Pilot Knob on September 27. This bloody engagement diverted Price from any move on St. Louis if he had planned such. He pushed on to Jefferson City, arriving there October 2. Finding Union troops entrenched, he circled the capital and moved on to Boonville without fighting.[31]

General Rosecrans called out the local militia on October 9 to serve within their own counties. Four days later he took the field personally to pursue Price. The Confederates were followed from Jefferson City by forces under Major General Alfred Pleasonton. Slowly Price's army moved westward toward the Kansas border. Here the Confederates became caught between Pleasonton and forces under General Curtis moving in from Kansas. Three days of fighting, climaxed on October 23 by the battle of Westport, sent Price and his men reeling down along the Missouri-Kansas line. Federal troops pursued them the entire distance. On October 30, Price's army re-entered the northwest corner of Arkansas from whence it had come.[32]

The last effort of the Confederates to win Missouri had failed completely. The moment invasion threatened, all the loyal people of the state, regardless of party, closed ranks to repulse it. Following the encounter at Pilot Knob, much of his courage seemed to leave Price. Thereafter he avoided a showdown until he was caught near the Kansas border. His failure to engage in effective action hindered whatever chance he might have had for large scale recruitment; secessionists still remaining in Missouri had suffered too much in a losing cause to flock to an obviously faltering banner.

By the time Price left Missouri, only a few days remained until the election. Colonel Fletcher, the Radical candidate for governor, had had little time to campaign because he had been at the front during most of the summer and throughout the fall invasion. His war service gave the Radicals excellent campaign promotion which they used to the utmost. The Conservative candidate, Thomas L. Price, now had two potent scores against him: his name and his failure to take an active role in the defense of the state although he held a general's commission in the militia.[33]

In the voting which followed, the Radicals made a clean sweep: Fletcher triumphed by a majority of approximately 40,000 votes; Lincoln received the state's electoral vote by not quite the same margin; eight of the nine congressmen elected were Radicals; the party carried both houses of the new General Assembly by a large majority; the proposal for a new state convention secured approval by a margin of 29,000; approximately three-fourths of the delegates chosen to make up that body were members of the Radical party.[34]

The Radical victory can be attributed to a number of factors. Disfranchisement under the test oath kept from voting many Missourians, most of whom would have supported the Conservative ticket had they been given the opportunity to do so. Nearly 52,000 fewer votes were cast in the 1864 election than in the one four years earlier. After the Baltimore convention the Radicals became the Administration party, a role which strengthened their appeal to the uncommitted element of the electorate. The lack of any concerted campaign because of the Price raid and the generally tumultuous conditions in the state tended to aid the Radical cause. The party had a more effective press than its opponents, and the comparative military records of the two gubernatorial candidates benefited their cause also.

Beyond all these factors was the simple one that Missourians generally felt the need for a change. The Conservatives had held the line throughout the war. But the nation and Missouri were entering a new era with new problems, especially new for a state previously committed to slavery. So Missourians voted for a new convention and placed in power a new party with new ideas to meet the new challenge. The failure of that party to bring forth a program which could win the support of many of its own members, let alone the continued approbation of the majority of Missourians, constitutes the story of Reconstruction in Missouri.

With the election returns in, it became but a matter of time before the Provisional Government should expire. The only major event of those final two months was the removal of General Rosecrans and his replacement with Major General Grenville M. Dodge.

Rosecrans had come under attack from a number of sources for his failure to prevent Price's invasion of Missouri. Attorney-General Bates, supported by a number of Missouri Conservatives, had urged his removal for some time, although Governor Hall interceded with Lincoln as late as November 5 seeking Rosecrans' retention. Bates disapproved of the Commander's extensive use of the provost marshal system with its interference with the civil courts. He later claimed that if the General had paid more attention to military affairs, Price's raid could have been cut short.

Rosecrans had come under fire from General Grant the year before at Chattanooga. Shortly thereafter, when Grant became general-in-chief, he desired a concentration of Union effort in Virginia and Georgia in 1864. Rosecrans' fears of conspiracy in the trans-Mississippi area irked Grant. His conviction deepened that Rosecrans was incompetent. The necessity for deployment of federal forces to Missouri because of the Price raid proved the final straw. These troops were badly needed in Tennessee where the Confederates under Major General John B. Hood threatened Nashville. The General-in-chief decided that Rosecrans must be replaced. When the War Department inquired what his new assignment should be, Grant shot back: "Rosecrans will do less harm doing nothing than on duty. I know no department or army commander deserving such punishment as the infliction of Rosecrans upon them." Thus, on December 9, Rosecrans went the way of his predecessors. Never again did he hold an active command.[35] Missouri was hard on all its military commanders; Rosecrans proved no exception.

On December 28, 1864, Governor Willard P. Hall delivered his biennial address to the recently elected Twenty-third General Assembly. He reviewed the situation which had led to the establishment of the Provisional Government, the problems that government had faced, and conditions in general within Missouri. The state had furnished 81,767 men to the federal army thus far. An additional 60,000 had seen service in the militia. Rising above factionalism, Hall appealed for cooperation by all groups within the state in order that the new convention might successfully carry out its work.[36]

Shortly thereafter the Provisional Government of Missouri passed from the scene. A unique establishment, it was the only government of its type in existence during the Civil War. All other state governments were either duly elected or militarily appointed. Yet the Provisional Government performed one of the most remarkable operations of the war. It had been established to provide an administration which could cooperate with the Union in ensuring the safety of Missouri. Nevertheless, it zealously upheld the state's cherished desire to administer its own affairs, both civil and military. Thus it became at one and the same time staunchly Unionist and an avowed defender of states' rights.

The extraordinary action of the state convention in establishing the Provisional Government can be legally justified only by the furthest stretch of the imagination. Yet the distraught times called for measures which would not be considered under ordinary circumstances. The Provisional Government was intended originally as a stopgap measure to serve until the fall of 1861. It received two subsequent extensions of life from the convention which created it and continued to hold power over Missouri until January, 1865. As a result the people were never given an official opportunity to express their approval or disapproval of what had been done. The first extension might plausibly be justified by the internal stresses of the moment, including Sterling Price's control over considerable parts of Missouri; the second can scarcely be defended as warranted, for conditions did permit the election of congressmen and legislators in the fall of 1862.

In the hands of the wrong leaders, this *de facto* administration could have produced a decided reaction against the very end it was designed to serve. Fortunately, it had strong leadership which realized the general sentiment of Missouri's people and sought to prevent the state's being swallowed up by an arbitrary Union military rule. The wisdom and courage of Hamilton R. Gamble and Willard P. Hall in the face of great obstacles kept Missouri faithful to the Union, provided it with some means of self-defense, and helped it weather the emancipation crisis which threatened to rend it apart. In the hands of these men and their associates the civil government continued to function in Missouri throughout the war even though much of the state remained in a condition of turbulence and violent unrest.

Different groups continually questioned the constitutionality of the action which brought the Provisional Government into existence and then continued it in power. Yet it quickly received the recognition of the Lincoln administration, which sought to cooperate with it to the fullest extent that circumstances would allow throughout the war. Even when the President questioned the conservatism of some of its leaders toward the end of the war, he never doubted their sincerity in the Union cause. He continued to uphold them as the legitimate power of the state. He realized, however, as many of them failed to do, that they were not keeping pace with the rapidly changing times. This was particularly true when the future of the Negro was involved. Lincoln's prediction that this conservatism would pave the way for the triumph of the Radicals proved well founded.

Paradoxically, the extreme dependence of the Provisional

Government upon the Lincoln administration handicapped it in carrying out its program and yet made its successes possible. During most of the war, Missouri's treasury was empty. Because of unsettled conditions taxes were difficult to collect. Indeed, the state was forced on two occasions to accept its own depreciated scrip for tax payments. Its major source of revenue became the federal treasury through funds designated mainly for the state militia. These made it possible for Missourians themselves to serve in putting down the guerrilla warfare which plagued their state. Without this money the Provisional Government could not have functioned effectively.

For all the cooperation of the Lincoln administration, the Provisional Government had to contend for authority with the federal military commander at St. Louis. During the life of the Provisional Government, the military department of which Missouri formed the major portion had eight commanders. One of these, Major General John M. Schofield, served on two different occasions. The insecurity of the military commanders was due, in each case, to their inability to leave the civil government and political affairs of the state alone. Each of them had his own ideas of what should be done to meet the persistent guerrilla warfare which plagued Missouri. As the state administration refused to succumb to the military authority, the resultant disputations between the two absorbed much of President Lincoln's time and attention. They sorely tried his phenomenal patience on several occasions. It is to his credit that he kept the two forces as well in balance as he did.

On January 2, 1865, with the inauguration of Thomas Clement Fletcher as the duly elected governor of the state, the Provisional Government of Missouri officially came to an end. Fletcher, in his inaugural address, looked forward with great anticipation to the new Radical era which had dawned upon Missouri. He forecast the end of the war by spring and consequently dealt largely with the issues of reconstruction. Fletcher urged a magnanimous policy by the victors. "In the name of

Truth, of Justice, of Freedom, and of Progress, God has permitted us a political triumph," the Governor boasted, "bringing with it the solemn responsibility of promoting those great principles by an enforcement of the fundamental law for securing the peace, happiness and prosperity of the people of the state."[37]

Four days later, the sixty-six members of the new state convention gathered in the Mercantile Library hall in St. Louis. Their deliberations were to have a profound effect upon the new age. Four years earlier, another convention had decided against secession in these same rooms. Now an entirely different group, made up for the most part of political unknowns, was meeting to plot Missouri's course for the future; only three of its members had helped make the earlier decision. Southerners and lawyers had dominated the meeting of 1861. The present membership found that not quite half of its number had origins in the free states and abroad. There were more farmers and physicians than any other interest groups. The 1861 convention had been dominated by a single personality, Hamilton R. Gamble; his antagonist of 1863, Charles D. Drake, emerged to such a position of power in this one that its final handiwork bears his name, the "Drake Constitution."[38]

With a large Radical majority, the convention had no difficulty organizing. It quickly settled to the work for which it had been called. The legislative act of 1864 authorizing the meeting had stressed three duties: (1) secure the necessary amendments to the state constitution which would provide more immediate emancipation; (2) assure by amendment that the elective franchise would be restricted to "loyal" citizens; and (3) consider other amendments which would promote the public good.[39]

Emancipation provided the issue on which the least difference of opinion existed. Referring all proposals on the subject to a special committee, the convention quickly disposed of the matter when that group reported on January 11. The committee avoided superfluous political philosophy in its short, simply worded ordinance declaring the immediate and unconditional emancipation of all slaves in Missouri. Only four negative votes were cast against the measure as the Radicals swept aside the work of 1863 in a matter of moments.[40]

Governor Fletcher formally proclaimed the convention's action the same day. Celebrations quickly broke out in St. Louis and spread throughout the state as the word carried to other communities. Even the four Conservatives who voted against the ordinance realized that the convention was but legalizing a condition that had existed in actuality for some time. The Union army had begun recruiting Negro soldiers the previous summer under orders from the War Department, and slaves were being freed under the confiscation measures of Congress. Emancipation had already come to Missouri.[41]

The General Assembly, by concurrent resolution, ratified the Thirteenth Amendment to the federal constitution abolishing slavery in February. Senator John B. Henderson had played a major role in its drafting. Thereby Missouri placed its stamp of approval on total and complete emancipation.[42]

Having witnessed the extent of their power in the passage of the emancipation ordinance, many of the Radicals began to think more clearly in terms of a general and thorough revision of the state's organic law to prevent some future legislature, which might not be so Radical, from upsetting the work of the convention. Charles D. Drake now moved increasingly to the forefront as the guiding light of the convention. Under his leadership, the ultra Radicals were determined by early February to commit the convention to the drafting of a completely new state constitution. Opposition manifested itself, but the Drake Radicals beat it down. On February 15, they passed, 29 to 19, a motion by their leader approving this new direction.[43]

The convention had already been working through an elaborate system of regular and special committees. Slowly the new document began to take shape. The total effect was drastic change to meet the altered conditions. Much of the work showed real thought and foresight.[44]

A detailed examination of the new constitution is beyond the scope of this work. Only the action of the convention designed to solidify the political control of the Radicals over Missouri will be discussed here.

By far the most controversial parts of the new constitution were those dealing with the "Oath of Loyalty" or the "Iron-Clad Oath," as it is sometimes called. The convention had specifically been delegated the task of providing for a restricted suffrage, so it authorized a special committee, with Drake as chairman, to study the matter and to report. Missouri had had a test oath since October, 1861, when the previous convention enacted one. Drake, in drawing up the new provisions, made them more stringent than the earlier requirements. He established a list of no less than eighty-six acts which must be denied under oath before a voter could qualify. Even the slightest sympathy for the Southern cause could bar one from voting. A state-wide system of uniform registration was established requiring that the "Oath of Loyalty" had to be taken each time the prospective voter registered. An oath to uphold the constitutions of Missouri and the United States was also required. Even then, the final determination of one's qualifications for the franchise rested solely with the registration officials, who might disregard both oaths.[45]

Opposition to Drake's proposals came from both the right and the left of the convention. The Conservatives sought, without success, to amend them so that the disqualifying acts of the oath would not be retroactive beyond December 17, 1861. Their reason referred to Governor Gamble's promise of amnesty in his August, 1861, proclamation and to the action of the previous convention in exempting from punishment those who had taken the test oath by the December date.[46]

The German extremists sought to include the Negro among those entitled to vote and hold office. They wished to eliminate the word "white" as a qualification for anything under the new document.[47] Most of the Radicals, including Drake, foresaw the difficulties involved in any such sweeping social change, and they opposed it from political considerations even if their beliefs permitted them to accept it.

The heated controversy set off by the Drake proposals on the franchise consumed two months of debate. Final approval did not come until April 1. There were few changes in the original.

The completed draft of the entire constitution passed on April 8, the seventy-seventh day of the convention, by a vote of 38 to 13. Several members who opposed it were absent. Most of the opposition came from the Conservatives and the Germans. Of the thirteen members who voted negatively, eleven refused to sign the final document.[48]

The General Assembly, in calling the convention, had made no provision for ratification of its work by the people. In the light of their drastic alterations of Missouri's basic law, the group decided to submit the new constitution to a popular referendum, however, and set June 6 for this election. No one was to vote who could not qualify under the "Iron-Clad Oath." By this means, the convention sought to eliminate "rebel opposition" which might defeat its handiwork.[49]

The Radicals had never forgotten their defeat in the judicial election of 1863. Now they sought to remedy the effect. Fearful lest the Conservative judiciary might try to upset their future plans, the Radicals introduced a resolution during the first week of the convention to provide for an overhaul of the judicial system. After due consideration by the committee on the judiciary, an ordinance was reported by its chairman, Henry A. Clover, one of the defeated Radical candidates of 1863. The provisions of this ordinance showed that the Radicals were determined to make a clean sweep of the existing court system: it would vacate the Supreme Court of Missouri; judges and clerks in all of the courts of the state, circuit attorneys and their assistants, county recorders, and sheriffs would lose their positions; all vacancies would be filled by the Governor until the next election for any particular position.

The ordinance established May 1 as the date when some eight hundred offices would be cleared of their incumbents and the new regime instituted. In spite of vigorous protests from the Conservative minority, the Radicals united to push the measure through, 43 to 5. The committee maintained that unless the three branches of government cooperated in harmony, "the working of the social system will be harsh, discordant and incapable of efficient result . . . and thereby may follow injustice, oppression, and wrong to the citizens of the State." In the more practical debate which followed, the Radicals simply reminded the Conservatives that they had acted similarly in December of 1861.[50]

Had Governor Fletcher been a more thoroughgoing Radical, the process of finding eight hundred replacements for the officers affected by this ordinance would have become the major task of his administration. As it was, he retained those whose loyalty could be proven and acted on the recommendations of the county Radical committees in other instances. Few of those affected made an effort to fight their ousters, but two of those who did created a major sensation.

The Missouri Supreme Court was the primary target of the ouster ordinance. The Radicals claimed its members had been elected fraudulently in 1863. The party's real fear was that the Court might upset some of the work of the convention. Justice Barton Bates had resigned during the convention, thus Justices John D. S. Dryden and William V. N. Bay constituted the Court when the May 1 deadline arrived. Two days earlier, Governor Fletcher appointed David Wagner and Walter L. Lovelace as their successors; A. W. Mead was retained as clerk of the Court.

The Court stood in recess at the time the change-over was scheduled to occur. On May 27, Justices Wagner and Lovelace called a special session for June 12. They issued an order against Mead for delivery to them of the Court's records. Dryden and Bay promptly handed down a counter-order. Mead, sympathetic to the displaced justices, went into the St. Louis Circuit Court where he secured an injunction against the new justices from a German judge who had earlier held the ouster ordinance unconstitutional.

When June 12 arrived, Dryden and Bay appeared at the Court chambers as usual and proceeded to conduct business. Wagner and Lovelace seemingly were incapacitated. An appeal went to Governor Fletcher, who sent a militia officer with an ouster notice to the Court. The two justices remonstrated that they considered the ouster ordinance unconstitutional, that their terms did not expire until 1869. The officer called the police, but the justices refused to leave the bench. Finally, they were dragged protesting from their places and taken before a local police judge who arraigned them on a charge of disturbing the peace.

A militia force now took charge of the Court. They seized the Court records from a protesting Mead and installed Wagner and Lovelace on the bench. In the months which followed, the new justices proceeded to uphold the entire Radical program.

The Conservatives protested in vain. They called a mass meeting in St. Louis to denounce Fletcher. They demanded his impeachment, but their involved legalistic arguments tended to lose their large audience. The Radicals replied that the whole affair was a Conservative plot to thwart the will of the people. Although charge and countercharge continued for some time, the Conservatives got nowhere.[51]

The Radicals meanwhile had completed their triumph with the ratification of the new constitution by the voting electorate. This had not been the easy task they anticipated. A bitter campaign developed against the "Draconian Code," as the Conservatives called the "Oath of Loyalty." Edward Bates, who had retired a few months earlier as attorney-general, wrote a series of articles opposing the new document. He branded it as an attempt to work a Radical revolution in the life of Missouri. Other Conservatives followed his lead in denouncing various aspects of the proposed revision.

Dissension now appeared in the ranks of the Radicals. Governor Fletcher initially opposed the document because he considered it too restrictive in its franchise qualifications. He intimated that he would like to see Negro suffrage included in its provisions. Many of the Germans agreed. Senators Henderson and Brown maintained a discreet silence. This dissension boded ill if it continued very long into the campaign.

Drake sought to make support of the constitution a test of party loyalty. Pressure was brought on the recalcitrant leaders through some of the Radical congressmen, who supported the constitution as the only hope of continuing in power. A conference was arranged in late April at St. Louis. From this meeting Fletcher, Brown, and Henderson emerged to lend their reluctant support to the constitution. None of them participated actively in the campaign which followed. Instead, Drake took the major role. Stigmatizing all opposition as rebel or Copperhead, he fought bitterly for the document which came increasingly to bear his name.

The outcome of the contest remained uncertain until the very end. Early returns seemed to indicate the defeat of the constitution. The Radicals lost St. Louis because of a large German defection coupled with a sizable Conservative vote. The final totals were not known for some two weeks after the election, when the military vote had been counted and produced victory for the constitution by a scant margin of 1,835 votes out of 85,769 cast.[52]

The closeness of this contest and the reasons for it boded ill for the Radicals in the years ahead. The "Oath of Loyalty" produced a great deal of friction as various contests of its legality were tried. The Radicals themselves divided on its retention. Ultimately it proved a major factor in splitting the party and bringing its downfall by the early 1870's.

The Conservatives went into temporary eclipse. They re-emerged at the beginning of the next decade to regain through the Democratic party a long-term lease on Missouri government. In 1875, this group replaced the Radical experiment with a new Conservative constitution which remained Missouri's basic law for the next seventy years.[53]

Footnotes

CHAPTER 1

1. Walter H. Ryle, *Missouri: Union or Secession* (Nashville, 1931), pp. 126-67.

2. Floyd C. Shoemaker, *Missouri and Missourians: Land of Contrasts and People of Achievements* (Chicago, 1943), I, 826; Sceva B. Laughlin, "Missouri Politics During the Civil War," *Missouri Historical Review,* XXIII (April, 1929), 423–24; (July, 1929), 583.

3. Buel Leopard and Floyd C. Shoemaker (eds.), *The Messages and Proclamations of the Governors of the State of Missouri* (Columbia, 1922), III, 33–37.

4. Walter B. Stevens, *Centennial History of Missouri (The Center State), One Hundred Years in the Union, 1820–1921* (St. Louis, 1921), I, 720–21; James Peckham, *General Nathaniel Lyon and Missouri in 1861* (New York, 1866), pp. 24–28; Thomas L. Snead, *The Fight for Missouri from the Election of Lincoln to the Death of Lyon* (New York, 1888), pp. 30–33; Basil W. Duke, *Reminiscences of General Basil W. Duke, C. S. A.* (Garden City, New York, 1911), pp. 42–43; *Missouri Democrat* (St. Louis), April 9, 1861.

5. *Laws of the State of Missouri. Regular Session, 21st General Assembly, 1860–1861* (Jefferson City, 1861), pp. 20–21.

6. *Ibid.; Missouri Statesman* (Columbia), January 4, 1861.

7. *Missouri Republican* (St. Louis), January 10 and February 10, 1861; *Missouri Democrat,* January 25, 1861; *Jefferson Inquirer* (Jefferson City), January 10, 1861.

8. Laughlin, "Missouri Politics," p. 592.

9. *Missouri State Convention Journal,* March, 1861, pp. 9–19; *Missouri State Convention Proceedings,* March, 1861, pp. 10–18.

10. *Missouri Republican,* March 5, 1861.

11. *Missouri State Convention Journal,* March, 1861, pp. 18–19.

12. *Missouri State Convention Proceedings,* March, 1861, pp. 11–20, 50–57.

13. *Ibid.,* pp. 55–58.

14. *Ibid.,* pp. 217–30.

15. *Ibid.,* pp. 237–45.

16. *Missouri State Convention Journal,* March, 1861, pp. 46–49.

17. *Ibid.,* pp. 49–62.

CHAPTER 2

1. Peckham, *Lyon and Missouri,* pp. 42–47; Snead, *Fight for Missouri,* pp. 114–18.

2. Peckham, *Lyon and Missouri,* pp. 30–32; Snead, *Fight for Missouri,* pp. 104–11; William E. Smith, *The Francis Preston Blair Family in Politics* (New York, 1933), II, 31; Duke, *Reminiscences,* pp. 38–40.

3. Ashbel Woodward, *Life of General Nathaniel Lyon* (Hartford, 1862), p. 236.

4. John McElroy, *The Struggle for Missouri* (Washington, 1909), pp. 41–48; Peckham, *Lyon and Missouri,* pp. 69–71; *The War of the Rebellion: Official Records of the Union and Confederate Armies* (Washington, 1880), Series I, Vol. III, 656–59, 668. (Hereinafter cited as *O. R.*)

5. *Ibid.,* Ser. III, Vol. I, 67–69, 82–83.

6. *Missouri Republican,* April 23–May 9, 1861; *Missouri Statesman,* April 26 and May 3, 1861; *Liberty Tribune,* April 26 and May 3, 1861.

7. *O. R.,* Ser. I, Vol. I, 668–69.

8. *Ibid.,* Ser. I, Vol. III, 667.

9. Stevens, *Centennial History of Missouri,* I, 721; *O. R.,* Ser. I, Vol. III, 668, 670.

10. Gist Blair Papers (Library of Congress), Frank Blair to Simon Cameron, April 18, 1861; Frank Blair to Montgomery Blair, April 19, 1861.

11. *O. R.,* Ser. I, Vol. III, 669–70.

12. John M. Schofield, *Forty-Six Years in the Army* (New York, 1897), pp. 33–34; McElroy, *Struggle for Missouri,* pp. 64–65; Galusha Anderson, *A Border City During the Civil War* (Boston, 1908), pp. 76–80.

13. *O. R.,* Ser. I, Vol. III, 675–76.

14. Anderson, *Border City,* pp. 87–88; Snead, *Fight for Missouri,* pp. 148–49; Duke, *Reminiscences,* pp. 43–44.

15. Leopard and Shoemaker, *Messages and Proclamations,* III, 384.

16. Stevens, *Centennial History of Missouri,* I, 729; Peckham, *Lyon and Missouri,* pp. 131–35; Snead, *Fight for Missouri,* pp. 162–63; *O. R.,* Ser. I, Vol. I, 649, 688. Cf. James O. Broadhead Papers (Missouri Historical Society, St. Louis), Allen P. Richardson to Broadhead, April 24 and 30, 1861.

17. *O. R.,* Ser. I, Vol. I, 689–90.

18. Snead, *Fight for Missouri,* pp. 162–63; Frank Moore (ed.), *The Rebellion Record* (New York, 1861), I, 59.

19. Peckham, *Lyon and Missouri,* p. 136; Snead, *Fight for Missouri,* pp. 167–68; Stevens, *Centennial History of Missouri,* I, 734; Duke, *Reminiscences,* pp. 45–50.

20. Broadhead Papers, "St. Louis During the War" (Manuscript by James O. Broadhead), pp. 60–61.

21. *O. R.,* Ser. I, Vol. III, 4–7; *Missouri Republican,* May 11, 1861; *Missouri Democrat,* May 14, 1861.

22. Broadhead, "St. Louis During the War," pp. 64–65; Stevens, *Centennial History of Missouri,* I, 738–39.

23. Snead, *Fight for Missouri,* pp. 172–74; McElroy, *Struggle for Missouri,* pp. 73–74; *House Journal, 21st General Assembly, Called Session,* pp. 52, 55; *Senate Journal, 21st General Assembly, Called Session,* pp. 76–77; Broadhead Papers, Richardson to Broadhead, May 11, 1861.

24. L. U. Reavis, *The Life and Military Services of General William Selby Harney* (St. Louis, 1878), pp. 355–56.

25. Robert Todd Lincoln Collection of the Papers of Abraham Lincoln (Library of Congress), Lyman Trumbull to Lincoln, May 15, 1861; *O. R.,* Ser. I, Vol. III, 369–74.

26. Snead, *Fight for Missouri,* pp. 181, 184–85; Broadhead Papers, Richardson to Broadhead, May 20, 1861; Thomas C. Reynolds Papers (Missouri Historical Society), "General Sterling Price and the Confederacy" (Manuscript by Thomas C. Reynolds), p. 28; *Missouri Republican,* May 14 and 16, 1861.

27. Lincoln Papers, Hamilton R. Gamble and James E. Yeatman to Lincoln, May 15, 1861; Hamilton R. Gamble Papers (Missouri Historical Society), Yeatman to Gamble, June 23, 1863.

28. *O. R.,* Ser. I, Vol. III, 9.

29. Reavis, *Life of Harney,* pp. 374–76; John G. Nicolay and John Hay, *Abraham Lincoln, A History* (New York, 1890), IV, 215–17; Gamble Papers, Yeatman to Gamble, June 23, 1863; Charles Gibson Papers (Missouri Historical Society), "Gibson Autobiography," p. 46.

30. *O. R.,* Ser. I, Vol. III, 374; Francis P. Blair, Jr., Papers (Library of Congress), Montgomery Blair to Ben Farrar or Frank Blair, May 17, 1861; Roy P. Basler (ed.), *The Collected Works of Abraham Lincoln* (New Brunswick, New Jersey, 1954), IV, 372–73.

31. Peckham, *Lyon and Missouri,* pp. 209–10; Reavis, *Life of Harney,* pp. 375–76.

32. *O. R.,* Ser. I, Vol. III, 374–75; Snead, *Fight for Missouri,* pp. 187–88.

33. Broadhead Papers, Broadhead to Montgomery Blair, May 22, 1861; *O. R.,* Ser. I, Vol. III, 376.

34. Peckham, *Lyon and Missouri,* cites excerpts from many of these letters which have since been lost, pp. 211–19; Broadhead Papers, Richardson to Broadhead, May 24, 1861; Richard C. Vaughn to Broadhead,

May 30, 1861; *O. R.,* Ser. I, Vol. III, 378; Lincoln Papers, Samuel T. Glover to Lincoln, May 24, 1861.

35. *O. R.,* Ser. I, Vol. III, 378–81.

36. Peckham, *Lyon and Missouri,* pp. 221–25; Snead, *Fight for Missouri,* pp. 192–97.

37. James S. Rollins Papers (State Historical Society of Missouri, Columbia), Rollins to Edward Bates, June 1, 1861; Lincoln Papers, John S. Phelps to Lincoln, June 3, 1861; *O. R.,* Ser. I, Vol. III, 381, 383.

38. Stevens, *Centennial History of Missouri,* I, 749–50; Snead, *Fight for Missouri,* pp. 199–200. Snead's version of the meeting includes the quotation used in the text and has been accepted by the majority of historians in their accounts of this conference. Blair's secretary, whose account appeared in the *Missouri Democrat* of June 13, 1861, and was copied by Peckham, quotes Lyon in a slightly different way: "Governor Jackson, no man in the State of Missouri has been more ardently desirous of preserving peace than myself. Heretofore Missouri has only felt the fostering care of the Federal Government, which has raised her from the condition of a feeble French colony to that of an empire State. Now, however, from the failure on the part of the Chief Executive to comply with constitutional requirements, I fear she will be made to feel its power. Better, sir, far better, that the blood of every man, woman, and child of the State should flow than that she should successfully defy the Federal Government."

39. Peckham, *Lyon and Missouri,* pp. 248–53.

40. Snead, *Fight for Missouri,* pp. 206–11.

41. *O. R.,* Ser. I, Vol. III, 11–19, 384–400.

CHAPTER 3

1. Peckham, *Lyon and Missouri,* p. 286; Broadhead Papers, Walter L. Lovelace to Broadhead, June 24, 1861; John B. Henderson to Broadhead, June 25, 1861; Jacob Smith to Broadhead, July 7, 1861; Bates to Broadhead, July 13, 1861.

2. William E. Parrish, *David Rice Atchison of Missouri: Border Politician* (Columbia, Missouri, 1961), pp. 216–17.

3. *Missouri Statesman,* August 9 and 23, 1861; Reynolds Papers, Memorandum of June 2, 1886.

4. Parrish, *David Rice Atchison,* pp. 219–20.

5. Arthur R. Kirkpatrick, "Missouri's Secessionist Government, 1861–1865," *Missouri Historical Review,* XLV (January, 1951), 127–37.

6. *Missouri State Convention Journal,* July, 1861, pp. 3–5. Thirty-two members were absent when the convention first met on July 22. Of these, fifteen failed to appear for any of the proceedings. These were men who either had followed Price or came from those parts of Missouri where conditions were so unsettled as to prevent their traveling.

7. *Missouri State Convention Proceedings,* July, 1861, pp. 5–13.

8. *Missouri State Convention Journal,* July, 1861, p. 5.

9. *Ibid.,* pp. 5–9.

10. This article provided: (1) "That all political power is vested in and derived from the people," (2) "That the people of this State have the inherent, sole, and exclusive right of regulating the internal government and police thereof, and of altering and abolishing their Constitution and form of Government, whenever it may be necessary to their safety and happiness."

11. *Missouri State Convention Journal,* July, 1861, pp. 9–11.

12. *Ibid.,* pp. 11–12.

13. *Ibid.,* p. 12; Gamble Papers, Bates to Gamble, July 16, 1861; Broadhead Papers, Bates to Broadhead, July 13, 1861.

14. *Missouri State Convention Proceedings,* July, 1861, p. 316; Broadhead Papers, Glover to Broadhead, July 27, 1861.

15. *Missouri State Convention Journal,* July, 1861, pp. 17–18.

16. *Missouri State Convention Proceedings,* July, 1861, pp. 63–67.

17. *Ibid.,* pp. 71–86.

18. *Ibid.,* p. 95.

19. *Missouri State Convention Journal,* July, 1861, pp. 20–22.

20. John F. Phillips, "Hamilton Rowan Gamble and the Provisional Government of Missouri," *Missouri Historical Review,* V (October, 1910), 6.

21. *Missouri State Convention Journal,* July, 1861, p. 25.

22. Phillips, "Gamble," pp. 1–5.

23. John F. Phillips, "Governor Willard Preble Hall," *Missouri Historical Review,* V (January, 1911), 69–79.

24. *United States Biographical Dictionary and Portrait Gallery of Eminent and Self-made Men.* Missouri volume (Kansas City, 1878), 675–76.

25. Leopard and Shoemaker, *Messages and Proclamations,* III, 411–14.

26. *Missouri State Convention Journal,* July, 1861, pp. 30–31.

27. *Missouri Republican,* August 1 and 13, 1861; *Missouri Statesman,* August 9, 1861.

28. Gamble Papers, Bates to Gamble, August 2, 1861.

29. *Missouri Republican,* August 1, 1861.

CHAPTER 4

1. Peckham, *Lyon and Missouri,* pp. 264–67; *O. R.,* Ser. I, Vol. III, 385.

2. Nicolay and Hay, *Abraham Lincoln,* IV, 401–2.

3. *Ibid.,* IV, 402; *O. R.,* Ser. I, Vol. III, 399; Smith, *Blair Family,* II, 56–57; Allan Nevins, *Frémont, Pathmarker of the West* (New York, 1955), pp. 535–36.

4. Leopard and Shoemaker, *Messages and Proclamations,* III, 512–17; Simon Cameron Papers (Library of Congress), Cameron to Gamble, August 3, 1861 (in Lincoln's handwriting).

5. *O. R.,* Ser. I, Vol. III, 416–17.

6. Peckham, *Lyon and Missouri,* pp. 298–317; Schofield, *Forty-Six Years in the Army,* p. 38; Gamble Papers, Samuel M. Breckinridge to Gamble, August 3, 1861; John M. Richardson to Gamble, August 10, 1861; Leopard and Shoemaker, *Messages and Proclamations,* III, 461; *O. R.,* Ser. I, Vol. III, 424.

7. *Ibid.,* p. 411; Smith, *Blair Family,* II, 60–62.

8. Schofield, *Forty-Six Years in the Army,* pp. 39–42. The original of Frémont's letter has never been found.

9. Gamble Papers, William A. Buckingham to Gamble, August 14, 1861; John T. Scharf, *History of St. Louis City and County* (Philadelphia, 1883), I, 507; Basler, *Works of Lincoln,* IV, 527.

10. Smith, *Blair Family,* II, 72.

11. *O. R.,* Ser. I, Vol. III, 423–24.

12. *Ibid.,* pp. 417–19; Robert T. Van Horn Papers (State Historical Society of Missouri), John Pope to Van Horn, August 9, 1861.

13. Wiley Britton, *The Civil War on the Border, 1861–1862* (New York, 1890), pp. 145–47; *Missouri Statesman,* July 26 and September 20, 1861; Gamble Papers, J. T. K. Hayward to Gamble, August 17, 1861; *O. R.,* Ser. I, Vol. III, 433–35, 456–61.

14. Leopard and Shoemaker, *Messages and Proclamations,* III, 519–20; *Annual Report of The Adjutant General of the State of Missouri,* 1863 (Jefferson City, 1864), 9; Samuel B. Harding, *The Life of George R. Smith* (Sedalia, Missouri, 1904), pp. 323–24.

15. Gamble Papers, Gamble to Lincoln, August 26, 1861.

16. *Missouri Republican,* August 31, 1861; William G. Eliot Papers (Missouri Historical Society), Bates to Eliot, August 19, 1861; Gamble Papers, Gibson to Gamble, August 19, 1861; Leopard and Shoemaker, *Messages and Proclamations,* III, 420; "Gibson Autobiography," pp. 43–44.

17. Gamble Papers, Gamble to Gibson, September 20, 1861; *O. R.,* Ser. I, Vol. III, 470.

18. Gamble Papers, Kelton to Gamble, August 2, 1861; Frémont to Gamble, August 3, 1861; Gamble to Frémont, August 6, 1861; Krum to Gamble, August 12, 1861.

19. *Ibid.,* Frémont to Gamble, August 18, 1861; Gamble to Gibson, September 20, 1861; *Missouri Republican,* August 31, 1861.

20. Gamble Papers, Frémont to Gamble, August 18, 1861; Lincoln Papers, Frank Blair to Montgomery Blair, August 21, 1861.

21. *Ibid.,* Frank Blair to Montgomery Blair, September 1, 1861. This letter mentions the letter sent through Gamble which the author has been unable to locate.

22. Schofield, *Forty-Six Years in the Army,* p. 49.

23. Lincoln Papers, Frank Blair to Montgomery Blair, September 1, 1861.

24. *Ibid.,* John How to Montgomery Blair, August 21, 1861; John Poyner to Lincoln, August 27, 1861; Montgomery Blair to Lincoln, no date, enclosing Glover to Montgomery Blair, September 2, 1861, and Broadhead to Montgomery Blair, September 3, 1861.

25. *O. R.,* Ser. I, Vol. III, 466–67.

26. Nicolay and Hay, *Abraham Lincoln,* IV, 416–17; Gamble Papers, Gamble to Gibson, September 20, 1861; Leopard and Shoemaker, *Messages and Proclamations,* III, 512.

27. Lincoln Papers, James Speed and Green Adams to Lincoln, September 2, 1861; Joseph Holt to Lincoln, September 12, 1861; Robert Anderson to Lincoln, September 13, 1861; Frank Moore (ed.), *The Rebellion Record* (New York, 1861–1868), III, 126–27.

28. *Missouri Democrat,* September 13, 1861; *Missouri Republican,* September 3 and 13, 1861.

29. *O. R.,* Ser. I, Vol. III, 469–70.

30. *Ibid.,* p. 477.

31. *Ibid.,* pp. 485–86; *Missouri Statesman,* September 20, 1861; Lincoln Papers, Glover to Lincoln, September 21, 1861.

32. *Missouri Republican,* September 12, 1861; Gamble Papers, Gamble to Gibson, September 14 and 20, 1861.

33. *Ibid.,* Gibson to Gamble, September 18, 1861; Gamble to Gibson, September 19 and 20, 1861; Bates to Gamble, September 27, 1861; Broadhead Papers, Bates to Broadhead, September 28, 1861.

34. Gamble Papers, William M. McPherson to Gamble, September 23 and 28, 1861; Bates to Gamble, September 27, 1861; Lincoln Papers,

Gamble to Lincoln, September 13, 1861; Frank Blair to Lincoln, September 15, 1861.

35. Gamble Papers, Bates to Gamble, October 3, 1861; Lincoln Papers, Gamble to Lincoln, September 18, 1861; Gamble to Montgomery Blair, October 5, 1861; Gamble to Bates, December 3, 1861.

36. *The Adjutant General's Report,* 1863, 11.

37. *O. R.,* Ser. I, Vol. III, 171–93.

38. Lincoln Papers, Glover to Lincoln, September 20 and 21, 1861; J. W. Schaeffer to Cameron, September 22, 1861; T. Blank to Montgomery Blair, September 24, 1861; Gamble Papers, Gamble to Gibson, September 20, 1861.

39. *O. R.,* Ser. I, Vol. III, 184–85; *Missouri Republican,* September 28, 1861; Gamble Papers, Bates to Gamble, September 27, 1861; Broadhead Papers, Bates to Broadhead, September 28, 1861.

40. Nicolay and Hay, *Abraham Lincoln,* IV, 412.

41. Basler, *Works of Lincoln,* IV, 513.

42. Smith, *Blair Family,* II, 75; Lincoln Papers, Montgomery Blair to Lincoln, September 14, 1861; *O. R.,* Ser. I, Vol. III, 477–79.

43. Nevins, *Frémont,* pp. 515–19; Nicolay and Hay, *Abraham Lincoln,* IV, 413–15; Tyler Dennett (ed.), *Lincoln and the Civil War in the Diaries and Letters of John Hay* (New York, 1939), pp. 133–34; Lincoln Papers, Jessie B. Frémont to Lincoln, undated note and two dated September 12, 1861; Basler, *Works of Lincoln,* IV, 517–18.

44. *Missouri Democrat,* September 18 and 24, 1861; Lincoln Papers, Frémont to Lincoln, September 18, 1861.

45. Gist Blair Papers, Montgomery Blair to Frémont, September 19 and 20, 1861.

46. Lincoln Papers, War Department to Frémont, September 19, 1861. Writing to Congressman Orville H. Browning three days later, Lincoln revealed: "There has been no thought of removing Gen. Frémont on any ground connected with his proclamation; and if there has been any wish for his removal on any ground, our mutual friend, Sam. Glover, can probably tell you what it was. I hope no real necessity exists for it on any ground." Basler, *Works of Lincoln,* IV, 531–33.

47. Gist Blair Papers, Montgomery Blair to W. O. Bartlett, September 26, 1861.

48. Nevins, *Frémont,* pp. 520, 526–27, 531; Lincoln Papers, Frank Blair to Lorenzo Thomas, September 26, 1861.

49. Gamble Papers, Gibson to Gamble, September 27, 1861; Bates to Gamble, September 27, 1861; Lincoln Papers, Gibson to Lincoln, September 27, 1861; Broadhead Papers, Bates to Broadhead, September 28, 1861.

50. Lincoln Papers, Lyman Trumbull to Lincoln, October 1, 1861; John How to Montgomery Blair, October 3, 1861; Samuel T. Glover to Lincoln, October 4, 1861; Charles G. Hulpine to Thurlow Weed, October 17, 1861; Cameron Papers, J. W. Schaeffer to Leonard Swett, October 4, 1861; *O. R.,* Ser. I, Vol. III, 511–13.

51. Basler, *Works of Lincoln,* IV, 549; Lincoln Papers, Curtis to Lincoln, October 12, 1861; Cameron to Lincoln, October 12, 1861.

52. *Ibid.,* Cameron to Lincoln, October 14, 1861.

53. *O. R.,* Ser. I, Vol. III, 540–49; Howard K. Beale (ed.), *The Diary of Edward Bates, 1859–1866,* The Annual Report of the American Historical Association for the Year 1930 (Washington, 1933), IV, 198. Cf. Gist Blair Papers, F. P. Blair to Bigelow, October 26, 1861.

54. Lincoln Papers, Elihu B. Washburne to Lincoln, October 17, 19, and 21, 1861; John G. Nicolay to Lincoln, October 17, 1861; Ward H. Lamon to Lincoln, October 21, 1861; John G. Nicolay Papers (Library of Congress), Nicolay to Lincoln, October 21, 1861.

55. *O. R.,* Ser. I, Vol. III, 553.

56. Lincoln Papers, Curtis to Lincoln, November 1 and 16, 1861; Leonard Swett to Lincoln, November 9, 1861; *Missouri Republican,* November 9, 1861; *Missouri Democrat,* November 12, 1861.

CHAPTER 5

1. Leopard and Shoemaker, *Messages and Proclamations,* III, 415–16; Gamble Papers, J. B. Gamble to Gamble, September 30, 1861; Gamble to J. B. Gamble, October 2, 1861; Curtis to Gamble, October 7, 1861.

2. *Ibid.,* Jo Davis to Gamble, August 22, 1861; John S. Phelps to Gamble, October 3, 1861; Broadhead Papers, Glover to Broadhead, July 29, 1861; Abiel Leonard to Broadhead, July 31, 1861; H. M. Woodyard to Broadhead, July 31, 1861.

3. Leopard and Shoemaker, *Messages and Proclamations,* III, 415–17, 521.

4. *Missouri State Convention Journal,* October, 1861, pp. 5–16.

5. *Ibid.,* pp. 23–25.

6. *Ibid.,* pp. 17–21, 25–26.

7. *Ibid.,* pp. 26–27.

8. *Missouri Republican,* November 1, 1861; Lincoln Papers, Gamble to Lincoln, October 30, 1861, and two undated; Montgomery Blair to Lincoln, November 5, 1861; Gibson Papers, Gamble to Gibson, November 7, 1861; *O. R.,* Ser. I, Vol. III, 565–66; Ser. I, Vol. VIII, 454–56; Basler, *Works of Lincoln,* V, 15; Gamble Papers, Gamble to Halleck, October 10, 1862.

9. *O. R.,* Ser. I, Vol. III, 567; Lincoln Papers, Hunter to Lincoln, December 23, 1861.

10. Allen Johnson and Dumas Malone (eds.), *The Dictionary of American Biography* (New York, 1932), VIII, 150–52; *O. R.,* Ser. I, Vol. III, 567; Ser. I, Vol. X, Part 2, 28–29.

11. *Missouri Republican,* November 19, 1861; Beale, *Bates Diary,* p. 201; Broadhead Papers, Bates to Glover and Broadhead, November 12, 1861; Gamble Papers, Gibson to Gamble, November 10, 1861.

12. *O. R.,* Ser. I, Vol. VIII, 378, 389; Johnson and Malone, *Dictionary of American Biography,* XVI, 452–54.

13. Gamble Papers, Gibson to Gamble, November 10, 1861; *Missouri Republican,* December 6, 1861, and January 16, 1862; Leopard and Shoemaker, *Messages and Proclamations,* III, 421–22; Lincoln Papers, Gamble to Bates, December 3, 1861. A copy of the receipt for the Treasury draft of $250,000, dated November 27, 1861, is in the Gibson Papers. Several cancelled checks for the militia are in the Gamble Papers.

14. Leopard and Shoemaker, *Messages and Proclamations,* III, 422.

15. *O. R.,* Ser. I, Vol. XIII, 8; *The Adjutant General's Report,* 1863, p. 13.

16. *Ibid.,* pp. 49–50.

17. Britton, *Civil War on the Border,* pp. 147–48; *O. R.,* Ser. I, Vol. VIII, 449; *Missouri Democrat,* December 21, 1861; *Missouri Republican,* December 29, 1861; Gamble Papers, Gamble to Halleck, December 24, 1861; Halleck to Gamble, December 26, 1861; Richard S. Brownlee, *Gray Ghosts of the Confederacy: Guerrilla Warfare in the West, 1861–1865* (Baton Rouge, 1958), pp. 42–47.

18. *O. R.,* Ser. I, Vol. VIII, 507–8, 829; *Missouri Republican,* February 4, 1862; Lincoln Papers, Halleck to Lincoln, January 6, 1862; Gamble to Lincoln, May 19, 1862.

19. *O. R.,* Ser. I, Vol. VIII, 546–47, 552–53; Rollins Papers, George C. Bingham to Rollins, January 22 and February 12, 1862; *Liberty Tribune,* March 7 and April 25, 1862; *Missouri Republican,* April 20 and May 12, 1862; *Missouri Democrat,* April 26, 1862; Brownlee, *Gray Ghosts of the Confederacy,* pp. 48–49.

20. *Missouri Democrat,* January 7 and February 11, 1862; *Missouri Statesman,* January 3 and 24, 1862.

21. *Congressional Globe,* 37th Cong., 2d Sess., p. 264; *Missouri Republican,* January 17, 1862; *Missouri Democrat,* January 21, 1862; Lincoln Papers, Thomas T. Gantt to Montgomery Blair, January 15 and 18, 1862; *Missouri Statesman,* January 31, 1862.

22. *Missouri Republican,* January 17 and February 21, 1862; *Missouri Statesman,* March 7, 1862.

23. Leopard and Shoemaker, *Messages and Proclamations*, III, 512–17; Gamble Papers, Gamble to Samuel Sawyer, August 5, 1861; E. B. Dobyns to Gamble, August 18, 1861; Horace L. Singleton to Gamble, August 26, 1861; Gamble to Chester Harding, August 27, 1861; Hamilton Gamble, Jr. to Gamble, August 27, 1861; *O. R.*, Ser. I, Vol. III, 463.

24. *Missouri State Convention Journal,* October, 1861, pp. 15–16; Lincoln Papers, Gamble to Lincoln, no date.

25. Gamble Papers, Halleck to Gamble, March 24, 1862.

26. Broadhead Papers, Broadhead to Bates, April 4, 1862; *O. R.*, Ser. II, Vol. I, 277.

27. Moore, *Rebellion Record,* III, 84; IV, 52, 129–30; *O. R.*, Ser. I, Vol. VIII, 557, 586–87, 832.

28. *Missouri Republican,* March 4 and 18, 1862; Gamble Papers, Halleck to Hall *et al.,* March 3, 1862.

29. *O. R.*, Ser. I, Vol. XIII, 8–10, 368, 409, 417.

30. *O. R.*, Ser. I, Vol. VIII, 59, 190–91, 462; Ser. I, Vol. XIII, 10.

31. *Ibid.*, pp. 10, 414, 515; Gamble Papers, Gamble to Thomas, June 9, 1862.

32. *O. R.*, Ser. I, Vol. XIII, 402–3.

33. *Ibid.*, pp. 446–47.

34. *Ibid.*, pp. 10–11, 505–6, 522–23; *The Adjutant General's Report,* 1863, p. 21; Gamble Papers, William D. Wood to Gamble, November 10, 1862.

35. *Ibid.*, Bates to Gamble, September 11, 1862; Gamble to Chase, September 17, 1862; Gibson to Stanton, October 3, 1862; Gibson to Gamble, October 3, 1862; *Missouri Republican,* December 5, 1862; *O. R.*, Ser. I, Vol. XXII, Part 2, 29.

36. *O. R.*, Ser. I, Vol. VIII, 431–32; Ser. I, Vol. XIII, 11–12, 459, 612, 691, 693, 700, 704, 736, 800; Lincoln Papers, Schofield to James S. Thomas, December 5, 1862.

37. Gamble Papers, Gamble to Robert A. Barnes, September 1, 1862.

38. *O. R.*, Ser. I, Vol. XIII, 13, 550–51, 664, 729–30; Gamble Papers, Ben Loan to Gamble, September 28, 1862; Gamble to Loan, September 29, 1862.

39. *Laws of the State of Missouri, Regular Session, 22nd General Assembly, 1862–1863* (Jefferson City, 1863), pp. 25–29.

40. Leopard and Shoemaker, *Messages and Proclamations,* III, 469–71; *Laws of the State of Missouri, Adjourned Session, 22nd General Assembly, 1863–1864* (Jefferson City, 1864), pp. 75–76.

41. *O. R.,* Ser. I, Vol. XIII, 513, 518–19, 534–35.

42. *Ibid.,* p. 534; Ser. I, Vol. XXII, Part 2, 119; Lincoln Papers, Glover to Montgomery Blair, August 6, 1862.

43. *O. R.,* Ser. I, Vol. XIII, 562.

44. Lincoln Papers, Frank Blair to Montgomery Blair, August 8, 1862. A partial explanation of Frank's charges against the Governor lies in Gamble's stand on emancipation at this time and in the action of the recent session of the state convention in continuing the Provisional Government in office for an additional two years. Both of these developments will be discussed in later chapters. By November, 1862, Frank had changed his mind somewhat on the value of the E.M.M., for he wrote Montgomery after the fall election that they had played a key role in keeping Missouri quiet during the voting period. Gist Blair Papers, Frank Blair to Montgomery Blair, no date, but obviously written in November, 1862.

45. *Liberty Tribune,* August 8, 1862; *O. R.,* Ser. I, Vol. XIII, 557–58.

46. Gamble Papers, Gibson to Gamble, August 14, 1862.

47. *O. R.,* Ser. I, Vol. XIII, 552, 561–63.

48. Brownlee, *Gray Ghosts of the Confederacy,* pp. 56–75, 92–102.

49. Lincoln Papers, Gamble to Lincoln, September 9, 1862; *Liberty Tribune,* August 29, 1862; *Missouri Republican,* September 6 and October 11, 1862; *Platte County Conservator,* September 20, 1862; *O. R.,* Ser. I, Vol. XIII, 618–19, 712–14.

50. *O. R.,* Ser. I, Vol. XXII, Part 1, 796–801, 821, 841–51; Part 2, 46–47.

CHAPTER 6

1. *O. R.,* Ser. I, Vol. XIII, 653–54.

2. Johnson and Malone, *Dictionary of American Biography,* IV, 619–20.

3. Schofield, *Forty-Six Years in the Army,* pp. 61–62; Gamble Papers, Schofield to Gamble, September 24, 1862; *O. R.,* Ser. I, Vol. XIII, 673, 719.

4. *O. R.,* Ser. III, Vol. II, 579.

5. *Ibid.,* pp. 658–61.

6. Lincoln Papers, Gamble to Halleck, October 10, 1862; Gamble Papers, Gibson to Gamble, September 30, 1862.

7. *O. R.,* Ser. III, Vol. II, 646–47.

8. Lincoln Papers, Gamble to Halleck, October 10, 1862.

9. *O. R.,* Ser. III, Vol. II, 702–4, 735–36.

10. Lincoln Papers, Gamble to Lincoln, November 17, 1862; Basler, *Works of Lincoln,* V, 515–16; Gamble Papers, Bates to Gamble, December 2, 1862; *O. R.,* Ser. III, Vol. II, 955.

11. *O. R.*, Ser. I, Vol. XXII, Part 1, 839–40, 878.

12. *Ibid.*, pp. 853–54, 878.

13. Lincoln Papers, Gamble to Montgomery Blair, September 24, 1862; Gamble Papers, Montgomery Blair to Gamble, September 27 and October 29, 1862; *O. R.*, Ser. I, Vol. XIII, 783–84.

14. Schofield, *Forty-Six Years in the Army*, p. 57.

15. *O. R.*, Ser. I, Vol. XXII, Part 1, 803–4; *Missouri Republican*, *passim*, September–October, 1862.

16. *O. R.*, Ser. I, Vol. VIII, 370, 465, 564.

17. *O. R.*, Ser. II, Vol. I, 810; Gist Blair Papers, A. Jacobson to Frank Blair, November 7, 1862; Gamble Papers, Wood to Gamble, November 10, 1862.

18. *O. R.*, Ser. I, Vol. XIII, 772–73.

19. *O. R.*, Ser. I, Vol. XXII, Part 1, 839; Part 2, 41. Cf. Lincoln Papers, Franklin A. Dick to Lincoln, December 19, 1862; Gamble Papers, Gibson to Gamble, January 4, 1863.

20. *O. R.*, Ser. I, Vol. XXII, Part 1, 884; Anderson, *Border City*, pp. 280–81.

21. John S. Grasty, *Memoir of Rev. Samuel B. McPheeters, D.D.* (St. Louis, 1871), pp. 122–49.

22. *Ibid.*, pp. 159–61; Lincoln Papers, McPheeters to Bates, December 23, 1862; Curtis to Lincoln, December 27 and 29, 1862; *O. R.*, Ser. I, Vol. XXII, Part 1, 877–78; Basler, *Works of Lincoln*, VI, 33–34.

23. Grasty, *McPheeters Memoir*, pp. 186–202.

24. *O. R.*, Ser. I, Vol. XIII, 12; Ser. I, Vol. XXII, Part 1, 801–3, 830.

25. *O. R.*, Ser. I, Vol. XXII, Part 1, 810–12.

26. Lincoln Papers, Gamble to Lincoln, December 5, 1862.

27. *O. R.*, Ser. I, Vol. XXII, Part 1, 826, 832–33.

28. *Ibid.*, Part 1, 888; Part 2, 17–18.

29. *Ibid.*, Part 2, 42–43.

30. Lincoln Papers, Citizens of California, Missouri, to Lincoln, January 1, 1863; Elijah H. Norton *et al.* to Lincoln, January 4, 1863; William A. Hall to Lincoln, January 7, 1863; James W. Sappington to John B. Henderson, January 7, 1863; *O. R.*, Ser. I, Vol. XXII, Part 2, 64; Schofield, *Forty-Six Years in the Army*, pp. 57–58.

31. Lincoln Papers, Gamble to Lincoln, February 4, 1863.

32. *Missouri State Convention Proceedings*, June, 1863, p. 231; Lincoln Papers, Gibson to Lincoln, February 23, 1863; Gamble Papers, Barton Bates to Gamble, January 21, 1863; Gamble to Curtis, February 9, 1863.

33. *Ibid.*, Schofield to Gamble, February 2, 1863; Schofield, *Forty-Six Years in the Army*, pp. 63–65; *O. R.*, Ser. I, Vol. XXII, Part 2, 88, 94–95.

34. Gamble Papers, Hamilton Gamble, Jr. to Gamble, March 6, 1863.

35. Beale, *Bates Diary,* p. 279; Gamble Papers, Hamilton Gamble, Jr. to Gamble, March 6, 1863; *O. R.,* Ser. I, Vol. XXII, Part 2, 152.

36. Edward Bates Papers (Missouri Historical Society), Bates to Charles Sumner, March 7, 1863; Bates to Gamble, March 19, 1863; *O. R.,* Ser. I, Vol. XXII, Part 2, 152.

37. Lincoln Papers, Henderson to Lincoln, March 23 and 30, 1863; William A. Hall to Lincoln, April 15, 1863; Gamble Papers, Henderson to Gamble, March 30, 1863. The Lincoln Papers contain fourteen letters and petitions dated between March 21 and 25, 1863, seeking Curtis' retention after the death of General Sumner.

38. Lincoln Papers, Curtis to Lincoln, March 23, 1863.

39. *Ibid.,* S. R. Filley *et al.* to Lincoln, May 1, 1863; Gamble to Lincoln, May 2, 1863; R. C. Vaughn to Broadhead, April 30, 1963; Glover to Bates, May 15, 1863; Gamble Papers, Bates to Gamble, April 23, 1863.

40. *O. R.,* Ser. I, Vol. XXII, Part 2, 277, 293; Basler, *Works of Lincoln,* VI, 210.

41. *O. R.,* Ser. I, Vol. XXII, Part 2, 277; Beale, *Bates Diary,* p. 294.

CHAPTER 7

1. Leopard and Shoemaker, *Messages and Proclamations,* III, 512.

2. Stevens, *Centennial History of Missouri,* I, 684–85.

3. *Congressional Globe,* 37th Cong., 2d Sess., pp. 1102–3; Nicolay and Hay, *Abraham Lincoln,* V, 201–9.

4. *Ibid.,* V, 211–14; *Congressional Globe,* 37th Cong., 2d Sess., pp. 1179, 1496.

5. Johnson and Malone, *Dictionary of American Biography,* V, 425–26; Charles D. Drake, *Union and Anti-Slavery Speeches Delivered During the Rebellion* (Cincinnati, 1864), p. 129.

6. Gamble Papers, April and May, 1862, *passim; Missouri Republican,* January 29, March 12 and 31, June 2 and 6, 1862; *Missouri Statesman,* May 16, 1862.

7. Leopard and Shoemaker, *Messages and Proclamations,* III, 525–26; *Missouri Republican,* May 6, 1862; *Missouri Democrat,* June 3, 1862.

8. Leopard and Shoemaker, *Messages and Proclamations,* III, 418–29.

9. *Missouri State Convention Journal,* June, 1862, pp. 13, 17–18.

10. *Ibid.,* pp. 15–16, 20–21, 29, 34, Appendix, 13–14.

11. *Ibid.,* pp. 29–31; *Missouri State Convention Proceedings,* June, 1862, pp. 178–200.

12. *Missouri State Convention Journal,* June, 1862, p. 32; *Missouri State Convention Proceedings,* June, 1862, pp. 211–16; Gamble Papers, Joseph W. McClurg to Gamble and Hall, June 12, 1862.

13. *Ibid.,* Archibald Gamble to Gamble, June 1, 1862.

14. *Missouri Republican,* June 14, 1862.

15. *Missouri State Convention Proceedings,* June, 1862, pp. 72–84.

16. Broadhead Papers, Glover to Broadhead, June 4, 1862.

17. Leopard and Shoemaker, *Messages and Proclamations,* III, 481–84.

18. *Missouri State Convention Journal,* June, 1862, pp. 45–47; Lincoln Papers, Gamble to Lincoln, June 21, 1862.

19. Gamble Papers, Henderson to Gamble, June 16, 1862.

20. *Missouri Republican,* June 17, 1862; *Missouri Democrat,* June 24, 1862.

21. *Ibid.; Missouri Statesman,* July 4, 1862; Charles D. Drake, "Autobiography" (Manuscript, State Historical Society of Missouri), pp. 736a–743.

22. William B. Hesseltine, *Lincoln and the War Governors* (New York, 1955), pp. 241–44.

23. Nicolay and Hay, *Abraham Lincoln,* VI, 108–12; Lincoln Papers, Wilson *et al.* to Lincoln, July 14, 1862; Noell *et al.* to Lincoln, July 15, 1862.

24. Nicolay and Hay, *Abraham Lincoln,* VI, 158–64.

25. Hesseltine, *Lincoln and the War Governors,* pp. 253–61; Gamble Papers, Bates to Gamble, September 19 and 21, 1862; John A. Andrew to Gamble, September 29, 1862.

26. Stevens, *Centennial History of Missouri,* I, 834; Shoemaker, *Missouri and Missourians,* I, 926.

27. *Ibid.,* I, 924–26; Lincoln Papers, Frank Blair to Lincoln, November 14, 1862. Cf. Gist Blair Papers, Frank Blair to Montgomery Blair, no date, but obviously written in November, 1862.

28. Leopard and Shoemaker, *Messages and Proclamations,* III, 430–50.

29. *House Journal, 22nd General Assembly,* pp. 129–41, 381–91; *Senate Journal, 22nd General Assembly,* pp. 115–40, 450–60.

30. *Missouri Republican,* February 6, 1863; Rollins Papers, Bingham to Rollins, February 16, 1863.

31. *Congressional Globe,* 37th Cong., 3d Sess., pp. 91, 207–9, 215–21, 302, 351, 625, 776–95, 903, 1295; Broadhead Papers, Henderson to Broadhead, December 27, 1862, and February 22, 1863.

32. Leopard and Shoemaker, *Messages and Proclamations,* III, 530.

33. *Missouri Republican,* May 14, 16, 21, 23, 1863; *Missouri Democrat,* May 20 and 25, June 1 and 5, 1863; Drake, "Autobiography," pp. 789–90.

34. *Missouri Democrat,* June 5, 1863.

35. *Missouri Republican,* June 6, 1863.

36. *Ibid.,* June 6 and 8, 1863; *Missouri Statesman,* June 12, 1863.

37. *Missouri State Convention Journal,* June, 1863, p. 3; *Missouri Democrat,* June 12, 1863.

38. Those parts of the message dealing with matters other than emancipation and the action taken upon them by the convention will be considered in Chapter 8.

39. Leopard and Shoemaker, *Messages and Proclamations,* III, 451–64.

40. *Missouri State Convention Proceedings,* June, 1863, pp. 10–20.

41. *Missouri State Convention Journal,* June, 1863, p. 12.

42. *Ibid.,* pp. 12–15.

43. *Missouri State Convention Proceedings,* June, 1863, pp. 78, 135.

44. *Missouri State Convention Journal,* June, 1863, pp. 27–28; *Missouri State Convention Proceedings,* June, 1863, pp. 264–65.

45. The *Proceedings* state Gamble's proposal as July 4, 1866, but the debate following clearly indicates this is incorrect.

46. *Missouri State Convention Proceedings,* June, 1863, pp. 283–91.

47. *Ibid.,* pp. 257–58; Eliot Papers, Schofield to Eliot, June 23, 1863.

48. *Missouri Statesman,* June 19, 1863; Schofield, *Forty-Six Years in the Army,* p. 71.

49. Lincoln Papers, Schofield to Lincoln, June 20, 1863. Cf. Rollins to Lincoln, June 12, 1863.

50. *O. R.,* Ser. I, Vol. XXII, Part 2, 331–32; Basler, *Works of Lincoln,* VI, 291.

51. *Missouri State Convention Proceedings,* June, 1863, pp. 329–30, 355.

52. *Ibid.,* pp. 330–45.

53. *Missouri State Convention Journal,* June, 1863, pp. 46–47.

54. *Missouri State Convention Proceedings,* June, 1863, p. 368. The final text of the ordinance was as follows:

SECTION 1. The first and second clauses of the twenty-sixth section of the third article of the Constitution are hereby abrogated.

SEC. 2. That slavery and involuntary service, except for the punishment of crime, shall cease to exist in Missouri on the fourth day of July, eighteen hundred and seventy; and all slaves within the State at that day are hereby declared to be free: *Provided, however,* that all persons emancipated by this ordinance shall remain under the control, and be subject to the authority of their late owners, representatives and assigns, as servants, during the following periods, to-wit: those over forty years of age, for and during their lives; those under twelve years of age, until they arrive at the age of twenty-three years; and those of all other ages, until the fourth day of July, eighteen hundred and seventy-six. The persons, or their legal representatives, who, up to the moment of emancipation, were the owners of the slaves thereby freed, shall, during the period for which the services of such free men are reserved to them, have the same authority and control over the said freed men, for the purpose of securing the possession and service of the same, that are now held absolutely by the master in respect to his slave: *Provided, however,* that after the fourth day of July, eighteen hundred and seventy, no person so held to service shall be sold to a nonresident of, or removed from, the State of Missouri, by the authority of his late owner, or his legal representatives.

SEC. 3. That all slaves hereafter brought into this State, and not now belonging to the citizens of this State, shall thereupon be free.

SEC. 4. All slaves removed by the consent of their owners to any seceded State after the passage by such State of an act of secession, and thereafter brought into this State by their owners, shall thereupon be free.

SEC. 5. The General Assembly shall have no power to pass laws to emancipate slaves without the consent of their owners.

SEC. 6. After the passage of this ordinance, no slaves in this State shall be subject to State, county, or municipal taxes.

55. *Missouri Statesman,* August 14, 1863.

CHAPTER 8

1. *O. R.,* Ser. I, Vol. XXII, Part 2, 293.

2. *Missouri Democrat,* May 22, 1863; Lincoln Papers, Austin A. King to Montgomery Blair, May 30, 1863; Schofield, *Forty-Six Years in the Army,* pp. 54–55.

3. *Missouri State Convention Proceedings,* June, 1863, p. 231; *Missouri Democrat,* June 27, 1863; *O. R.,* Ser. I, Vol. XXII, Part 2, 373–74.

4. *Ibid.,* p. 366.

5. Basler, *Works of Lincoln,* VI, 253, 326, 338; Lincoln Papers, Richard McAllister to Lincoln, July 13, 1863; Schofield to Lincoln, July 14, 1863.

6. *Ibid.,* Gamble to Lincoln, July 13, 1863.

7. Basler, *Works of Lincoln,* VI, 344–45.

8. Leopard and Shoemaker, *Messages and Proclamations,* III, 462–63.

9. *Missouri State Convention Journal,* June, 1863, pp. 15, 25–26; Schofield, *Forty-Six Years in the Army,* p. 72.

10. *Ibid.,* pp. 72–73.

11. Leopard and Shoemaker, *Messages and Proclamations,* III, 502–4.

12. *Missouri Democrat,* June 17, 1863.

13. *Missouri Republican,* June 18 and July 2, 1863.

14. *O. R.,* Ser. I, Vol. XXII, Part 2, 315; Broadhead Papers, Henderson to Broadhead, May 30, 1863; Rollins to Broadhead, June 8, 1863; Drake, "Autobiography," pp. 878–81; *Missouri Democrat,* June 17, 1863.

15. *O. R.,* Ser. I, Vol. XXII, Part 2, 290–92, Schofield, *Forty-Six Years in the Army,* p. 71.

16. *O. R.,* Ser. I, Vol. XXII, Part 2, 315.

17. *Ibid.,* pp. 428–29, 450–51; Broadhead Papers, Abram Comingo to Broadhead, August 20, 1863.

18. Brownlee, *Gray Ghosts of the Confederacy,* pp. 118–25; *O. R.,* Ser. I, Vol. XXII, Part 1, 579–93.

19. *Ibid.,* pp. 573, 576; *Missouri Republican,* August 28, 1863; *Missouri Democrat,* August 24, 1863.

20. *O. R.,* Ser. I, Vol. XXII, Part 2, 475, 479, 482–84.

21. *Ibid.,* Part 1, 572–74; Part 2, 552.

22. *Ibid.,* pp. 472–73; Brownlee, *Gray Ghosts of the Confederacy,* pp. 125–26. George Caleb Bingham, the noted artist and Missouri's state treasurer, had long been dismayed by the violence which Kansans perpetrated on the border population. Now he immortalized Ewing's action with his famous painting, "Order Number Eleven," which depicted in vivid terms the process of eviction.

23. Gamble Papers, Hall to Gamble, August 31, 1863; *O. R.,* Ser. I, Vol. XXII, Part 1, 574; Schofield, *Forty-Six Years in the Army,* p. 83.

24. *Missouri Republican,* July 22, 1863; Gamble Papers, Bates to Gamble, August 3, 1863.

25. Bates Papers, Gamble to Bates, August 10, 1863.

26. *Missouri Republican,* August 12 and 31 and September 21, 1863.

27. *Missouri Democrat,* July 31, 1863.

28. *Ibid.,* September 2 and 4, 1863; Drake, *Speeches,* pp. 271–307; Drake, "Autobiography," pp. 911–13.

29. *Ibid.,* pp. 915–17; *Missouri State Times* (Jefferson City), September 12, 1863.

30. *O. R.,* Ser. I, Vol. XXII, Part 2, 547; Schofield, *Forty-Six Years in the Army,* pp. 84–86.

31. *O. R.,* Ser. I, Vol. XXII, Part 2, 546–65.

32. Nicolay and Hay, *Abraham Lincoln,* VIII, 224; *O. R.,* Ser. I, Vol. XXII, Part 2, 574–75; *Missouri Democrat,* October 5, 1863.

33. Lincoln Papers, Rollins to Lincoln, September 8, 1863; Hay to Lincoln, September 11, 1863; Rollins to Bates, September 13, 1863; Broadhead to Bates, September 22, 1863; Gist Blair Papers, Rollins to Montgomery Blair, September 12, 1863; Gantt to Montgomery Blair, September 30, 1863; Rollins Papers, Montgomery Blair to Rollins, September 21, 1863;

Bates to Rollins, September 26, 1863; Broadhead Papers, Bates to Broadhead, September 26, 1863; Beale, *Bates Diary,* p. 308; Dennett, *John Hay Diaries,* p. 96.

34. Nicolay and Hay, *Abraham Lincoln,* VIII, 214–20.

35. Drake, "Autobiography," pp. 924–25; Nicolay and Hay, *Abraham Lincoln,* VIII, 216–20.

36. Schofield, *Forty-Six Years in the Army,* pp. 89-91.

37. Dennett, *John Hay Diaries,* pp. 108, 135.

38. Basler, *Works of Lincoln,* VI, 499–504.

39. *Missouri Republican,* October 21 and 23, 1863.

40. *O. R.,* Ser. I, Vol. XXII, Part 2, 585–86, 667–68.

41. Lincoln Papers, Gamble to Lincoln, October 1, 1863.

42. Gamble Papers, Archibald Gamble to Gamble, September 29, 1863; Leopard and Shoemaker, *Messages and Proclamations,* III, 533–39.

43. Basler, *Works of Lincoln,* VI, 526–27.

44. *O. R.,* Ser. I, Vol. XXII, Part 2, 677–78.

45. Lincoln Papers, Loan to Stanton, October 12 and 13, 1863, with affidavits; Schofield to Lincoln, November 9, 1863; Basler, *Works of Lincoln,* VI, 543–44.

46. *The Adjutant General's Report,* 1863, 51–52; *O. R.,* Ser. I, Vol. XXII, Part 2, 667–68.

47. *Missouri State Convention Journal,* June, 1863, p. 33; *Missouri Republican,* August 26, 1863; *Missouri Democrat,* September 4, 1863.

48. *Missouri State Times,* October 24, 1863; *Missouri Republican,* November 1, 1863; *Canton Press,* November 12, 1863; Broadhead Papers, Bates to Broadhead, October 24, 1863.

49. *Missouri Democrat,* November 9 and 25, 1863; *Missouri Republican,* November 9 and 11 and December 2, 1863; Lincoln Papers, Schofield to Lincoln, November 9, 1863.

50. *House Journal, 22nd General Assembly, Adjourned Session,* pp. 20–21; *Senate Journal, 22nd General Assembly, Regular Session,* pp. 40, 210; *Missouri Republican,* November 18, 1863.

51. *House Journal, 22nd General Assembly, Adjourned Session,* pp. 20–21; *Senate Journal, 22nd General Assembly, Regular Session,* pp. 40, 210; *Missouri Democrat,* August 5 and 12, 1863; *Missouri Republican,* November 20, 1863; Broadhead Papers, Richardson to Broadhead, March 3, 1864.

52. *Missouri Democrat,* November 16, 1863; *Missouri Statesman,* November 20, 1863.

53. Guy J. Gibson, "Lincoln's League: The Union League Movement During the Civil War" (unpublished doctoral dissertation, University of Illinois, 1957), pp. 332–33, 348.

54. Dennett, *John Hay Diaries,* pp. 135–36.

55. Nicolay and Hay, *Abraham Lincoln,* VIII, 471.

56. Schofield, *Forty-Six Years in the Army,* pp. 107–8; Nicolay and Hay, *Abraham Lincoln,* VIII, 472.

57. *Ibid.,* VIII, 472–74; Schofield, *Forty-Six Years in the Army,* p. 106; *O. R.,* Ser. I, Vol. XXXIV, Part 1, 188.

58. Eliot Papers, Halleck to Eliot, January 31, 1864.

59. Gamble and Hall had been particularly irked by Schofield's sanctioning of Ewing's Order Number Eleven. A short time earlier they had seriously considered removing him as commander of the E.M.M. when he ordered that group to abide by the federal policy of not returning runaway slaves who came into their lines. Only their knowledge that Schofield in turn would cut off all supplies from the E.M.M. and thereby make it totally ineffective prevented their doing this. Gamble Papers, Hall to Gamble, August 10 and 31, 1863; Gamble to Hall, August 15, 1863.

60. *O. R.,* Ser. I, Vol. XXII, Part 2, 281.

CHAPTER 9

1. *Missouri Statesman,* November 20, 1861; Leopard and Shoemaker, *Messages and Proclamations,* III, 477–80, 504–10.

2. *Missouri Republican,* December 21, 1863, January 15 and 18, and February 1, 1864.

3. Grace G. Avery and Floyd C. Shoemaker (eds.), *The Messages and Proclamations of the Governors of the State of Missouri* (Columbia, 1924), IV, 27–28.

4. Beale, *Bates Diary,* pp. 328–29.

5. *Missouri Democrat,* February 1, 1864.

6. Avery and Shoemaker, *Messages and Proclamations,* IV, 28.

7. *Laws of the State of Missouri. Adjourned Session, 22nd General Assembly, 1863–1864* (Jefferson City, 1864), pp. 24–26; *Missouri Democrat,* December 7, 1863, and February 19, 1864; Rollins Papers, Hall to Rollins, February 5, 1864.

8. *Missouri Democrat,* February 24 and 26, 1864; Drake, "Autobiography," p. 951.

9. Nevins, *Frémont,* pp. 573–74.

10. Broadhead Papers, Thomas H. Allen to Broadhead, November 16, 1863; Alexander J. Reid to Broadhead, December 21, 1863.

11. Gist Blair Papers, R. J. Howard to Montgomery Blair, December 28, 1863; *Missouri Statesman,* January 8, 1864.

12. *Missouri Democrat,* April 13, 1864; *Missouri Statesman,* May 27, 1864.

13. *Missouri State Times,* April 9, 1864.

14. *Missouri Democrat,* May 30, 1864; *Missouri Republican,* June 6, 1864; Drake, "Autobiography," p. 952.

15. Beale, *Bates Diary,* p. 373; Nicolay and Hay, *Abraham Lincoln,* IX, 62.

16. *Missouri Democrat,* June 10, 1864; *Missouri Republican,* June 13, 1864.

17. Smith, *Blair Family,* II, 246–67. Cf. Lincoln Papers, Glover to Montgomery Blair, May 27, 1864; Montgomery Blair to Lincoln, June 2, 1864; J. A. Hay to John Hay, June 8, 1864. There is some strong although indirect evidence that Lincoln actually encouraged the seating of the Radical delegation to thwart a full-fledged movement for Frémont in Missouri. William F. Zornow, "The Missouri Radicals and the Election of 1864," *Missouri Historical Review,* XLV (July, 1951), 368–69.

18. *Missouri Republican,* May 16, June 17, and September 9, 1864.

19. *Ibid.,* September 2 and 26, and October 31, 1864; *Missouri Statesman,* September 9, 1864; *Missouri Democrat,* June 10 and 27, 1864; Lincoln Papers, Nicolay to Lincoln, October 18, 1864.

20. *O. R.,* Ser. I, Vol. XXXIV, Part 2, 49.

21. *Missouri Statesman,* February 26, 1864; *O. R.,* Ser. I, Vol. XXXIV, Part 4, 194–95, 294–96.

22. *Ibid.,* pp. 581–82.

23. *O. R.,* Ser. I, Vol. XLI, Part 2, 158–59.

24. *Missouri Republican,* July 18, 1864; *O. R.,* Ser. I, Vol. XLI, Part 2, 190, 393–94.

25. Lincoln Papers, Broadhead to Bates, July 24, 1864; Broadhead Papers, Bates to Broadhead, July 30, 1864; Beale, *Bates Diary,* p. 415.

26. Lincoln Papers, Nicolay to Hay, June 29, 1864.

27. Brownlee, *Gray Ghosts of the Confederacy,* pp. 206–8; Hesseltine, *Lincoln and the War Governors,* pp. 364–65; Dennett, *John Hay Diaries,* pp. 187–92; Basler, *Works of Lincoln,* VII, 379, 386–88, 436; *O. R.,* Ser. I, Vol. XXXIV, Part 3, 42, 62, 107, 381, 416.

28. *Missouri State Times,* July 30, 1864; *Missouri Republican,* July 27, 1864.

29. Avery and Shoemaker, *Messages and Proclamations,* IV, 35–36.

30. *Missouri Democrat,* September 28 and October 7, 1864.

31. *Ibid.,* September 28 and October 12, 1864.

32. Broadhead Papers, Army journal kept by member of Price's army during the raid; *O. R.,* Ser. I, Vol. XLI, Part 1, 307–17.

33. *Missouri Democrat,* September 30, 1864; *Missouri State Times,* October 1, 1864. Thomas L. Price was unrelated to Sterling Price.

34. Shoemaker, *Missouri and Missourians,* I, 934–36.

35. Broadhead Papers, Bates to Broadhead, July 30, August 13, and October 17, 1864; Lincoln Papers, Hall to Lincoln, November 5, 1864; Beale, *Bates Diary,* pp. 593–94; *O. R.,* Ser. I, Vol. XLI, Part 4, 389–90, 672, 716, 742–48, 811–12; William M. Lamers, *The Edge of Glory: A Biography of General William S. Rosecrans, U.S.A.* (New York, 1961), pp. 420–21, 433–38.

36. Avery and Shoemaker, *Messages and Proclamations,* IV, 8–25.

37. *Senate Journal, 23rd General Assembly, Regular Session,* pp. 34–40.

38. Laughlin, "Missouri Politics During the Civil War," *Missouri Historical Review,* XXIV (January, 1930), 270–71.

39. *Laws of Missouri, 1863–1864,* p. 25.

40. *Missouri State Convention Journal,* 1865, pp. 16–17, 25–27.

41. Avery and Shoemaker, *Messages and Proclamations,* IV, 256; Anderson, *Border City,* pp. 345–48.

42. Shoemaker, *Missouri and Missourians,* I, 578, 941.

43. *Missouri State Convention Journal,* 1865, pp. 14, 89–90; *Missouri Statesman,* January 13, 1865.

44. Shoemaker, *Missouri and Missourians,* I, 946–47, contains a good analysis of the 1865 constitution.

45. 1865 Missouri Constitution, Article II. These oaths were also required of all officers and directors of corporations, teachers, trustees, attorneys, jurors, bishops, priests, and ministers.

46. *Missouri State Convention Journal,* 1865, p. 57.

47. *Ibid.,* pp. 47–48, 77, 138, 147–48.

48. *Ibid.,* pp. 247–48.

49. *Ibid.,* Appendix, pp. 275–76, 283.

50. *Ibid.,* pp. 97–98, 156–57.

51. Thomas S. Barclay, "The Liberal Republican Movement in Missouri," *Missouri Historical Review,* XX (October, 1925), 46–53.

52. *Ibid.,* 31–44. For the Bates letters see Beale, *Bates Diary,* pp. 571–612.

53. Barclay, "The Liberal Republican Movement in Missouri," *Missouri Historical Review,* XX (October, 1925), 3–78; (January, 1926), 262–332; (April, 1926), 406–37; (July, 1926), 515–64.

Bibliography

I. United States Public Documents

Biographical Directory of the American Congress, 1774–1949. Washington, 1950.

Congressional Globe. Thirty-seventh Congress. Washington, 1862–1863.

War of the Rebellion: Official Records of the Union and Confederate Armies. 4 series, 70 vols. Washington, 1880–1902.

II. State Public Documents

Annual Report of the Adjutant-General of the State of Missouri. 1863, 1864. Jefferson City, 1864–1865.

Avery, Grace G. and Floyd C. Shoemaker (eds.). *The Messages and Proclamations of the Governors of the State of Missouri*. Volume IV. Columbia, 1924.

Journal of the House of Representatives of the State of Missouri. Twenty-first through Twenty-third General Assemblies, inclusive. Jefferson City, 1861–1866.

Journal of the Missouri State Convention Held at Jefferson City and St. Louis, March, 1861–June, 1863. St. Louis, 1861–1863.

Journal of the Missouri State Convention Held at St. Louis, January 6–April 10, 1865. St. Louis, 1865.

Journal of the Senate of the State of Missouri. Twenty-first through Twenty-third General Assemblies, inclusive. Jefferson City, 1861–1866.

Laws of the State of Missouri. Twenty-first and Twenty-second General Assemblies. Jefferson City, 1861–1864.

Leopard, Buel, and Floyd C. Shoemaker (eds.). *The Messages and Proclamations of the Governors of the State of Missouri*. Volume III. Columbia, 1922.

Proceedings of the Missouri State Convention Held at Jefferson City and St. Louis, March, 1861–June, 1863. St. Louis, 1861–1863.

Proceedings of the Missouri State Convention Held at St. Louis, January 6–April 10, 1865. St. Louis, 1865.

III. Manuscripts

Attorney-General. Personal Papers, 1861–1864. National Archives, Washington.

Edward Bates. Papers. Missouri Historical Society, St. Louis.

Francis P. Blair, Jr. Papers. Library of Congress.

Gist Blair. Papers. Library of Congress.

James O. Broadhead. Papers. Missouri Historical Society, St. Louis.

Simon Cameron. Papers. Library of Congress.

Civil War Papers. Missouri Historical Society, St. Louis.

Charles D. Drake. "Autobiography." State Historical Society of Missouri, Columbia.

William G. Eliot. Papers. Missouri Historical Society, St. Louis.

Hamilton R. Gamble. Papers. Missouri Historical Society, St. Louis.

Charles Gibson. Papers. Missouri Historical Society, St. Louis.

Robert Todd Lincoln Collection of the Papers of Abraham Lincoln. Library of Congress.

John G. Nicolay. Papers. Library of Congress.

Thomas C. Reynolds. Papers. Missouri Historical Society, St. Louis.

James Sidney Rollins. Papers. State Historical Society of Missouri, Columbia.

George R. Smith. Papers. Missouri Historical Society, St. Louis.

Robert T. Van Horn. Papers. State Historical Society of Missouri, Columbia.

IV. Published Collections

Basler, Roy P. (ed.). *The Collected Works of Abraham Lincoln.* 9 vols. New Brunswick, New Jersey, 1953–1955.

Beale, Howard K. (ed.). *The Diary of Edward Bates, 1859–1866.* The Annual Report of the American Historical Association for the Year 1930, IV. Washington, 1933.

Diary and Correspondence of Salmon P. Chase. The Annual Report of the American Historical Association for the Year 1902, II. Washington, 1903.

Drake, Charles D. *Union and Anti-Slavery Speeches Delivered During the Rebellion.* Cincinnati, 1864.

Johnson, Allen, and Dumas Malone (eds.). *The Dictionary of American Biography.* 20 vols. New York, 1928–1936.

Moore, Frank (ed.). *The Rebellion Record.* 12 vols. New York, 1861–1868.

Nicolay, John G., and John Hay (eds.). *The Complete Works of Abraham Lincoln.* 12 vols. Cumberland Gap, Tennessee, 1894.

United States Biographical Dictionary and Portrait Gallery of Eminent and Self-made Men. Missouri volume. Kansas City, 1878.

V. NEWSPAPERS

All of the newspapers listed here are in the library of the State Historical Society of Missouri at Columbia.

Canton Press, Canton, Missouri, 1863.

Jefferson Inquirer, Jefferson City, Missouri, January, 1861.

Liberty Tribune, Liberty, Missouri, 1861–1865.

Missouri Democrat, St. Louis, Missouri, 1861–1862 (weekly), 1863–1865 (tri-weekly).

Missouri Republican, St. Louis, Missouri, 1861–1865.

Missouri Statesman, Columbia, Missouri, 1861–1865.

Missouri State Times, Jefferson City, Missouri, 1863–1864.

Platte County Conservator, Platte City, Missouri, 1862.

VI. UNPUBLISHED THESES AND DISSERTATIONS

Gibson, Guy J. "Lincoln's League: The Union League Movement During the Civil War." Unpublished doctoral dissertation, University of Illinois, Champaign, 1957.

Kirkpatrick, Arthur R. "Missouri, the Twelfth Confederate State." Unpublished doctoral dissertation, University of Missouri, Columbia, 1954.

March, David D. "The Life and Times of Charles Daniel Drake." Unpublished doctoral dissertation, University of Missouri, Columbia, 1949.

Peterson, Norma L. "B. Gratz Brown, the Rise of a Radical, 1850–1863." Unpublished doctoral dissertation, University of Missouri, Columbia, 1953.

Rosin, Wilbert H. "Hamilton Rowan Gamble, Missouri's Civil War Governor." Unpublished doctoral dissertation, University of Missouri, Columbia, 1960.

VII. ARTICLES

Barclay, Thomas S. "The Liberal Republican Movement in Missouri," *Missouri Historical Review,* XX (October, 1925), 3–78; (January, 1926), 262–332; (April, 1926), 406–37; (July, 1926), 515–64.

Fitzsimmons, Margaret L. "Missouri Railroads During the Civil War and Reconstruction," *Missouri Historical Review,* XXXV (January, 1941), 188–206.

Harding, Samuel B. "Missouri Party Struggles in the Civil War," *The Annual Report of the American Historical Association for the Year 1900,* I (Washington, 1901), 85–104.

Herklotz, Hildegarde R. "Jayhawkers in Missouri, 1858–1863," *Missouri Historical Review,* XVII (July, 1923), 505–13; XVIII (October, 1923), 64–101.

Kirkpatrick, Arthur R. "Missouri's Secessionist Government, 1861–1865," *Missouri Historical Review,* XLV (January, 1951), 124–37.

Laughlin, Sceva B. "Missouri Politics During the Civil War," *Missouri Historical Review,* XXIII (April, 1929), 400–26; (July, 1929), 583–618; XIV (October, 1929), 87–113; (January, 1930), 261–84.

Loeb, Isidor. "Constitutions and Constitutional Conventions in Missouri," *Missouri Historical Review,* XVI (January, 1922), 189–246.

March, David D. "The Missouri Radicals and the Re-election of Lincoln," *Mid-America,* XXIV (July, 1952), 172–87.

McDougal, H. C. "A Decade of Missouri Politics—1860 to 1870—from a Republican Viewpoint," *Missouri Historical Review,* III (January, 1909), 126–53.

Parrish, William E. "General Nathaniel Lyon. A Portrait," *Missouri Historical Review,* XLIX (October, 1954), 1–18.

Phillips, John F. "Governor Willard Preble Hall," *Missouri Historical Review,* V (January, 1911), 69–82.

———. "Hamilton Rowan Gamble and the Provisional Government of Missouri," *Missouri Historical Review,* V (October, 1910), 1–14.

Potter, Marguerite. "Hamilton R. Gamble, Missouri's War Governor," *Missouri Historical Review,* XXXV (October, 1940), 25–71.

Shackelford, Thomas. "The Shackelford Amendment," *Missouri Historical Review,* I (January, 1907), 121–28.

Smith, William E. "The Blairs and Frémont," *Missouri Historical Review,* XXIII (January, 1929), 214–60.

Stevens, Walter B. "Lincoln and Missouri," *Missouri Historical Review,* X (January, 1916), 63–119.

Switzler, William F. "Constitutional Conventions of Missouri, 1865–1875," *Missouri Historical Review,* I (January, 1907), 109–20.

Thomas, Raymond D. "A Study in Missouri Politics, 1840–1870," *Missouri Historical Review,* XXI (January, 1927), 166–84.

Williamson, Hugh P. "Willard P. Hall, Lawyer, Lawmaker, Statesman," *Journal of the Missouri Bar,* XVII (April, 1961), 170–73.

Zornow, William F. "The Missouri Radicals and the Election of 1864," *Missouri Historical Review,* XLV (July, 1951), 354–70.

VIII. Books

Adamson, Hans C. *Rebellion in Missouri: 1861: Nathaniel Lyon and His Army of the West*. Philadelphia, 1961.

Anderson, Galusha. *A Border City During the Civil War*. Boston, 1908.

Bay, William V. N. *Reminiscences of the Bench and Bar of Missouri*. St. Louis, 1878.

Britton, Wiley. *The Civil War on the Border, 1861–1862*. New York, 1890.

Brownlee, Richard S. *Gray Ghosts of the Confederacy: Guerrilla Warfare in the West, 1861–1865*. Baton Rouge, 1958.

Carr, Lucien. *Missouri: A Bone of Contention*. Boston, 1888.

Connelley, William E. *Quantrill and the Border Wars*. Cedar Rapids, Iowa, 1910.

Dennett, Tyler (ed.). *Lincoln and the Civil War in the Diaries and Letters of John Hay*. New York, 1939.

Duke, Basil W. *Reminiscences of General Basil W. Duke, C.S.A.* Garden City, New York, 1911.

Eliot, Charlotte C. *William Greenleaf Eliot: Minister, Educator, Philanthropist*. Boston, 1904.

Filley, Chauncey I. *Some Republican History of Missouri*. St. Louis, 1898.

Grasty, John S. *Memoir of Rev. Samuel B. McPheeters, D.D.* St. Louis, 1871.

Gray, Wood. *The Hidden Civil War: The Story of the Copperheads*. New York, 1942.

Harding, Samuel B. *The Life of George R. Smith*. Sedalia, Missouri, 1904.

Hesseltine, William B. *Lincoln and the War Governors*. New York, 1955.

Hume, John F. *The Abolitionists*. New York, 1905.

Lamers, William M. *The Edge of Glory: A Biography of General William S. Rosecrans, U.S.A.* New York, 1961.

Leftwich, William M. *Martyrdom in Missouri*. 2 vols. St. Louis, 1870.

McElroy, John. *The Struggle for Missouri*. Washington, 1909.

Monaghan, Jay. *Civil War on the Western Border*. Boston, 1955.

Nevins, Allan. *Frémont, Pathmarker of the West*. New York, 1955.

Nicolay, Helen. *Lincoln's Secretary: A Biography of John G. Nicolay*. New York, 1949.

Nicolay, John G. and John Hay. *Abraham Lincoln, A History*. 10 vols. New York, 1890.

Parrish, William E. *David Rice Atchison of Missouri: Border Politician*. Columbia, Missouri, 1961.

Peckham, James. *General Nathaniel Lyon and Missouri in 1861*. New York, 1866.

Randall, James G. *Constitutional Problems Under Lincoln.* New York, 1926.

Randall, James G. and David Donald. *The Civil War and Reconstruction.* 2d ed. Boston, 1961.

Reavis, L. U. *The Life and Military Services of General William Selby Harney.* St. Louis, 1878.

Rombauer, Robert J. *The Union Cause in Saint Louis in 1861.* St. Louis, 1909.

Rusk, Fern H. *George Caleb Bingham.* Jefferson City, Missouri, 1917.

Ryle, Walter H. *Missouri: Union or Secession.* Nashville, 1931.

Scharf, John T. *History of St. Louis City and County.* 2 vols. Philadelphia, 1883.

Schofield, John M. *Forty-Six Years in the Army.* New York, 1897.

Shoemaker, Floyd C. *Missouri and Missourians: Land of Contrasts and People of Achievements.* 5 vols. Chicago, 1943.

Smith, Edward C. *The Borderland in the Civil War.* New York, 1927.

Smith, William B. *James Sidney Rollins.* New York, 1891.

Smith, William E. *The Francis Preston Blair Family in Politics.* 2 vols. New York, 1933.

Snead, Thomas L. *The Fight for Missouri from the Election of Lincoln to the Death of Lyon.* New York, 1888.

Stephenson, Wendell H. *The Political Career of General James H. Lane.* Topeka, 1930.

Stevens, Walter B. *Centennial History of Missouri (The Center State), One Hundred Years in the Union, 1820–1921.* 3 vols. St. Louis, 1921.

Switzler, William F. *Illustrated History of Missouri from 1541 to 1877.* St. Louis, 1879.

Trexler, Harrison A. *Slavery in Missouri, 1804–1865.* Baltimore, 1914.

Williams, T. Harry. *Lincoln and His Generals.* New York, 1952.

———. *Lincoln and the Radicals.* Madison, Wisconsin, 1943.

Woodward, Ashbel. *Life of General Nathaniel Lyon.* Hartford, 1862.

Wooster, Ralph A. *The Secession Conventions of the South.* Princeton, New Jersey, 1962.

Zornow, William F. *Lincoln and the Party Divided.* Norman, Oklahoma, 1954.

Index

ST. LOUIS, MO.